The Bills Are *Due*

Rob Thompson

Outskirts Press, Inc.
Denver, Colorado

Cover image full rights obtained
www.shutterpoint.com

Photos license obtained from pro look photos
www.prolookphotos.com

Photos courtesy of Robert L. Smith Orchard Park New York.

Outskirts Press, Inc.
http://www.outskirtspress.com

ISBN: 978-1-4327-2854-0

Library of Congress Control Number: 2008934431

Outskirts Press and the "OP" logo are trademarks belonging to Outskirts Press, Inc.

PRINTED IN THE UNITED STATES OF AMERICA

Table of Contents

Foreword

Joe DeLamielleure, was born in Detroit Michigan in 1951. He was an All-American at Michigan State and was the last pick in the 1st round of the 1973 NFL Draft. Joe was an All-Pro six times and a six time Pro Bowler. No recognition was greater then his enshrinement in the NFL Hall of Fame in 2003. I remember Joe D. as a fierce offensive lineman and did my best to emulate him, although the result was a rather poor. *Now thirty years later he and I have become associated for a different reason.* He still plays a fierce game, although his opponent this time is the National Football League Players Association and its treatment of retired players, players from other eras, players who built this modern game.

In an excerpt from an Associated Press story from June of 2007 that appeared on the website of ESPN, retired NFL players told members of Congress that; "*...playing professional football has left them with broken bodies, brain damage and empty bank accounts*." That day a number of former players spoke before the House Judiciary Committee, telling tales of dementia, multiple surgeries, financial ruin *and* in some cases homelessness.

My goal of The Bills Are Due is to show the reader that, prior to the mid-eighties, NFL salaries were horrendous compared to what we see today. I want to educate readers on what the players who built this league have had to go through since they have retired and since they have begun to age. There is no glory when the glory days are over and many stories will show that.

This book will give you the voices of those who played in three very distinct eras in Buffalo Bills history. They are the AFL years of the 1960s, the record setting years of the 1970s and the Super Bowl years of the 1990s. To provide you with an understanding of what the older players are now facing I asked Joe DeLamielleure to describe it.

Joe good evening, could you give us some quick background on when you were growing up?

Sure Rob. I was born and raised in Detroit Michigan. I went to St Clement High School on the east side of the city. I was close to Reggie's high school but we were considered a suburb.

Did you, Paul Seymour and Reggie McKenzie know each other in high school?

Yes we did, we all knew each other. I played against Paul in high school. We knew *of* each other but we didn't really meet until we were in college. Paul and Reggie went to Michigan and I went to Michigan State. As a matter of fact Paul and I've known each other since the fifth grade. Paul was All-State, one of the best athletes in the Michigan I wasn't surprised he went number one in the draft.

Did you play both ways in high school?

Yes. We all played all sports. Paul Seymour and I were All-Catholic and All-State in basketball and football.

What did you play on defense?

Linebacker, and I was a fullback on offense.

You didn't start playing guard until you went to Michigan State?

That's right and not until my sophomore year. On the freshman team I played tight end and linebacker because we weren't eligible for varsity. When I began to play guard, I made All-Big-Ten the first year. I actually played both ways as a freshman in college.

What other colleges were looking to sign you out of high school?

It seemed like everyone. I actually went to Super Bowl III, the Jets and the Colts. The University of Miami flew me down there to see the game and to talk me into signing. We could make trips like that back in those days. I was recruited everywhere, and I took every trip I could too. I went to - Boston College, Holy Cross, and Purdue. You name it and I went there.

You stayed home in Michigan though? Why did you choose Michigan State?

Duffy Daugherty. He was the *only* reason I went to Michigan State.

He's quite a story all by himself.

Yes he is. My dad wanted me to go to Michigan to play for "Bo" Schembechler, but my dad said he couldn't *pronounce* Schembechler. Then he wanted me to go to Notre Dame and play for Ara Parsegian, but said he was a phony because he discovered he was a Protestant coaching at a Catholic university.

Good one.

Dad said go to Michigan State because Duffy's a Catholic and we can trust him. So, I went to State.

What did you study in college?

I graduated with a major in Criminal Justice and a minor in Psychology.

You were drafted in 1973 at the end of the 1st round.

Yes sir. Seymour was the 7th overall and I was 26th, two 1st round picks, kind of cool since we had known each other since we were kids. Lou Saban was a Big-Ten guy so he took a lot of Michigan and Michigan State guys - Reggie, Paul and myself. He *wanted* a running game.

Who from the Bills scouted you?

Ralph did. Ralph actually called me on draft day. He said that I was the only one he ever called. I don't know if he was kidding me or not but he always said that.

I was looking at the 1970, '71 and '72 seasons and it seemed to me that, when Lou Saban came in, the Bills were going to make the shift from a throwing to a running team.

That's right. Lou hired Jim Ringo who blocked as part of Lombardi's power sweep and he drafted Donnie Green from Purdue. They made Paul tight end and with that they had a Big-Ten line. Well, Mike Montler was from Colorado but was born in Ohio.

Big-Ten by birth.

Yea. I knew Ringo too. He had coached me in the Senior Bowl and knew that I could run. He told me that we were going to run the Green Bay sweep; we had the team for it.

Four yards and a cloud of dust?

Instead of Jim Taylor, we had O.J. Simpson, simple. The ball carrier would get around the end and have a bunch of guys out in front. It wasn't complicated at all. That's all it was, the Green Bay sweep. Lou had all Big-Ten blockers who could run block.

That first year I didn't know *what* we were going to do. We were 0-4 in the preseason, so nobody had a clue. When I went home after camp, I was asked what was the difference between Michigan State and the Bills and I said, “Simple. It was O.J.” It was clear that O.J. was a cut above everyone else.

Lets go to the last game of the 1973 season against the New York Jets. O.J. was in a position to break two records that day - Jim Brown's single-season rushing record, and he could become the first to reach 2,000 yards. Did O.J. break Jim Browns record over you?

Well, it was a sweep. 27 is what it was called. It was over the left side. I told him to just follow me. He did and he got the yards and the record.

The play was called 27?

That's right. We only had eight plays. It was pretty simple - 26, 27, 28, 46, 47, 29, 10 and 11. That was Ringo's offense.

Were 46 and 47 for Jim Braxton?

10 and 11 were Braxton's, but literally it was just eight plays.

There were no complicated blocking schemes?

It didn't matter what the schemes were. It was a simple sweep. We had roles and we perfected those roles. I have never seen any team *since* either to be as good as we were with the sweep.

Jim Ringo was great at what he did! When Ringo went to the Rams, Erik Dickerson rushed for 2,000 yards too. When Ringo went to New England, they had two backs rush for a thousand yards each. Then he went to New York and Freeman McNeil had his great seasons. The reason O.J. did what he did and we did what we did was because Jim Ringo was a master at the running game. Ringo was Vince Lombardi's center and a power blocker on the sweep that gave Jim Taylor all those good years. Ringo really knew what he was doing when it came to the running game.

He was a master line coach too because *he* had been a center. I mean his record speaks for itself. He's in the Hall of Fame and he coached four Hall-of-Farmers - Jackie Slater, Ron Yary, John

Hannah and myself.

Do you think the condition he had in the last years of his life is attributed to his playing days?

Most definitely. *He* played sixteen years in the league. Actually it was quite different than now, most coaches now in the league never played at the professional level. Lou Saban played. He was captain of the Cleveland Browns. Stan Jones played. Jim Ringo played. They were our coaches. Few head coaches now never played at *this* level.

Lou was the best coach I ever had, hands down. If you speak to many of the guys from back then, they'll say the same thing. I don't understand why he is not on the Wall of Fame at the stadium because, when you think of the AFL Championship teams and the Bills of the '70s, you think of Lou Saban.

Absolutely. He was the coach I remember from when I was a kid. It was a shock to look up one day and he was no longer there. Like the players, we always expected Lou Saban to be on the sidelines. What was your first impression as a rookie at training camp?

I knew about Lou because he had coached me in that Senior Bowl. So I came into camp knowing a little. My wife was pregnant and Lou said to me the most important thing is *your* wife, *not* the game. So, when you have to go, just go. To me that was the best type of coaching. He knew what was best for each player. Paul wasn't married and he knew how to treat Paul. Lou treated each player as a person and like they mattered.

I loved training camp. I would have played for free for Lou Saban. He understood the players. He knew that O.J. was probably the best running back ever to play the game, other than Jim Brown, and he was going to build a team around him that would be able to show him off.

If Lou had not come in, what would have happened to O.J.?

I think they would have traded him. I know he wasn't real happy until Lou got there and he didn't do anything *until* Lou got there.

That's certainly what the statistics show. Those I have spoken to believe O.J. would have been traded too. Joe, let's skip ahead to the real issue behind much of your work now, and that's making the lives of former NFL players easier.

Okay sure Rob, thank you.

I recently read a story saying the NFL will be releasing its updated disability program for retired NFL players. Did you see that?

I did. *They* haven't done anything at all! It's sugar coating, all that talk and they're not going to do anything. They *delay*, *deny* and hope we *die*. That is their approach to the retirees. It's so confusing that no one can make sense of it. Because of *it*, because of *them*, the guys who built the league are not being taken care. Those guys *built* the league! They are the ones who worked hard so the players in today's league can be multi-millionaires. First, and probably most important, is that we have a lousy union, the worst union in professional sports by a long shot. Not only do we have a lousy union but we also have a lousy union leader in Gene Upshaw, and that's putting it mildly. All they have to do is to improve the pensions for everyone, *that's* what we're asking.

Gene Upshaw has been in power longer than Fidel Castro. That's why I call him, *Fidel*, some folks call him the Pope. How does anyone challenge Fidel or the Pope? I certainly am not saying that those two are equal, but I want to point out that it's near impossible to fight the establishment. Simply put, the NFL, is not going to take care of the former players although we *were* the guinea pigs for the league. We were the guys who played on Astroturf that's now *torn* up because it's unsafe. Once the league saw how bad Astroturf was, they tore it up! Those of us who played on it, we are the ones with knee, hip and ankle problems.

We had inadequate helmets that caused concussions that went misdiagnosed, or, at best, nobody knew about them. We had crappy helmets and bad fields; nobody knew what they were getting into when they played on Astroturf. Now all these guys have hip and knee problems. There are dementia problems because the facemask was being used to tackle; some coaches were *teaching* players to tackle head on head. Nobody even knew what a concussion was when we played. You get one now, you're out for one or two weeks. If you got one when we played, you went right back into the game.

It's an absolute disgrace in my opinion Rob. The NFL is a multi-*billion* dollar industry built by guys who didn't make that much money but who were happy playing. They didn't know the consequences either because many of the guys who played early on didn't even wear facemasks, so when they were introduced; everyone just tackled with them. That damaged a lot of players. Two of the greatest centers ever to play the game are dead from forms of dementia, Mike Webster and Jim Ringo.

You don't need a rocket scientist or some special committee to tell you about what causes brain injuries. We *know* what causes them. It's from being hit in the head all the time. Now, finally, because there are enough of us complaining and there are so many injured, we see how failed our disability compensation is and that we're not being taken care of. We're just supposed to sit here and take what the NFL hands out? No sir! They did all the experiments on the players from the '60s, '70s and '80s to be where they are now.

We're going to fight for as long as it takes. Gene Upshaw, in my opinion, should be ashamed of himself. He is a disgraceful union leader. He threw all the guys he played with under a bus while he, as the head of the union, makes $6.5 million dollars a year. He is not going to do a thing to help the older retired player, he doesn't care about them.

Conrad Dobler said, and I quote, "Gene Upshaw is an ass-hole with a brain somewhere between the size of a head of lettuce and a head of cabbage." Without exception many believe he is a tremendously poor leader who doesn't care at all about the former players.

I won't call him names but I will say that Gene Upshaw has thrown the guys he has played with under a bus for the sake of a dollar. He's all about money and I have no respect for him at all, absolutely none. He *said* he was going to break my neck. First of all, he won't be able to do it. He says things that he can never do all the time. He just doesn't ever do anything he says he *would* do or threatens to do. I'll call him Pinocchio to keep it clean.

That story came out last year after we first talked, Joe. I'll paraphrase what Upshaw said; "You think I'm going to invite him to dinner, no I'm going to break his..."

Yea, he was going to break my goddamn neck. Then when he sees me, he says, "Oh no! It was just a misunderstanding. I would never mean to say it that way." What type of guy would say that behind someone's back and then denies it when he met him face-to-face. He's a phony, pure and simple.

What instigated that?

I've been complaining about him forever. I've never liked him *or* respected him. I never even voted for him. In 1974, we wanted him out. Current players probably wouldn't be able to tell you how much money Upshaw makes. If you tell them that he makes more than 93% of the players in the league, they probably would feel that there's nothing they can do about it. If they complain about it, they *migh*t be out of the league. Upshaw makes $6.5 million a year and he is just a puppet for the owners. That's all he is.

Tom Condon and Gene Upshaw are in this together. They just *have* to be, and Condon *has* to be the brains behind the operation because I don't think that Upshaw is smart enough to orchestrate this thing by himself.

Explain who Tom Condon is for the readers please.

Tom Condon played for the Kansas City Chiefs and was their player representative. He also sits on the disability board. He must love free agency because he's the agent for over a *hundred* NFL players *and* for Gene Upshaw. There is definitely a conflict of interest here and have a wolf in the hen house. Upshaw is not going to do anything for us and our pensions are not going to get any better unless Congress steps in.

Here's another example. What did we hear all last year when it came to drug testing for HGH, steroids? Baseball is all over that issue but *Upshaw* says we have the gold standard for drug testing in professional sports, won't test for HGH. Come on! There's no HGH in football? Come on Fidel! These guys aren't 340 pounds because of Little Debbie's.

In the NFL, Gene Upshaw answers to no one. He *is* the Pope. He can do whatever he wants. What the retired players need to do is to entirely break away from the NFL because we will never have anything. We, the guys who built this league in the '60s, '70s and up through the early '90s, are on our own. We just need to take care of ourselves, because Upshaw and the league wont.

You would think the guys who played when we played and who are now coaches would step up to the plate on our behalf. Marty Shottenheimer, Bill Cowher, Jim Haslett – when they were coaching, got their money and now they don't care about anybody else. They're not going to step in and help anybody. They're not going to kill their golden goose. Anything they can do to screw the former players they will do.

The camaraderie between the players is great don't get me wrong. *It's* a great game but it was a horrible business for those who played in the '60s, '70s and '80s. Bottom line is it's just terrible now for many of us.

If you could wave your hand and give the former players an ideal package what would it be?

Some said giving former players a vote in union activities would be a good idea. Since the NFL has been granted antitrust status by Congress, pulling that status would be a good idea. But having a retirement system that matches baseball would be ideal.

Isn't the average pension in baseball is around thirty-five thousand dollars and the NFL is just over twelve thousand dollars, just above the poverty level.

Yes. The NFL is smaller than baseball. *They* travel less and play one-tenth the number of games but the NFL grosses *more* and pays *less* than baseball. We want the NFL to give us good pensions. We will be fighting disabilities forever unless they make the changes. If you're under age fifty, you're not going to get anything.

I did take a look at some of the other interesting side-by-side comparisons of the NFL and MLB and want to thank former Bill Jeff Nixon for this.

- *A ten year player in the NFL at the age of sixty-two gets $32,000 while a ten year player in major league baseball gets $175,000.*
- *Average salary in the NFL is $1.4 million while the average salary in major league baseball is $2.8 million.*
- *The salary for the union chief executive in baseball is $1 million while in the NFL Gene Upshaw make $6.7 million a year.*

Do you think these new, young guys would be upset if the knew how much Upshaw was making?

No. They wouldn't. What we want is *our* pensions to be taken out of the sub-poverty level. Upshaw makes $6.5 mill while others, who built this league long before he played, make a few hundred bucks a month. The average life span of an NFL player is fifty-seven. I don't care what anybody says, it's fifty-seven. They know we're going to die. Look at all those who died well before age fifty - Payton, Alzado, Mike Webster. Even the Bills - Jim Braxton, Bobby Chandler, and John Leypoldt who died at 40.

The motto of the Shriners football game is; *"Strong legs run so that weak legs may some day walk."* We *have* to be the voice for those nobody will listen to. I'm just a lineman. They won't listen to me and *I'm* in the Hall of Fame. If someone is in the league a couple of years and is severely injured, certainly no one will listen to them. We have to do what we can for them as well. The league has forgot those players from all those great years and it's a shame. It's bullshit!

Joe, when I first read of stories of Conrad Dobler, Donnie Green and Willie Wood, I was generally shocked. We grew up with you.

You were the heroes for us little kids. We hung your posters and collected your football cards and we have never forgotten you. I spoke with Joe Ferguson last week just prior to his returning to his treatment in Houston and he was surprised at how many cards and emails he had received from people in western New York. I said, "Joe, no one will ever forget you or the Bills of that era." For lack of a better word, we had a special bond with one another.

Rob, when you were a kid you knew all the players. You knew their positions and probably their statistics too. It's because we were always there.

Absolutely! You guys were always there from one year to the next.

It was a different era, a different time. Most people in this country now just want to be entertained. News items such as the war in Iraq, the economy, or even the election are just background noise. People just want to be entertained. Football is entertainment and so is the endless supply of video games. Right now it's a league of interchangeable parts. A player is with a team two to three years at the most. Then they renegotiate their contract so the agents can take an ever-increasing cut of the pie. Tom Condon is the biggest of them. It will be a real mess a decade from now.

It doesn't matter if a player has produced on the field. Now it's just the art of the renegotiation. If the agent can make the kid sound good and if the kid can be marketed well by the league, then some team will sign him for whatever is asked.

The league, the union and its leadership all seem to be about money. So, do you think the Bills will move to Toronto because of the lack of it?

Wow! I don't know. I like Mr. Wilson. I was fortunate to have played for two great owners, Ralph Wilson and Art Modell of the Cleveland Browns. I love them both. They are good, decent, kind men and the league is squeezing them to a breaking point. The NFL may not be squeezing Mr. Wilson as much as the city of Buffalo is being squeezed, and that's a joke.

The city of Buffalo has sold out most every game for almost a decade. They haven't been in the playoffs in *nearly* a decade, and now they may have to move the team because the league isn't making as much as they can off of the city. That's a joke! The Buffalo Bills, because of their fans, are one of the greatest sports franchises in history. It would be like moving the Green Bay Packers.

It's all about money then?

Yes. It's unbelievable but it is. The current players should get down on their knees everyday and *thank* the former players like us for being dumb enough to keep Gene Upshaw in office.

A question that many *should* ask is why should free agents make so much money? A team is spending millions on a player who may have only spent a couple of years in the league and may not have had any success at all. It's insane. Most of them haven't done anything and they get three or four million-dollar bonuses alone. These guys are millionaires at twenty-two. How can you deal with that and with them?

I agree. Most haven't completed college and most are millionaires when they are barely old enough to drink.

Well, God bless them! But they have ruined the league. Joe Ferguson said TV can make anything great, and he's right. When the USFL came out twenty years ago, many said those guys aren't any good. I was watching the USFL and I said bullshit. I watched Reggie White, Steve Young, and Jim Kelly. These guys were great but the media was telling us they weren't. The only difference was that they weren't wearing the NFL uniform and didn't have NFL marketing.

Joe that attitude goes back sixty years for the NFL. In the late 1940s, they resisted the All-American Football Conference and in the late 1950s, the NFL resisted the American Football League calling Len Dawson, Jack Kemp and Lance Alworth NFL rejects. What I think made the AFL successful was television. You and Joe Ferguson are right about how something, whether it be a mediocre NFL star, a professional team or a war, is portrayed by television will form the publics opinion. Hasn't free agency added to this mess?

Free agency, I think it is killing the league while those who built it suffer. I will beat this into the ground but we were the guinea pig society for the league. The owners said artificial turf was the best thing to play on at the time. It was the cheapest that's for sure but it was concrete with rubber on it and in Buffalo it froze. What you have now is a bunch of guys with hip displacement and the league's *not* going to pay for it because they say that it's not football related. C'mon!

Donnie Green, one member of our *Electric Company,* now lives in a homeless shelter. He's not going to say anything bad about anyone because that's not him. Perhaps, if the league and the union had better prepared him, he would be in a different situation but they didn't. There are so many guys who have had it as bad and some even worse than others, but the truth is we played on unsafe fields wearing unsafe equipment. They were giving us salt tablets when we were sweating too much. It's not or wasn't the coaches fault because nobody knew, but now they *do* know and for those who were the guinea pigs, they should make it right but they won't.

I compare what we went through to cigarette smoking fifty years ago. Nobody knew what the effect of cigarette smoking was but now they do. They tell us now don't smoke because it will cause cancer and any number of other things. The lawyers of the country got together and saw a payout was possible. They won a lawsuit against the tobacco industry.

Nobody knew about the conditions we played under until *now,* when many suffer from the injuries sustained from such primitive conditions. The NFL says that it has 10,000 former players on pension. That's bullshit too because there are, and forever will be, only 2,800 former players receiving a pension. The average life span is fifty-seven as I have said. Few ever become old enough to collect a full pension, and more are dropping dead every day. Upshaw is a liar about most everything and is, in my opinion, scamming those who built this league out of their remaining dignity.

One of the biggest scams is the league tells us that we can collect our pension at forty-five or we can take it at fifty-five. But what they say is that, since the average lifespan of an NFL player is fifty-seven, why not take it at forty-five. A lot of guys did this because they believed what they were told by the union, but what the union did not tell those players is that when they took their pensions at forty-five, they lost their disability.

You have become one of the national voices for the former players and I think it is important that you know we fans see your work, and that we too speak but with our wallets. This aside, what is one thing you remember about Buffalo?

Rob I think the fans related to the players back then and the players related to the fans. That doesn't exist anymore. We lived *outside* the gated communities. The fans were part of the team, the twelfth man. That's why the fans are on the Wall. When I played, I was on a bowling team, we were part of the community we had that bond with the fans. I don't see how that can possibly exist in today's game. I love the city and have so many friends there. We are up there often because of my business commitments. When I remember those days, I often miss them, I love the city and the fans but I really feel so sorry for those guys who played when I did and got hurt and now have nobody to turn to. I tell you this Rob - I will fight until I die to make it better for those who built this league.

Introduction

The bills are due.

They most certainly are and in more ways than one. Seemingly they always were, always are and always will be.

We hear this phrase every month as we sit at the kitchen table, hoping that what comes in is enough to cover what must go out. Overdrafts and monthly budgets, however, are not what this book is about.

The bills are due.

These simple words can be heard all throughout the hidden and not so hidden valleys of western New York State when each year the hint of fall first touches the sky.

The *Bills* are due.

We *hear* these words every year.

We *say* these words every year.

We sincerely mean it when we say the Bills are due and that ***this*** year will be the Bill's year.

We never get sick of hearing these words nor do we get worn out from the give and take, the "*this* should be the year" conversation with our coffee-counter neighbors.

Whether we work a farm in South Lima, a store in East Aurora or a school in Henrietta, the fall season of each year shakes with the ghosts of games past and is warmed by the hopes for what next Sunday will bring.

"This has to be the year, it just *has* to be!" those ghosts echo.

"This *has* to be the year!" - the ghost's echo that is repeated from town to town, coffee-counter to coffee-counter.

This time of year arrives slowly though.

The summer came to us ever so slowly as we were sitting in 4th grade classrooms, but it *did* come and earthly interests were reborn and refocused. Those summer days moved along and we all did what youths of summer do as long as there has been youth of summer. We were caught up in a nether world. A world filled with sky, trees and bamboo, with days moving at a sprinter's gait. We soon crossed that imaginary boundary of time and began to dread the first day the yellow school bus came over the hill. There was a plus side to seeing that bus though. There was a good with the bad. The good being *those* first games were close.

As we sensed that our summer vacation was nearing an end and the leaves began to fall, the smell of football joined the symphony of senses. From grocery stores, to college campuses, to front porch swings, in head-nodding unison, everyone agreed - the Bills are due.

Nervous and trembling, we stepped onto a school bus full of new faces. Calmed only by Sunday's approach, the game of the week was our goal.

We all know just how much the school week dragged as we learned who did what on what date, and why A + B *always* equals C, but Sunday was our weekly reward for all *that* mess.

That bus brought us home in Friday's twilight sun. Then Saturday mornings came and, from Mt. Morris to Lancaster, Geneseo to Caledonia, we became part of hustle-and-bustle-filled days. We knew everything had to be done on Saturday, for Sunday, *oh,* Sunday, it was going to be one hell of game.

Sunday mornings dribbled alive. As a kid, Sunday mornings were a time when emotions were yanked in opposing directions with as equal a force as anything God has created. Sunday mornings meant that yes, we were just one day away from another school week, but it also meant that we were mere hours away from the kickoff of the game of the week.

The roads that dot the small towns across the Southern Tier were, at first, anxious with last minute errands but they grew still as fresh donuts and Sunday papers were brought home.

TV Guides were hurriedly sought out, opened, and scoured to discover what games would be aired, most times with delight, but sometimes with nausea because the Cowboys would, once again, be a featured game.

The radio played atop John Deere's on Sunday afternoons when the harvesting could not wait. We, who picked the potatoes by hand, agreed the Bills were due. This would be the season when it all would happen in *just* the right way.

We coughed up the dust of the muck as the pre-game show neared and we turned at the next hedgerow, and *just* for a moment, the coughing diesel outdid Van Miller.

We whose work was already done woke up then, and now, hours before kick off. We thumbed the over-stuffed Buffalo News or the Democrat and Chronicle as we heard the bacon sizzle.

We read the *expert* opinions of why one team would win and we read why *they* would lose.

We washed the car, took the trash out, and made last minute runs to Wal-Mart or Martins. We walked the dog around the neighborhood making sure he was set, as we met and greeted others on similar Sunday morning countdowns of their own.

We came home to a living room slightly askew as family members, young and old, finished last minute tasks and found the seats they claimed each game day.

We would seek our favorite pre-game show, not the national cookie-cutter stuff but the true-blue in-your-face two-hour rock radio network. We wanted to be told about what they *should* be doing to win and not about what rookie was holding out or what end zone celebration to expect from one particular receiver of infamous note. "Who cares," we would say.

All the years of bad luck, dropped passes, terrible calls and just missed kicks were forgotten as the pre-game show and interviews with alumni brought smiles and good memories back to the family room.

Final phone calls were made.

The dog insisted on one last trip around the back yard.

The wife insisted *we* accommodate the dog.

Lunchtime neared and friends came. If we were lucky, we plopped next to our sweetie on the couch and awaited the game. If we were really lucky, our sweetie didn't mind the game or our plop. She would set lunch out on the coffee table in front of us both, or, perhaps, I would order out from just down the road.

We turned down the volume on the wide screen and turned on the radio, fumbling for the best reception until, at last, we reached the best in both possible worlds, and returned to the couch.

The radio told us what the hell the real problem was with the Buffalo Bills and that frankness would bring us back to momentary reality. For just a moment or two, we wondered if it would *ever* be the Bills year.

Some of us agreed with such frankness while others, sincere and gray-haired, doubted the newcomers' words as to what the problem was. Was it defense, or was it offense? The old timer knew what was wrong and would happily tell them, they just had to ask.

Grandma sat with grandpa, remembering the first game in 1960 while across town, some grandma will sit alone this year remembering *all* the seasons past.

Meanwhile, the potato harvester rolled on as background timpani to our football wishes, to a happy, successful day on the field.

We sat in the chair of our choice, alone or with our favorite girl, through handholding moments, exultant in having made it to another Sunday afternoon.

Some of us enjoyed the early baseball months but, in the back of our minds, we always heard the rolling rumbles of two-a-days.

We tasted the sweat. We heard the whistle. We saw the games begin, if only in our minds.

As training camp was only weeks away and talks began to swirl of trades, signings and retirees, we silently nodded to ourselves the reassurance; "*This* would be the year, this *had* to be the year! *This* would be their year; *this* would be their time; it would happen *this* year." We all knew it!

The harvester rolled on.

Many times though, as the months of early winter wore our noses raw, we would see that yet another year would end much like all those before it.

"Wait until next year!" we said. "Next year will be our year. It just *has* to be!"

We *all* said this.

We *all* heard this.

We *all* wished this and, for many of us, we passed this wish on to our children and grandchildren. A wish unfulfilled to some degree, but a lifetime of love and respect for the game and its players has been spread to a new generation of fans. Though we may not have seen a title in our lifetime, we have done our part for the next generation of fans. This book is a book of memories. It is a where are they now? It is a where are *we* now? It is a book of memories and recollections of their lives and of ours.

The seasons all come together in the living rooms across the Western New York counties made strong by man and by old man winter. Regardless of age, financial position in life or knowledge of the game, the true blue, honest, hard-working and dedicated fans of the Buffalo Bills stick by the red, white, and blue of Orchard Park, year after year. We are forever the optimists.

Whether we work a first, second or third shift we set aside time to watch our Bills even through the worse of seasons. Their history is *our* history; they are part of our lives.

We recall events in our own lives by what the Bills did that year.

From the time we were old enough to speak our views in homeroom, to scribbling the number of our favorite player on a t-shirt in crayon, we knew that *this* year was the Bills year.

We did come close a couple of times, we certainly did, but the enjoyment of the game never left us, even after *we* came up just short. There is no room for fly-by-night fans in Buffalo. They need not apply here in the Queen City.

This book is written by a fan and for the fans of the Buffalo Bills. This book is written for those of us who, this year, will enjoy our fortieth season of Bills football. It is also written for those who soon will sit down to their very first NFL game of the week.

The Bills Are Due is not a book where one's eyes will glaze over by wholesale usage of X's and O's. This book will not try to dazzle the reader with detailed explanations of slant patterns, nickel packages, or why the H-back will succeed. The Bills Are Due will not attempt to recall, third and fourth hand, the problems of some long forgotten play and the trickle-down effects on history. *However*, when at all possible, when such a memory *must* be recalled, I will have the players involved tell the tale.

The intent of this book is to entertain fans of every era and of every level of knowledge of the game. I hope that it will bring back fond, long-dormant memories of this special time of year and the game we so love, and of when we were young and too busy being young to care about much else. The interviews and opinions have been written *just* as they were spoken, editing did not change that.

It is the goal of this book to remember the players of yesterday, the Buffalo Bills of our youth and to share with you a little of their lives now. It is my wish that this book will instill in all of us a greater appreciation of America's *real* game and a newfound respect for those who built it. Those who played for hundred dollar game checks while working second jobs will be remembered by this book. Those who played for one team most of their careers will be remembered. Those players who didn't charge an eight year old for an autograph will be remembered. Those who delivered to America, through hardship and through dedication to team, teammates and community, this game we now so love, will be remembered.

A simple thank you is not enough to the alumni who made this book possible. To their kindness and helpfulness and to the memories they gave us all, thank you. To Phil Bracchi, my term paper is now complete, thank you for waiting. To my wife Kendra let us live the next twenty-five making up for the first twenty-five we missed I love you.

Dedication

For his tremendous strength in overcoming many of life's obstacles and doing so without wavering from his strong faith in God, family and friends this book is happily dedicated to Joe Ferguson.

Chapter 1
My Day

"Each new Sunday meant a brand new challenge,
rich with new opportunities, a time for achievement,
a time for purpose, a time for glory." (1)
-John Facenda-

John Facenda—will it ever be possible for any us who remember Elvis being alive to forget the voice of John Facenda?

The NFL and John Facenda seemed one and the same. In words, he could share with the world what our hearts felt about one game, one play or one player. Many called him the voice of God. He could say what we all felt and dreamed about the game; he was our weekly explanation point and he is still the spokesman for its history. The story that he told had been written long before this nearsighted, portly fan ever sat in front of any Sunday afternoon game of the week. John Facenda was the game's history teacher to many of us.

However, does the game's history still matter?

Do those who built this game still matter?

The tales of Lambeau, Three Rivers and Riverfront were just being passed on to me as I came of age. John Facenda was sharing tales of the autumn wind, of Raiders, and numerous stories of courage and self-denial when I was short and bald.

History has no meaning especially when it's ignored. As this writer age's it appears that history has little relevance to a nation increasingly interested only in self.

The same is true for the game of football. As I've aged, I have found myself caring more about its history than I do about its current form.

History is unique, it is both fiction and non-fiction depending on what author you choose to read. History generates questions for those desiring an answer and the opposite is true for those who don't have an interest. Whenever a question is posed though, it creates other questions and this book did just that. I had many questions to ask about the game and didn't know how or even whom to ask.

When did the game start?

Why is a touchdown six points?

Why are there five linemen?

With each of these questions *more* questions were created.

Was a touchdown worth more or less points at one time?

Why a field goal?

The game did not begin the day my rear end sat in front of the television set for the first time. There *was* a beginning, and I wanted to know about it.

As a young boy growing up in Western New York, I'd sit inches from our Zenith, watching endless replays of should-have-been completions and touchdowns that just got away. I was wide-eyed at what I saw. And after every replay, I'd turn to my brother and ask why, as my glasses slid down my nose.

He'd answer in a way that older brothers do. As I sat there on the floor, I was mere inches away from Sonny Jerguson tossing to Charley Taylor and Terry Bradshaw tossing to Lynn Swann. "Why were they so good?" I asked. "Did they always play football?"

I had to squint, adjusting the greatly overused rabbit ears but I saw it all. I scooted closer to that hand-me-down Zenith, much to my mother's dismay. I saw Bob Griese and Paul Warfield, Ken Stabler and Cliff Branch and, of course, Joe Ferguson and J.D. Hill.

"Did they always play football?" I asked again.

"What did they do when they were my age?"

The voices of the game told it in a way my storybooks never did. The players lived it; I dreamed it; and John Facenda made the tales dance like no poet ever could. Even today, years after his death, he still is the voice of the NFL -for *me*.

When I was young, in the early '70s, there were only three television networks, a handful of colored televisions sets and, for better or worse, only Walter Cronkite. Like the news and so much else in the world during that time, the NFL existed only on CBS or on Monday Night. The NFL existed for us kids on television and in our imaginations as we scribbled the numbers of our favorite players on blown out undershirts. We always did what we could to bring the game closer to us and us to it.

For me, football was in the back yard of Claude Moses. That's where all my buddies and I became *our* heroes; we became the after-school, muck-covered gridiron greats. In our imaginations, John Facenda did our own back yard play-by-play with an undercurrent of chuckles filtering through overstuffed pine trees from the same Claude Moses watching us from his folding chair.

The football cards I collected by the thousands and the pennants I hung around my room. The magazine articles I cut out and taped in scrapbooks. My brother's old high school helmet painted in the color of the Kansas City Chiefs. All of this brought me closer to the game. That's what made me part of the NFL brotherhood of fans. I lived and loved the game of football in this way. These feeble attempts and youthful participation are what we small-town, poor-town young kids of the early seventies had and that's all we needed.

From Monday to Saturday, we all lived the game in our collections and in our backyards. In our Friday lunchroom chats, we defended our team and we made bold predictions as to what they would do that forthcoming Sunday afternoon. We, the younger version of the bold brotherhood, on Saturdays battled the parentally mandated chores and bed times. We did what we had to because kickoff was just hours away.

Up and down the one-street hometowns, others and I drew close to the 19" screens. It was a membership, that brotherhood of fans, and I *paid* my dues weekly. *That* membership, however, was changed when at ten years old I entered an all-new level of appreciation.

The year was 1974. What a year that was. Nixon was both in and out of the White House. Both Democrats and Republicans said the troops would be home by Christmas and both were wrong.

Chinatown and *The Longest Yard* were competing for our movie dollar. Elvis was still Elvis, and the American south found an all-new anthem with the release of Leonard Skynard's, *Sweet Home Alabama.* The annual Jerry Lewis Labor Day Telethon, yellow school buses and backyard football games marked the end of that summer as I began to hate girls a little less. 1974 was quite a year.

We survived those hard-fought 70 to 69-tumbling bumbling Garden Street mud bowls to go to school and back to Mrs. Boyd's 4th grade class. Football was our daily respite too as the weekend drew close and so too did our NFL game of the week. Our backyard games were classics, from end arounds, to blocked punts, broken noses, shattered knees and my belly-jiggling-hoochie-momma-twist end zone dances. We wore our blown-out hand-me-down jerseys and played with footballs years past their prime on neighbors' yards that were strewn with rocks, uneven sod and reeking of leaking septic tanks.

Before we knew it, the Sunday sun knocked on our window and there were chores to be done and bacon to be burned. We fumbled through the aforementioned TV Guide and almost inevitably found the game of the week consisted of the team I hated then and now, the Dallas Cowboys, the leagues ego.

We did our best to make the game real in South Lima, New York. TV made the NFL more real; the voices, the sounds, the smells made the game real and our imagination cemented it all together into a well-rounded fan-of-the-game experience. The voices and my imagination were how I knew the game back then.

But as I said, 1974 was going to be different for one day in September "Santa" came early, carrying tickets for two to a Buffalo Bills home game. Looking back these three decades since, I think that nearsighted boy cried that day when he held those tickets.

I couldn't believe I was going to a game.

I didn't even know it was possible.

Sunday October 20th was so far away.

I held tickets to a real game!

I called my friends!

I told the kids in our backyard games!

I told the kids across the lunchroom table only to have them smirk.

I told my pals in Mrs. Boyd's 4th grade class.

I *even* told Mrs. Boyd herself because I was so excited.

The anticipation was incredible and it grew as the days dragged on.

I couldn't concentrate in school and I couldn't sleep. I could eat though. *That* was never a problem.

Watching every game in the interim was torture.

My throat was drying up by the hour.

My palms were sweaty as the calendar dribbled on.

That October afternoon was never going to get here. I knew it.

School got in the way of my day dreaming of the Sunday yet to be. I was excited and paranoid all at the same time; I was even crampy in the most unpleasant of ways. All the worst fears began floating through my ten year old, shaved, bi-speckled head. Everything that could go wrong was going to go wrong and I knew it! I just knew it!

Mom would change her mind and not let me go!

My brothers' station wagon would catch fire!

The game would be canceled!

A blizzard, a flood, a plague of locusts or some other pestilence would befall Western New York!

Worst of all, *I* would be grounded!

But eventually, after living through hyperactive imagination, wide-awake nightmares and 4th grade math tests, that day in October 1974 did come. All the excitement that could be conjured up had passed and I was now ready.

I'd prepared the week before, showing everyone what I'd wear, then change my mind a dozen times each day. Dinners would be gulped. The final days slowly dribbled by. I'd pee a thousand times if I'd pee once.

Though the Bills were 4-1 at that time of the 1974 season, there was the nay Sayers. The doubters from all over the NFL and from the local I-know-everything sports reporters who were promising a 4-10 season or, at best, a 7-7, and, of course, the two annual losses to the Miami Dolphins. But I knew better.

Nobody, then or now, listens to such voices of the well-coiffed sports guy, for a real fan has his mind made up before he ever buys a newspaper or turns on the nightly news. Nothing mattered to me because the Bills were due and I wanted to be part of it all and thanks to Santa, I would get my chance.

I was better prepared then any TV sports guy. How dare he say such things as I heard him say at times! I would thumb the sports sections and watch the standings as if I was fully invested in Wall Street. Who was injured? Who was going to start and who wasn't? Both teams received the fullest of my 10-year-old scrutiny. This was to be the Bill's year and we would witness history. I just knew it.

The clock ticked and the cuckoo let us know the hour had arrived. I'd slept little. When the sun of that cool, fall morning woke the family, I was sitting on the chair in the hallway, skullcap planted firmly, my glasses crooked, cracked and dirty as hell.

It was Sunday, October 20, 1974. It was the Buffalo Bills vs. The New England Patriots. I'd been up for hours, fully dressed, waiting for the sun and older brother to rise.

"Is it time to go?" I asked brother Scott as he stumbled by.

"Is it time?" he asked. "Time, for what?" he said, torturing his near-sighted sibling.

"Did you take out the garbage?" Dad demanded, while knocking the skullcap off my head.

I mumbled in response.

I pounced downstairs and was forced by Dad to eat every ounce of a cereal I hated while again slapping the skullcap free. I did finish *it* though, dribbling much to the awaiting black lab under the table.

My breakfast was done and I sat at the kitchen door with my skullcap pulled down, *tight* this time.

My brother came downstairs not saying a word.

"Shovel the drive-way, feed the dogs, take out the garbage and wash the dishes!"

"Shovel the driveway?" I asked with my eyes. It was a snow free day.

Orders came from all directions and from family members with questionable levels of authority.

I was bouncing about, half-assing task upon task, praying to myself and mumbling just slightly louder for 1:00 to arrive. I performed all the chores as quickly and as poorly as could be expected of any ten year old under extreme dictatorial conditions and reassured my father that the garbage had indeed been taken out.

Laughter followed his last instruction, as did a crisp $5.00 bill for spending money. I grabbed it and a bag stuffed with sandwiches and orange cupcakes for our road trip to Orchard Park. The station wagon horn beeped as I ran tripping down the front steps.

"Let's go!" barked brother Scott, backing out of the driveway without me. "What's taking you so long?"

He'd stop the car then pull forward as I reached for the doorknob. I ran ahead to the passenger door again as he once more pulled further ahead, just out of reach. At last I got in and we hung a left, heading to Route 15. My hat was crooked but my hands were full of Mom's bologna and cheese sandwiches and smashed orange cupcakes.

The olive green wagon rumbled down South Lima Road, belching its way through a bad muffler. We headed over to Geneseo, then on to Batavia, through Tonawanda and, finally, in to Orchard Park and Rich Stadium. The trip was both long and short and I had to pee badly.

It was real!

I was really there!

Rich Stadium was right in front of me.

Cars! My God there were cars everywhere!

I think too it was the first time I said @#*& without being smacked.

There were traffic jams and it was the first time I'd ever seen a police officer directing traffic. Some of the words I heard coming from the drivers who were words I'd only heard coming from the older kids working that South Lima muck.

The parking lot was a city unto itself. I'd never seen so many cars at one time in one place, not even at the Lakeville Drive-Inn. We paid what ever it took to get a spot as far away from the stadium as we possibly could. Scott's $5 resulted in what had to be a seventeen mile walk to the stadium gates.

The stadium was a dot in the distance but we were part of a parade as we, with thousands of others, marched our way toward those gates.

We could hear the roar of the crowd. It grew louder with each of our steps. We could smell the food, and *some* could taste the beer in the air.

"Why does the air smell like Uncle Jim?" I asked sheepishly.

"Uncle Jim's a football fan too, smart ass," Scott barked in reply.

There was music playing from unseen bands. There were shouts and screams by the thousands for numbers I'd only seen on TV.

We made our walk through a mass of Western New Yorkers, up ramps, stairway-to-stairway, going up and down at the same time, until; at last, we found our seats. It was unbelievable. We were just a handful of rows up from the goal posts. We were in the end zone!

WOW! My eyes couldn't take it all in.

Scoreboards! Lights! Music! Even referees!

Our end-zone neighbors welcomed us aboard.

I was wide-eyed and growing accustomed to it all as that day would and did forever change me. Just then, as the seats began to fill up, a slow rumbling roar exploded, running east to west and north to south at the same time. It was a signal to us Rich Stadium rookies to rise.

I remember I was sitting there surrounded by the end zone veterans and confused by that roar as my brother grabbed my head and forced it toward the tunnel. The roar *was* a signal. *They* were coming out. The game had been made real for me.

"Look," he said. "There's J.D. Hill and Jim Braxton, and Joe Ferguson is over there. See, he just took off his jacket!" There was Paul Seymour and Bobby Chandler talking to Lou Saban as John Leypoldt kicked right at us.

"Is that Bobby Moore?" I asked Scott.

"Yes, it's Ahmad Rashad now, I think," he said.

"Joe DeLamielleure. He'll go somewhere *that's* for sure," a retired high school hero behind us bragged.

My brother turned and nodded.

There was Montler, McKenzie and # 32 was right there behind them all.

"Don't *ever* forget 1973, Robbie," my brother demanded.

It was a subtle reminder that what happened just a year earlier with these guys was indeed electric, and something that will mark a cornerstone of the NFL for generations to come.

Scott. I've *never* forgotten 1973 or *that* day in 1974, I assure you. Nor have I forgotten so many other times you shared with your baby brother.

The excitement was tremendous and, just as soon as the cheers began to lessen in intensity, boos started. Then other words came that some parents might deem inappropriate even by today's level of raunchy lyrics and wholesale debauchery.

They came out too! They were running onto the field like they actually stood a chance against our Buffalo Bills. *Those* guys, the New England Patriots, led by Chuck Fairbanks were running onto the field with as arrogant an attitude I hadn't seen since the last Cowboy win. The boos bounced across the chilling Rich Stadium turf as Jim Plunkett tossed wobbly screens to Darryl Stingley and Steve Schubert dropped more than he scooped up.

"We're going to kill 'em," I whispered.

The cheers and the questionable four-letter comments covered my whisper and then soon ended. The teams separated. The national anthem was sung. The captains met at sparring distance. The Patriots won the coin toss; *they* would get the ball first.

A few moments later the crowd roared as if thunder was coming from across that Great Lake. It then engulfed us all as John Leypoldt met the ball. Everyone stood as the kick was returned to the 25-yard line. The first play from scrimmage had arrived. We had to stand on our seats just to see.

Plunkett came to the line and barked commands.

"It's going to Reggie Rucker I bet," my brother declared.

There was shifting. Jim Plunkett was pointing this way and that way. Then BAM! It was under way. That guy Hannah pulled and it was *BAM* all right. Sam "The Bam" Cunningham with a quick hit was in the Bills secondary.

A gasp arose from Rich Stadium. Krakau will get him. No! Well, Robert James was right there! It wasn't to be, as the first play from scrimmage saw Sam Cunningham sprint 75 yards, giving the Patriots the lead, just seconds into the game.

I was heart broken. This was not something I had expected. I swallowed hard. I could hear the jeers of my lunchroom mates as they all pointed to their TV screens and laughed as my team was getting whooped.

Sam Cunningham had taken the air out of Rich Stadium and took a degree of juvenile pomposity out of me with that run down the sideline. We all sat briefly to collect ourselves. No fear though, we have # 32. The crowd thought and hoped as one as the whisper around the stadium affirmed that there was plenty of time left.

John Smith kicked off and we were given our turn. We all stood again as Joe Ferguson barked commands of his own. We would be fine as our Bills danced the 32 Waltz down the field.

It was O.J. left, O.J. right and Braxton up the middle behind Green, Foley and Montler. First down after first down, and then, with a quick flick of the wrist, Joe Ferguson hit tight end Paul Seymour and the Bills delivered their comeback blow.

With I-told-you-so glee, I laughed back at the faces of my lunchroom mates, even harder as our defense stood strong against the Patriots attempted rebuttal.

It was our turn again and the offensive line turned the power on, as we all knew they would. I watched as, a few moments later, Ferguson delivered to O.J., and he gave us a 29-yard touchdown sideline dash. Leypoldt was blocked though.

Before the 1st quarter was over the Bills had another and a commanding 20 to 7 lead. I sat back and with a hotdog filled face, laughed at my Livonia Elementary lunchroom peers.

Lake Erie began to wail as the first half bounced toward a happy conclusion. The temperature was dropping and I had to go to the bathroom every five minutes. We stood to get a quick jump on concessions and that inevitable beer rush.

We heard a roar as we crept down the ramp. I saw the catch of what could have only been a play action pass by Ferguson. The result a 40-yard catch and run by the former Wolverine Paul Seymour. O.J. had established the run and now the passing game was working. It was going to be a glorious Monday morning.

We had a 27-14 half-time lead. We were going to kill ‘em as I’d so declared upon first taking my seat. Pride and fellowship enveloped hotdogs, beer, and urinals alike, as we too were given a fifteen-minute respite.

The second half began as a sense of euphoria had overcome most of us. The game was a one, two, three punt by both teams, our nerves began to be tested. Could we hold on?

The Patriots came close as Sam Cunningham scored his 3rd touchdown of the day and, with a last second toss to Reggie Rucker, the Patriots made it seem closer then it was.

We waited for the final whistle. It came and we received what we had hoped for, what our pride knew we would have. We had won and I'd known we would all along. The Bills came out on top, 30-28, thanks to the toe of John Leypoldt.

That day was my first NFL game in person. It was a memorable day because of the game and because it wouldn't be long before my brother Scott left home for good and my role as little brother forever changed.

That particular year, 1974, the Buffalo Bills would finish 9-5, making the playoffs for the first time since the merger. They fell however, to the eventual Super Bowl Champions Pittsburgh Steelers in the divisional playoffs.

That *one* October day will never be forgotten. It is so crystal clear and that excitement that ten-year-old boy felt comes back each time I set foot into an NFL stadium. Each time, perhaps only for a brief moment, I'm taken back to that October day when that nearsighted boy sat laughing alongside his brother.

I would sit in those end zone seats several more times with Scott and once, years later, with my Dad. Memories of those special moments with them hold greater importance now as my walk has begun to slow. My Dad is now many years passed, and time and distance has, to some degree, separated my brother and I. Yet the memories given that ten-year-old boy all those years ago stand strong as my brother and I watch each other grow increasingly gray.

I share with you some nice memories for me as a kid. Those moments are filled with love, respect and tremendous happiness. I also share with you the type of reverence for some of the real greats I saw play the game on those Sunday afternoons. They were my heroes and, I dare to suggest, probably your heroes too.

It is now my turn to give a little something back to the players of yesterday who did so much for me. To the memory of Jim Braxton, Bobby Chandler and John Leypoldt and all those who made Sunday afternoons like no other time in America's sports scene - this story is about and for you.

The Bills Are Due will show how, through fan support, the Buffalo Bills of the AFL became the Buffalo Bills of the NFL.

The Bills Are Due will show you how the NFL seemingly is just for profit now. Greed now rules the league. It's become a profit now at the expense of everything and let the chips fall where they may style of business. "To hell with player, fan, city and history," Roger Goodell and Gene Upshaw are saying for the sake of this profit.

This book will show that, yes, corporate money is nice but it is ultimately the fans that bring the game to a city and keeps the team in a city. If the league reaches a point where the franchise city no longer matters to the NFL, will the cities themselves become free agents? Can a franchise be put up to the highest bidder? I want you to learn, laugh and remember.

This book is written to get those concerns out to those who may not be aware. The Bills Are Due has also been written to entertain you in perhaps ways that no football book has before. Come with me and relive yesterday.

So without further delay let us, just for a handful of moments return to my first NFL game, October 20, 1974, The Buffalo Bills vs. The New England Patriots. Tight end Paul Seymour scored two touchdowns that day, the first two of his career. It turned out that Paul would score only three in his career; his best NFL day was *that* day when my brother and I sat in those end zone seats of Rich Stadium.

Chapter 2
Paul Seymour

"Virgil Caine is the name, and I served on the Danville train.
'Till Stonewall's cavalry came and tore up the tracks again..."(1)
-Joan Baez-

Paul Seymour came from one of the great football families in the state of Michigan. His brother, Jim, was a receiver at Notre Dame and still holds the school record for most receiving yards in a game, 276 yards with 3 touchdowns. Paul's cousin, Phil, was a defensive standout at the University of Michigan as well.

Paul Seymour, as mentioned, is a University of Michigan alumnus so as I prepared for our sit down, I thought it would be wise if I didn't bring up, in any way, shape or form, the greatest upset in the history of College football, Appalachian State's defeat of Paul's beloved Wolverines which had taken place on opening day 2007.

Paul, Michigan doesn't have to play the Mountaineers this year do they?

Oh, shit. I hope not! Is that the first question you have Rob? Nothing better?

Yeah, Paul, I have a few but I had to ask it. There is no Michigan on the Mountaineer's schedule next season by the way.

Good. I know Reggie wants to play them every homecoming for the next hundred years, but I'd sooner never seen them again. That was an ugly, ugly day!

Michigan, finished up okay, 8 and 4?

Yes. They won the Capital One Bowl in Orlando.

You're a native of Michigan?

I am, I grew up as a kid in Royal Oak listening to folk music and became an old man listening to folk music. Older, I should say.

Folk music?

I love it. Why?

I thought you would be a Purple Haze or Grand Funk Railroad guy, something like that.

Oh *no* folk music is it. Michigan, I *love* Michigan - born, raised and retired here. I grew *up* in Royal Oak, a Detroit suburb. Royal Oak had quite a history. You're a history guy, right Rob?

My major was in history.

Royal Oak didn't become a city until the twenties. There was a Catholic priest who lived and worked there, but the town was Protestant and was pissed off at some of the things he was doing. So the KKK, who was active there, just went over and burned his church down. In those days when the KKK wanted to scare the shit out of people, they burned things down. I think his name was Coughlin. He raised money on his radio show to build a new church. Burning his church down didn't calm him down any and his radio show became popular all over the country, but he was really pissing people off. He was against everybody. The Vatican even told him to shut up at one point.

(In researching Charles Coughlin, I discovered he had a radio show that each week had millions of listeners. His political views began to be seen as Anti-Semitic, essentially blaming the Jewish people for the state of affairs in Europe. To some degree, it appeared he was supporting Adolph Hitler. When FDR took office, Coughlin did support some of his early New Deal reforms but later became more anti-administration in tone. Roosevelt believed in freedom of speech but believed it was limited when it came to the public airways. New regulations and on-air restrictions eventually forced Coughlin off the air).

What did you do as a kid?

A kid?

Yeah.

I slept, ate, watched TV.

Thanks, real informative Paul.

I liked being a kid and I did what kids do. I played. I loved all sports - basketball, baseball. I never stopped growing though. I liked basketball a lot. I attended Royal Oak High School. I was as big as I am now almost, 6-4, 6-5 maybe, and I played wide receiver. But thought basketball was the direction I would go.

You were big for a high school wide receiver.

Yes I was. When they threw to me, I caught it. I was used mostly as a blocker though. High schools never did throw the ball much then and when I blocked someone they went down.

You were a blocking receiver?

That's true. I could run a route and knock someone on his ass at the same time long before I got to Michigan.

You know, when I was a kid-playing ball in the backyard, I was a big fat kid, I pretended to be "Bubba" Smith, when we played. Who did you admire or want to be like?

Bubba Smith! You *were* huge Rob.

A belly- jiggling pro I was.

I followed the Lions, of course, being from Detroit. What else, right? I wanted to be like Bobby Layne, Yale Lary and Tobin Rote. He was there, too, when they won the title in 1957. Ron Kramer was from the University of Michigan so I followed him, both when he was with the Packers and Lions. When we could, we'd watch the Browns on television. The Browns always seemed to win. Around that time Jim Brown was taking over the league. Folks would watch the Browns, just to see what Jim Brown did.

I watched those players and I tried to take in what they were doing on the field and use it during my high school years. I tried anyway.

Did you like school or was it something to do while waiting for the next game?

High school was okay. I didn't shine with the grades but did pretty well on the football field and with the girls, of course.

You know Paul I was a stud myself, so hot no girl ever came near me.

That's hot all right.

When did colleges start coming around looking to recruit you?

My senior year, maybe my junior, I started to hear from them. One day at practice my coach, Al Fracassa, came to me and said there was a scout from the University of Buffalo who wanted to talk to me about coming to Buffalo to play football. I must have had a dumb look on my face, because the coach asked me what's wrong.

Buffalo! What's a Buffalo? "Where is Buffalo," I asked coach. I'm pretty sure I was serious too. I had no idea where Buffalo was. Coach told me just go talk to them. *Be* polite, just talk to them and see what they have to say.

"All right," I said.

I went over and talked to him, found out where Buffalo was and said I wasn't interested. I knew I wanted to stay in Michigan. Reggie (McKenzie) and I were both recruited by Michigan's "Bump" Elliott; we were part of his last recruiting class. "Bo" Schembechler would inherit Reggie and me.

There was no other school that interested you?

Oh sure there was. I'd briefly considered Michigan State. Joe D. and I played against each other in high school and he was there. We'd known each other since we were kids. He went there but it was going to be Michigan for me.

Did you play much as a freshman?

No. As a freshman I wasn't allowed to play. We weren't eligible so I was third string behind Jim Mandich.

I stood around as a sophomore, too, in 1969. With Mandich and Dan Dierdof there, I didn't get much of an opportunity then either. In 1970, Jim Mandich was drafted by the Dolphins so I was given some play as a tight end and got some work at the split end position too. In 1971, my junior year, I was given my chance. The St. Louis Cardinals had drafted Dan Dierdorf in the 2nd round. He was the first from Michigan to go in the draft that year so both Reggie and I started.

Was your first year a good one?

It *was* a good year. We knocked the shit out of some teams that year.

I saw that in five games in 1971, you outscored your opponents 264-14. What the hell is that? Have you ever felt guilty about whooping up on those teams that year?

Hell no, Rob. It was great. Our defense was probably ranked number one in the country. Reggie had made All-American and we were undefeated going into the Rose Bowl.

How did the Rose Bowl turn out for you?

You know how it turned out Rob. That day sucked. We lost to Stanford by 1 point, a last second field goal.

In 1972, Reggie was gone and "Bo" moved me to right tackle. He told me that he believed I had a better chance at making it in the pros as a tackle rather than a tight end. I disagreed with him. I liked "Bo" though, so I did what he wanted.

1972 was still a good year, 11-1 overall. You were All-Conference and All-American. When did you think you had that shot at the NFL?

I don't think a lot of folks know this but my older brother, Jim, had played at Notre Dame and was drafted number ten in the 1st round of the 1969 NFL draft, the same year O.J. was drafted. Jim referred me to an agent and he presented my case to a couple of teams. I went in the 1st round of the 1973 draft. I don't know for sure but Jim and I may be the only brothers who were both drafted in the 1st round.

Did you receive any letter from NFL teams, saying that you might be drafted?

Nope. Nothing. I just got a call afterwards telling me I'd been drafted, saying it was Buffalo. So I was off to Buffalo as their *first* pick. I didn't want to play there in college but as a pro I'd make the move. It was a good thing that college scout, way back when, told me where Buffalo was because that's where I was headed. It was ironic thinking about it. I didn't want to go there after high school but it seemed the city was bound and determined to see my face.

Did you know what you were getting into in Buffalo?

I did. I looked to see what they had and couldn't help but get excited. I saw that we could be good and have fun at the same time. I gave it some thought and realized that Reggie McKenzie was already playing there and that O.J. Simpson was in the backfield. It was easy; I was looking forward to it. I was looking forward to reuniting with my old college teammate and with Joe DeLamielleure coming from Michigan State; it was going to be a hell of a time. It was like a reunion in a way.

You guys turned out okay.

Yeah, we did all right.

Rob, I have to tell you this story. It started my first day of training camp. There was this guy named Joe L. Sullivan who came to camp that year as a free agent. Joe didn't look like much of a ball player either. He dropped everything thrown to him and kicked to him. He couldn't block and never ran out of a tackle, so he was cut, obviously.

The next year camp started and in walks Joe. He looked in even worse shape than the year before and we just rolled our eyes. During camp he dropped everything and had the crap knocked out of him over and over, so Joe was cut.

The *next* year camp started. All the rookies and free agents were there and sure enough, there sat Joe Sullivan. I couldn't believe it so I walked up to him and said, "Joe, what the shit are you doing? You know you're not going to make it. Why are you here?" I've never forgotten his answer;

"Oh, I *know* I'm not going to make it. This just gets me out of the house, and besides, I like drinking with you guys."

Unbelievable.

Shit. I've never forgotten Joe. I sometimes wonder where he ended up.

I can think of better ways to spend my summer other than having Jim Cheyunski knock the shit out of me just for fun. For the Bills to get a high pick in 1973, 1972 had to be a bad year. It was, 4-9-1.

No, it wasn't too good.

Looking at the numbers from 1972 - Dennis Shaw threw for over 1,600 yards but had 17 interceptions, J.D. Hill had nearly eight hundred receiving yards. Lou Saban was back and he was putting a good team in place so the next couple of years could be good ones. Because of the 1972 finish, the Bills had a number of high picks. They took you and Joe DeLamielleure in the 1st round, and with their 3rd pick they chose the quarterback out of Arkansas, Joe Ferguson.

I guess I'd say I'm happy they had a bad season in 1972, because I, at least in a small way, am part of the history of the league. I signed with the Bills. It was a *huge* contract too - $30,000 signing bonus and a base salary of $23,500. My first year, 1973, couldn't have been better. Well, we could have beaten the Dolphins but regardless it still turned out great.

You said coming to Buffalo was like a reunion?

Yes, it was. The situation was that we three - Joe, Reggie and I - knew each other. Joe and I played each other in high school and for both of us to go in the 1st round, to the same team *was* pretty cool. We were all from Detroit and knew each other going damn near back to elementary school.

You could play a couple of positions. Where did you fit in under Lou Saban?

I had played tight end in high school and in my first couple years at Michigan, but in my junior year I was moved over to tackle. The Bills though seemed to be looking for an addition to their offensive line, so my experience as a big receiver who could block down field came in handy.

Jan White had retired as tight end and the Bills were effectively without one, so, shortly after the start of training camp, Lou told me that I would be their tight end. He knew I could block and catch and that I was flexible. That might account for me being such a high first round draft choice that year.

With O.J. Simpson in the backfield and the game plan being the run, I understood that I was going to be a more or less a third tackle and occasionally serve as a safety valve receiver. As a rookie, that would suit me just fine.

How long did it take for the offense to realize that 1973 could be special?

We, the offensive line, knew that we were going to be good in 1973. All we had to do was to look at the guy next to us and we knew we were going to be entertaining to say the least. Reggie, Joe, Donnie, Foley, Montler. What a group. It was my rookie year but, with the line the Bills already had in place, *it* could be a championship team. With the others such as Bobby Chandler and J.D. Hill, we were telling the defenses around the league to stop us. That's all they had to do was stop us.

We all fit together great. We had Joe starting at quarterback, rookie or not. He won the job after a couple of games and we felt comfortable with him back there. Anyway, he had O.J. in the backfield. O.J. had the best blocking back ever to play the game, Jimmie Braxton, back there too. I *really* miss him. He was one of the best lead blockers I ever saw, and he died way too young.

So was the game plan from the first day of training camp simply the run?

Yes, it was. We knew what Lou was all about. We liked Joe Ferguson but the game plan for 1973 was clear - run, run and run some more. With the line we had and O.J. in the backfield, shit, why not run the ball. Our first game in'73, O.J. ran for over two hundred yards, maybe two hundred and fifty or more, against the Patriots so the potential was there from that first game.

Our focus that year, like every team, was to win each game. We lost both games to the Dolphins, of course. It pissed everybody off, but after the halfway point in the season, we beat Kansas City, we were 5-2 and O.J. had already gained over a thousand yards.

Was there a time when the line said 2,000 was possible?

I don't know of one such moment, but we all silently knew that we could do just that. Reggie, I think, went around shouting; "Two grand, two grand!"

Did Lou Saban change the game plan at any point when the possibility of a two thousand yard season for O.J. became a possibility?

No, Lou kept everything the way he had planned it right from the start of training camp. We were going to run and run and run. Every now and then Bobby, J.D. or I would catch one but we were going to be a running team.

After beating Kansas City at the halfway point, we felt good for a couple of days because we had a shot at the playoffs. But, POW! We had a three game losing streak and were 5-5 with just four games left. We finished with four wins and a 9-5 record. It was in week thirteen, when we beat the Patriots, that we believed, or, *I* really believed, that O.J. could get two thousand yards the following week against the New York Jets. He'd need a good game.

That next week, against the Jets, we had a lot to think about - playoffs, keeping O.J. healthy, breaking Jim Brown's record and going for 2,000. O.J. was going to need another two hundred yard day to break 2,000 and everything turned out the way it was supposed to, I guess. I wish we had made the playoffs though.

The Jets were having a hard year but they still had Namath and John Riggins. They always played hard and we still had to win for a chance at the playoffs. I remember the atmosphere. It was New York

City. There was all the national attention being paid to the game. It was drizzling and the field was a snow and slush covered mess.

O.J. needed sixty yards to catch Jim Brown and on our first drive he gained almost of all of that. It was on our second drive, a sweep, when Joe D. pulled and I threw a chop block, a chop block is like throwing your body into a tree, it knocked the stars out of me, but O.J. got it. He had broken Jim Browns record and we had most of the 1st quarter to still go.

Looking at that game, the 1st quarter ended in a tie. Then O.J. had a touchdown and Bill Cahill had a punt return for a score, giving the Bills a lead at half time. Jim Braxton put you up 28-7. When did the 2,000 yards begin to loom?

I think Joe Ferguson was told by a public relations guy on the sidelines that O.J. needed fifty, or so, for two thousand and Joe told us. We went out and O.J. got it with a couple of minutes left in the 4th. It took some time for us, me, I guess I shouldn't talk for the other guys, to understand that it was part of history. I was just a young rookie.

1973 was a team effort and I really mean team. The lead blocker for O.J. was Jim Braxton. As I said earlier, he was one of the greatest unrecognized full backs in the history of the NFL. I don't know if 2,003 yards would have been possible if Jimmy hadn't been the lead blocker once O.J reached the outside.

Did you think that 2,003 yards was just the first step for the Bills in the years to come?

We hoped so. We missed the playoffs in '73, however. The Steelers were the wild card team, if I remember correctly. Some of the guys did think that we sacrificed a win in exchange for the record. I don't know about that.

I have heard that before so I looked at the losses that year. Only one was by three points or less and that was to Cincinnati so run or pass wouldn't have mattered in a three touch down loss, I don't think.

We wanted to win and were pissed if we didn't.

Most of us had come from the Big-Ten and in that conference the run game was the primary way of moving the ball. These guys came to the NFL as well-seasoned run block specialists. Coming into the NFL with a couple of years run blocking experience in major college football would mean a great deal to a team that had O.J. Simpson in its backfield. With me being turned back into a tight-end, I knew that, more or less, I'd primarily be used as a third tackle, an additional blocker for O.J. and Jim Braxton. No one could stop us.

Jim Braxton was a great guy, a great teammate and a friend to everyone. O.J. and the Bills were damn lucky to have him. Jim wasn't always healthy but, when he was, I don't think there was anyone better then Jim.

I remember one game against the Steelers. The play was to have our line split at the tackle and guard with Jim being the lead block up the middle with O.J. behind him. Jimmie went through and knocked Joe Green right on his ass, in no uncertain terms. *That* was pretty cool, so we ran it again and again, pissing Joe Green off all day long. Jim was a great guy to have around on and off the field. I miss him a lot. Too many died way too young - Jim, Bobby Chandler, John Leypoldt, our kicker. Way too young.

That's true. I remember how old I felt when Walter Payton, or Johnny Unitas or Lyle Alzado died. What is your memory of O.J.?

O.J. was an okay guy. He was a good teammate and certainly shared the credit for that 1973 season with all of us. He was good about that but, overall, he was a decent guy, until he started to get too full of himself.

Your best year was 1975?

Statistically Rob it probably was 1975. I was still being used primarily as a third tackle and O.J. ran for nearly 1,900 yards. I ended that season with twenty receptions and about three hundred yards. But I began to see the writing on the wall and 1976 was a real ugly year. We won two games, and then went on a ten game losing streak. It was getting near the end for me, and my feet were getting real bad. Jim Ringo replaced Lou before the season was over in 1977. During those two years, I think, we only won a total of five games. Bobby Chandler was the go to guy. I think I had only a couple of catches in '77; we were in a rebuilding phase, to say the least.

Chuck Knox came in 1978.

Yeah, that was to be all for me. My feet were bad and the artificial turf wasn't helping. Getting stepped on by everyone all those years didn't help either. I knew 1978 was going to be bad news; Chuck Knox came over from the Rams and became head coach.

You went off to the Steelers?

Yeah. Chuck Knox and I didn't get along and he traded me to the Pittsburgh Steelers for Frank Lewis. The Steelers gave me a chance. They waited to see if I could pass the physical but I couldn't and so I was done.

Back to Michigan?

Yup. Back to Michigan. After football, I was lucky to find a job that put up with me for over twenty years until they decided one day that I was no longer needed as much as I thought I was.

We've all had jobs like that. That's why I choose to remain gainfully unemployed. Any thoughts about the Bills eventually moving to Toronto?

That would be a sad time. Buffalo is a great city. Yes, Buffalo is a small market, maybe too small for the NFL in today's world, but let's face it, it's all about money. I would think that the NFL wouldn't want a team lost to Canada though, but I wouldn't be surprised that sometime soon Las Vegas isn't awarded a team.

The Las Vegas Bills?

Sure why not. But Buffalo is a great city and I want the Bills to stay there. The Buffalo Bills are so much part of the league's history. When I was a high school kid, I struggled to find Buffalo on a map. Now I can't get back there enough. I love the fans, the games; we raised a lot of hell at times, some I can share and many that will probably never be shared. But I will give you one more. We were coming back from a road game - New England I think. It was raining. We came off the plane. The busses were to one side and the police escort cars with all their flashing lights were to the other side. We were getting onto the busses when, all of a sudden, J.D. Hill had sneaked off, hopped into one of the cop cars and, with lights flashing, drove it all over the Buffalo airport with a dozen pissed off cops following him. It's hard to believe he did that back then. J.D. is a preacher now out in Arizona.

To be part of history, part of *The Electric Company,* I am really proud of that. I am back here in Buffalo as often as I can be, for signings, alumni weeks or just visiting old grounds. I love the place especially now that I can find it on a map.

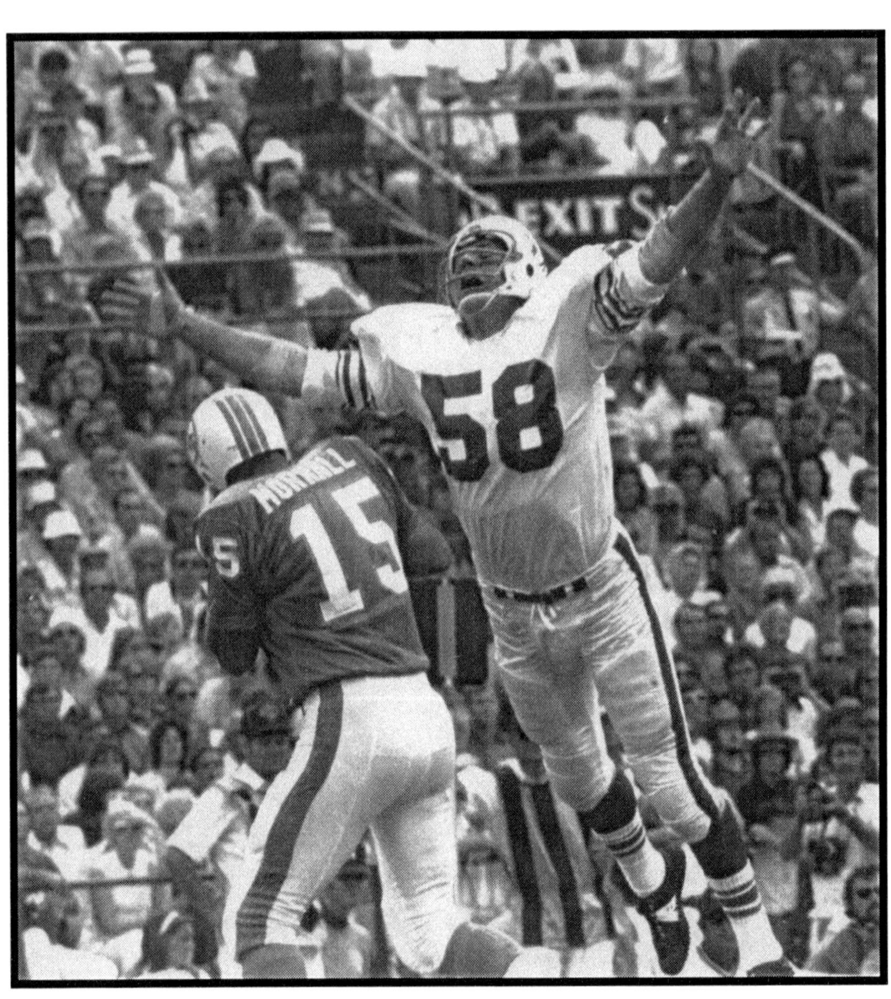
EXIT
58
15

Chapter 3
Mike Stratton

"We don't hire linebackers that aren't mean."
-Buster Ramsey -
Time Magazine December 1957 (1)

The National Football League had been successful in defeating their first challenger in the post war years, the All American Football Conference or AAFC. I will be brief but you should know the AAFC was formidable. It was the AAFC that gave Buffalo their first professional team of note the Buffalo Bisons owned by James Breuil of Frontier Oil. The AAFC had many great players most notable were Otto Graham, Lou Groza and Dante Lavelli all from the Cleveland Browns. The Browns were without question the best of AAFC teams. The AAFC did force the NFL to expand and just prior to 1950 three teams were admitted to the NFL, the Cleveland Browns, Baltimore Colts and the San Francisco 49ers. To learn more about the AAFC I encourage you to read Pigskin by Robert W. Peterson.

The NFL establishment showed little respect for the AAFC. There was *an* ego that came from the NFL that showed they were not susceptible to challenge. That chip was knocked off their shoulders by the AAFC as three teams, now historical in their own rights became part of the NFL. The AAFC showed that the NFL could be challenged but it showed too that something was missing, perhaps marketing *was* that something. Marketing of professional sports forever changed when television was introduced. It is simple business, but the demand for entertainment increased as more people began to be entertained by not only television, but also radio, the movies, music and much more.

A sport is entertainment and football was approaching baseball as the top game across the nation. Television and football were wed and the demand for football grew. The demand for expanding the NFL began in the late 1950s. The NFL said no once again, the NFL was a good old boys club, however, once gain, a group of businessmen took it upon themselves to challenge the NFL. Led by Lamar Hunt from Texas the American Football League was born in 1959 and Ralph Wilson, a Detroit businessman was granted a franchise for the city of Buffalo. The AFL though greatest of challengers to the NFL but in my opinion would never have succeeded if not for television.

Buffalo had their team. Ralph Wilson only had to look to the sidelines of the Detroit Lions for his first coach, “Buster” Ramsey. During his stints as a defensive line coach with the Cardinals “Buster” is credited with inventing the linebacker blitz. Until this point, only linemen would blitz, he called it the *red dog*. “The object of the red dog was simple,” he said. “You either the sack the quarterback or rush the pass plays, sending more rushers than the offensive line can handle.” Ralph Wilson hired Ramsey as the Bills first coach.

The 1960 season would be fourteen games long with the Bills opening up against the New York Titans at the Polo Grounds in New York. Sammy Baugh coached the Titans at the time and they allowed the Bills only nine first downs and a total of 113 yards, with 39 total passing yards in that first game, resulting in a loss 27-3. The defense was respectable that season as they concluded the season with 49 total turnovers, 6 games with five or more, and 8 turnovers in a November game against the Los Angeles Chargers and their quarterback Jack Kemp. The Bills, with their first year behind them, had a third place finish in the division with a 5-8-1 record.

The second AFL draft was held in November and concluded in December of 1960 after a total of thirty rounds. The Bills selected third that year with Ken Rice, out of Auburn, as their first pick and Billy Shaw, from Georgia Tech, their second selection. Remember that the reason the AFL drafted early was to get a jump-start on the NFL. The NFL, though, also drafted many of the same players the AFL had, thus leaving it up to the player to decide where they would play. An example is, Billy Shaw was drafted in the later rounds of the NFL draft by the Dallas Cowboys but chose to go to Buffalo because he could play guard.

The first couple of seasons saw the Bills with a combined 11-16-1 record so in 1962 a new assistant came to the Buffalo Bills from the Boston Patriots, Lou Saban. His job was to build a winner, pure and simple. Lou Saban had his eyes set on Glenn Glass a wide receiver from the University of Tennessee. Glass was capable of playing both defensive back and flanker. The Bills took Glass as their second pick in that 1962 draft and the Chicago Bears of the NFL drafted Glass in the 17th round. The Bills wanted Glass in Buffalo badly and they knew that in order to prevent him from going to the NFL, additional voices of encouragement were needed. In hopes of getting Glass to come to Buffalo, the Bills drafted another Tennessee Volunteer, Mike Stratton.

Rob I guess "Buster" was using me as bait.

The story makes it sound that way. How are things in Tennessee, Mike?

Beautiful as usual, Rob.

Tennessee is one of my most favorite places. I love the Smokey's that's for sure. Were you born there in Tellico Plains?

No. Actually I was born in Vonore, a little town that sits on the Tennessee River.

Vonore. That is not far from North Carolina is it?

No sir it's not far at all. It's about twenty-five miles up the river road to North Carolina.

What did you do growing up? I know what I would have done there in small town Tennessee.

Oh, we did everything. I don't remember the war much but I was coming of age when the '50s got rolling. I fished, hunted, played from sun up to sunset and, when I had nothing else to do, I did go to school. Rob, Tellico was a very small area. The big city was up the river thirty miles or so away. We did what kids do, or used to do anyway. We'll never see days like those again in *this* video-game age, I guess. We didn't even get our first TV until I was a junior in high school, in 1956. I remember that when we didn't have a TV, we would have to walk up the streets to the neighbor's house to watch it there. They loved to watch wrestling, so that and Groucho Marx are what I saw.

School when used properly can be a productive hobby. Growing up in a small town myself I know what you mean. Did you go to Tellico Plains High School?

Yes I did, it wasn't real big either.

Did you play both ways?

I sure did. You had to in those days. We had to play ways in high school. We only had eighteen of us so on the team so we had to play everything.

You played tight end, right?

Yes, tackle, defensive end and special teams I played every position it seemed. Bill Spurling was my head coach in high school. One day when I was a senior, he said he was going to take me up to Knoxville, and we weren't going to leave without a scholarship. I thought that, since he was also a Baptist preacher, he would have to ask forgiveness for such a far-fetched wish.

It worked out well though.

Yes sir, it did.

Were any other colleges looking at you then?

No, I don't think so, Tennessee was my choice.

Who was the coach at Tennessee then?

Bowden Wyatt. He had come from Wyoming.

Could you start as a freshman?

No one could as freshman. We played three freshman games of our own. Then the next year, the sophomore year, you were eligible for the varsity. If I recall correctly, Bowden's biggest win at Tennessee was against LSU. We had stopped Billy Cannon late in the game. That ended an almost two year winning streak for the Tigers. My time at Tennessee was great. I really liked it. I liked the environment, I wanted a good education and I was getting that, plus playing a game I loved was a big plus.

Mike, you told me the story about your first talk with Lou Saban.

Yeah. It was just after my final game as a senior. We had finished up at Vanderbilt and I received a call from Lou Saban. The AFL was going to have an early draft that year to get a jump-start on the NFL. I had gotten from Lou saying that the Buffalo Bills had drafted me.

Did that come as a surprise?

Yes it did; it really did.

You were drafted in the 13th round that year.

Yes. I think I was 13B. I didn't even make the A squad. Lou Saban was more interested in getting Glenn Glass, our wide receiver to come to Buffalo.

Glass was the second pick that year behind only Ernie Davis.

Yea he was. Lou felt that I might be able to add some encouragement in getting Glenn to sign with the Bills. Glenn *did* sign but, because of injuries in college, it just didn't work out for him there. He did get along, though, with "Buster" Ramsey, the Bills' first coach and when "Buster" left the Bills he eventually picked him up at both Philadelphia and Pittsburgh. Glenn ended up playing defensive back. Come to think about it I think "Buster" was the one responsible for drafting me. Lou Saban was the player personnel guy at the time.

They both wanted you to encourage Glenn to come to Buffalo. I think you were bait Mike.

Bait might be too harsh Rob but I think "Buster" and Lou wanted me to do what I could to encourage Glenn to come to Buffalo.

What other teams were considering you?

I don't think any were. I was banged up and on crutches when I got that phone call from Lou Saban. He said that the Buffalo Bills wanted to draft me. He said he was at the airport and he wanted to talk to me for a few minutes. Could I meet him there at one of the hotels? So I borrowed a buddy's car, drove to the hotel and met with Lou. He was understandably concerned when he saw me get out of the car on crutches. I had to reassure him that it was only a sprain and that I'd be okay in a couple of days. "Mike, we want you to play in Buffalo," Lou told me.

"Okay," I said. We talked and when I left him at the airport, we had an agreement that I would show up in Buffalo on the first day of training camp that summer.

Out of Glass, Davis and you, you'd be the only one to actually play for the Bills.

Yes sir I was.

So there were no such things as mini-camps and voluntary conditioning?

Oh, no. We were given a date, told to be there on that day and that's when we showed up.

Just a few months earlier "Buster" Ramsey had been the head coach of the Bills. That's whom I thought I'd be playing for. When I get there, however, I found out that "Buster" was gone and Lou Saban was the new head coach.

I looked at the AFL drafts of 1960 and 1961 and it seemed that the Bills were looking to build an offense. The number of halfback and offensive line selections were high compared to defensive picks. Did you have an idea of what direction they would be going?

Well, it's hard to tell. Scouting back then was a lot different. I'm sure they had a spot for me. I hoped they did anyway. I was just happy to get a shot at playing anywhere, but "Buster" was gone when I got to Buffalo that summer.

Do you remember what that first day was like?

Oh, yes. It's hard to forget. I got up to Buffalo that first day of camp and there were over a hundred of us competing for thirty-three spots. Teams weren't allowed to have more than that. With that large number, there wasn't even enough equipment for everyone so we had to go out onto the field in shifts.

So you shared equipment?

Yeah. They had a group that went out at 9:00. Then when they came off, we'd go out at 10:30 or so. When someone came off, we had to fight for pads and helmets that fit, and most times *nothing* fit real well.

Did you have any idea what role you might have with the team?

No I didn't. When I get to camp in July, Lou Saban had been promoted to head coach and the team was divided up into groups, - veterans, draftees and free agents. It was tackles here, receivers over there and linebackers in another line. I walked around and went up to Lou. I asked where he wanted me and he had *no idea* who I was, none what so ever. He said, "Kid, just go ahead and get in any line." They didn't even have me listed on any roster. *That* didn't give me a lot of hope but I was determined to show that that I could play.

Training camp was based, I think, out of the Roycroft Inn, and we practiced at Knox Polo Field. I don't know for sure but we were in East Aurora at that time. That first day, many of us just stood around throwing the ball back and forth in the parking lot, waiting to be told what to do next.

I was trying everything - tight end, offensive tackle, defensive tackle. I just wanted to show Lou I could play and was willing to play *anywhere* I could to get a job, so, I did my best to get out onto the practice field anytime I could.

I began to look around the next few days and saw that when the Bills added Ernie Warlick, who had all those great years in the Canadian league, I wasn't going to get much of a chance to catch any balls as tight end. They tried me at defensive end for a while. I was okay, but when a bunch of linebackers started to drop by the wayside, they moved me to linebacker. I became a linebacker with the hands and speed of a receiver.

The rest I guess is what football folks call history. I was a linebacker with the instincts of a tight end. I could watch the quarterback's eyes like a receiver, so my ability to anticipate a throw helped me in getting a real quick six interceptions in my first year.

Did you wish in those early days that you had gone to the NFL?

Rob, as I mentioned, I was just so elated to be playing anywhere in pro-football and Lou Saban *did* give me a chance to play, but not at tight end. That disappointed me some because I'd been a tight end in college and thought I was pretty good at it.

Things might have been a lot different if you had been a tight end instead of a linebacker. Keith Lincoln might have appreciated you playing a different position.

Yeah, probably so. The AFL was just the right thing for a guy like me because it gave so many of us a chance to play. Our defense just played so well together and it was coming together all at the right time.

I remember this one time; maybe it was in '64 or 1965, I can't remember the exact year. We were good as a team. We had some *real* good years. We *had* the championship, so one time, Harry Jacobs, John Tracey and I decided that we were entitled to a raise and we were going to sit out until we got it. Sitting out awaiting a raise was different in 1964 than now.

Mike Stratton was a hold out? Did you get what you were looking for?

Well, we all decided that we were going to ask for $1,500 dollars and Ralph didn't respond. Then we asked for $1,000 and still nothing from Ralph. Then we asked for $500. Ralph Wilson came and handed us each $500 and we all went back out onto the field.

So you guys held out for $500? Well, you guys already had at least one ring so Ralph could've come up with an extra five hundred for you.

Yup we thought so too.

That isn't exactly like these twenty-three year olds who have accomplished nothing and hold out for millions, is it?

No sir. It was a lot different.

The 1966 AFL Championship game against the Kansas City Chiefs was the Bills third straight title game. Frankly put, that was a pretty ugly game.

That was the Super Bowl I year. You know, Rob, I've never seen the film of *that* game. I would really like to because my memory plays tricks on me sometime. Even though we had some absolutely horrendous plays, I think, overall, we played a good game. If my mind serves me right, we may have sacked Len Dawson 7 or 11 times that day.

They scored first but we came right back on a long throw to someone to whom I don't remember now.

It was Elbert Dubenion.

Yes, Elbert. The Chiefs got the ball and we had them pinned deep when Dawson threw a pass right into the arms of one of our defensive backs that dropped it. *That* play hurt us. Anyway, we lost it, the game. It just didn't seem to be our day. If we had won that game, we would have been better competition for the Packers in the Super Bowl, at least for their style of play. The Packers seemed to be a team that would tell you what they were going to do. They'd almost point to the hole daring you to stop them. Our defense was good enough that we knew we *could* stop them.

I'm a fan in my forties now and I've seen the Bills at all levels of success - 2-12 seasons, the Super Bowls. I've really seen a change in the type of player; the most glaring change I see is what a player expects from the team. Do you think some of the new, younger guys could have competed in your era?

Oh sure, but I also think that, most certainly, some of the players from my time could play today. I think it could go both ways. It is an entirely new ball game now. The most difficult adjustment the players of *today* would have to make playing in our time would be stamina. In my era, there just wasn't any relief. We had to play on a thirty-three-man squad. You had to practice and play hurt. There was no platooning of players in and out. There were no third and short or second-down linebackers then, no short yardage specialists. Stamina would be the biggest problem for a lot of these young guys.

I hadn't looked at it that way; I have seen any number of times that guys are now becoming winded during an extended no huddle drive.

Exactly, and that is with substitutions coming on and off the field.

Mike, you were around in 1968 and 1969 when O.J. came to town. What do you remember of that time?

I remember this one thing maybe more than anything else. In 1968, we had a terrible season. We were getting beat pretty bad right from the first game. Lamonica had handed it to us in the second game of the year when we were in Oakland.

He sure did - 48-6.

That sounds right. Thanks for reminding me Rob. It was the last game of the season and we were playing the Oilers in the Astrodome. We had won only one game that year and had one tie. I think we beat the Jets. It was half time in that last game and I think we were ahead. Even so, our fans booed us as we went into the locker room at half time because, if we had won, we may not have been able to draft O.J. Simpson.

That was unusual, being booed by our fans for being ahead. We *did* accommodate them and lost the game by a few touchdowns. Then we came back in '69 and *O.J.* was there. He was a tremendous athlete, the best runner I have *ever* seen, before *or* since. He was the best the league ever had in ability, strength and, when he wanted to be, he was a pretty good blocker.

Do you think there was a threat of O.J. going to an NFL team in 1968?

If the there were still two drafts in 1968 as there had been in the early years of the AFL, I think there would have been no doubt that O.J. would have gone to an NFL team. I don't know whom but I think he would have gone elsewhere.

I have looked at the NFL season in 1968. The team with the lowest productivity was the 2-12 Atlanta Falcons, so, O.J. could have very well been a Falcon if not for the common draft.

I do think so. Yes.

You even played against Namath a couple of times.

Oh, sure. We would always pick off one or two off of Joe. As a matter of fact, that horrible year in '68, the year we only won one game, that win came against the New York Jets. The year the Jets went on to win Super Bowl III, when Joe made that bold prediction. We got our only win against them.

What do you think of the Bills potentially moving to Toronto?

That would be a real shame. I don't think the NFL wants Buffalo to lose the team but Buffalo is not made of money. The people of Buffalo don't have a real stake in the team, money wise. It's Ralph Wilson's family that has stake in it. Money is what it is all about now. I hope it doesn't happen, but I have to say this that it is all about money now. I am truly fortunate, in many ways. I was truly fortunate to have played my days in Buffalo. We, I, could not have been better treated anywhere else like I was treated in Buffalo. Buffalo is an incredible city. It has incredible people and even today, after all these years, when I come up there, we are treated wonderfully.

What do you remember about Jack Kemp?

I have always been stunned, in a way that Buffalo ended up with Jack Kemp because he is one of the true geniuses of the game. Sid Gilman let Jack slip away on the waiver wire. Jack had a gun for an arm. He could, out and out, hum the ball on a rope.

Rob, Jack Kemp was great. He did it all in the game. We went through some tough years and he had a couple of tough injuries, but he brought Buffalo back-to-back Championships. There was one thing, however, that often made many of us shake our heads. There were times when the game was well in hand and we had just come off the field. We were tired and trying to catch our breath for the last series or two, and Jack would still be flinging the ball around. It was his use of the clock that sometimes aggravated me.

He had seasons with twenty or more interceptions.

That's what I mean. I love Jack but we'd no sooner have our helmets off when he'd be three and out and we were back on the field. You had too many interceptions, Jack. It was never as bad as that, I'm sure. We would never have done what we did without Jack but sometimes Jack; you didn't let us catch our breath.

66

Chapter 4
Billy Shaw

"The heroes of the '60s, like the game itself, seem larger than life size."(1)
-John Facenda-

I should preface the following few pages by saying that Billy Shaw is from Georgia and has, quoting my wife, "the *cutest* of southern drawls." So as you read on, please keep that in mind, as my writing ability will fail to reveal that.

Billy thanks for this. How do you see the NFL of today?

Rob, I loved Buffalo and I think the fans loved us during those years. The affection that we had for each other showed, because we played some pretty *bad* football at times. But the fans *and* many of us were friends and that made it fun. There was a genuine *bond* between the fan and player during that time. I don't know if that exists anymore.

Other than the money and all the peripheral things, is that bond the biggest difference?

I believe so. No doubt the money is unbelievable compared to what we made, but the closeness of the fan and the player is missing. It's nothing like what it was. There were times when I was hurt with a broken nose or banged up leg or something when fans would call the house and ask if I was going to be okay. Sometimes they'd even bring stuff by the house or drop cards off. You'll never see that again.

No, none of that.

No, and it's unfortunate in a way, because it takes away the fan to player bond that *we* had in the championship years.

I remember when I was a kid we had a sense that we were closer to the players than what it seems now. Maybe it was because we knew every player's name year after year. Now everyone wants to be a star. That may account for the loss of interest.

I can see how that's possible now Rob.

How about when you were a kid, ten or so, what did you do?

When I was ten? Shoot that was a long time ago.

At least ten years right?

Yeah, at least. When I look around now at everything, things were so much different than back when I was ten, or when my children or you were ten at your first game, Rob. So much has changed. I grew up in the south and was a teenager during the fifties. Everything was *so* much different. Life for us really was family, church, and school. The outside world was something that didn't really impact us. We couldn't touch the world and it couldn't touch us. That's how we felt.

Like it was for us in South Lima.

I was born in Natchez, Mississippi in 1938, so *I* was ten in 1948. What I grew up on wasn't video games or television. It was my family, church and school. Everyone in town knew each other. When someone was sick we all helped one another. We *all* supported one another when we were having hard, bad times. Then again, when we kids got in trouble, the whole town knew about that too. We had neighbors whooping us before our parents got hold of us.

That wouldn't happen today, would it?

No, it sure wouldn't.

How old were you when you got interested in football?

I was seven when the war ended and, for better or worse, we couldn't go back to being just a small town. There was so much more than football. Football was just a game and not really an interest for most of us. The NFL was the pro league everyone spoke of and, every now. But in Mississippi, the football that people followed was college football.

Natchez was a real small town. At the start of the Second World War, work was hard to find so my family moved to Vicksburg just a few miles up the road. The area had been hard hit by the depression like the rest of the country but with the war, jobs could be found a little easier in bigger towns.

There weren't any televisions then so our world, again, was the church and our family. Everyone knew everyone else and they certainly knew what the other folks across the street were up to. Word of mouth proved to be the entertainment so many looked forward to and *so* many mastered, I'd say.

That has to be something about South Lima too, nothing but bleeding gums.

I never saw a football game for a lot of years but, because there were some good radios, I listened to a game whenever I could. What folks knew of football came from the radio or from high school games. What we heard on the radio was college football. Not much NFL made it down to Vicksburg. We listened to Ol' Miss, Mississippi State, and Alabama. Listening to those college games, that's what really created my interest.

Did the pro game interest you at that age?

No, Rob, not really. When we read the newspapers or listened to the sports news, we heard about the NFL and some of the players but like most other things, they were a world away from small town Mississippi. The college game and the cross-state rivalries is what made the game fun for everyone and brought it to every house. There was nothing like Ol' Miss and Mississippi State, or Auburn and Alabama. We could drive by those campuses. We could even go to a game, if we were lucky. We couldn't do that with the NFL.

When did you first play?

I played my first organized game with the gray "Y," part of the YMCA. They made me quarterback, *quarterback* of all things. That was my first experience with organized football. By playing the game and by listening, I became a fan of football. That allowed me to enjoy the fans more when I became a professional. Many of us were fans of the game first and that helped keep that bond with the fans.

Did you follow a college team?

As a kid, I followed the teams that were nearby or teams that had local guys on them. My favorite player was George Morris. He was from Vicksburg so he was a local guy. George, he went on to play at Georgia Tech. and later with the San Francisco 49ers. I was getting older and I played in High School, Jett High School at first and transferred in my senior year to Central.

Both ways right?

Oh yes. We had to play both ways then. There was cross-town rivalries and even cross-state competition between the high schools, too, not just the colleges, because Mississippi is a small state. The teams and the players all knew each other. Richard Price was considered by everyone in Mississippi as the top player in the state, and I guess I was right behind him in the minds of many, too.

Number two in Mississippi?

Yeah, number two in Mississippi. I was young and full of myself and *acted* like I was young and full of myself. I didn't *like* being number two. Both of us were courted by the same state schools but I thought, why be number two in Mississippi, when I could be number *one* in Georgia, and they had a pretty good coach there with Bobby Dodd. If George Morris did okay there, then Billy Shaw would be just fine over in Georgia.

Everyone in football could see what Bobby Dodd could do to motivate young players. He had won a couple SEC championships and the national championship in 1952. I think he'd come to Georgia Tech in the forties and was one of the first coaches the school had. He had a number of bowl games but what showed most of all was that he really cared about his players. He always believed that if a player was promised a scholarship but couldn't play because of an injury, that player should still be allowed to use the scholarship and complete his education.

There aren't many coaches like that anymore. How many players that leave college early ever go back to complete their degree?

Sad, I know. Things like that mattered to young guys at a time when education is what was important, not whether or not professional football was an option. If a player knew that an education was important to their future and *their* coach knew that too, the player, more times than not, would give their all on the field and we did that for Bobby Dodd. He gave his players his all and we gave him our all.

There were only a dozen NFL teams at that time anyway so the likelihood of making the pros were slim for most college players, don't you think?

I do. A guy would really have to be a stand out. The NFL was the only league and they had just a few teams. There were the Giants, the Bears, the Packers and the Cleveland Browns who were then the big boys in the NFL.

So you went to Georgia Tech?

Yes sir, I did. I'd play guard and defensive tackle.

There were some tough years at Georgia Tech in the late '50s.

Yes sir we had a few, lost the Gator Bowl in 1959.

When you were playing in college, did you look at NFL players to emulate?

I did admire Lou Groza. With few teams in the NFL, finding a player to admire wasn't hard and since the champion always seemed to be the Cleveland Browns, I seemed to drift toward Lou Groza.

A guard liked a kicker?

Yes, sir. He was from Ohio. His family was immigrants. He'd served his country in the Army and besides being the All-Star kicker for the Browns; he also started most of his career as an offensive tackle.

There's this story Rob. One year, Lou Groza comes down to Georgia Tech. The Browns had a number of injuries on their offensive line so Bobby Dodd called Lou and asked him to come down to Atlanta and look at some of his linemen. Coach Dodd had the track record of wins and he believed his line was good enough for the pros. Lou Groza did look at a bunch of us. He had us go through some drills and when we finished up, he took us all aside. I'll never forget what he said to me; "Shaw," he said. "You're quick.

You have a strong desire for the game. You seem motivated but you'll never make it because you just don't have the size."

Coming from someone you admired, that had to be hard?

It was. It made me mad as hell too. I thought okay. I'll show him when I get the chance. I would show Lou Groza some day. He went back to Cleveland and I went back to Georgia Tech.

You began to have a sense that you could have a shot at the pros about that time?

Yes, 1959 or 1960. It was about halfway through my senior year in college when I started to believe that there was a going to be a real shot for me to play professional football. A friend of mine had told me that there was going to be a new league so that meant more of us would have a chance. I was a little apprehensive because I remembered the AAFC but the AFL seemed different.

It was the expanded use of television, I think.

TV was a difference, but players and money was always good to have too. Bobby Dodd helped guide me, I'd have to say. He had told me that I could make it at the pro level. Another opportunity came for me at the college All-Star game in my senior year. Otto Graham was my coach.

The All-Stars played the defending NFL champion at that time, right?

Yes. In '58 they had beat the Lions. Otto Graham coached this game for a few years. He beat the Packers under Lombardi a few years later.

One day before the all-star game, I was practicing at defensive end in the game and Houston Antwine, out of Southern Illinois, was playing on the offensive line. Otto said we were both playing terrible so he switched us with one another. Houston went to tackle and I played guard. I played guard for good.

So after that it was watching the draft?

Yes sir. I had played both ways in high school and played both offense and defense at Georgia Tech so I could've been drafted for either side of the ball. The Dallas Cowboys were looking for a linebacker so they drafted me 184th overall in the 1961 NFL draft. They knew I could hit and had the speed to cover the run and pass, and they could convert me.

Why did you decide to take a chance with a new league and with Buffalo than with the Dallas Cowboys?

Well, it came down to where I thought I would have a chance to play. The Buffalo Bills made me an offer to play regularly and to probably to start as guard, so they drafted me in the second round to do just that. Personally, *I* wanted to play guard, *not* linebacker. Besides, Bobby Dodd felt I could have a better chance in the pros by playing guard so I signed with the Bills. The Dallas Cowboys would hold my rights in case the AFL flopped and, to tell you the truth, Rob, they may still hold my rights still today.

No mini camps like today?

Oh, no. We were told when to show up at training camp. There was a hundred guys trying for about thirty-five spots. Let me tell you this. I was a rookie in a pro camp and I was getting ready for my first exhibition game, a game against the Cleveland Browns. Being a rookie, we knew the place to make a good impression on the coaches was on special teams so everyone went all out. I felt like I was going to make the team anyway, and maybe I could hold back on special teams a little, but not in *that* game.

Now on the kickoff, when we received the ball, my job was to take out the kicker and on that day I would take pleasure in doing just that. The Browns kicker was, of course, Lou Groza. I'm proud to say that I reintroduced myself to him that day, so to speak. Lou had said I would never make it and I wanted to show him that I *had* made it.

That was the start of it all, that first exhibition game against the

Browns. When I could take out an All-Pro. I knew I could play and had earned a place on the Buffalo Bills.

What do you remember about your first regular season game?

I don't remember much, other than it *was* a loss. I do remember the game at the Polo Grounds, though, against the Titans, the second game of the season and my first win. The first win is always remembered. For a kid from a small town to go onto the famous Polo Grounds and play was very memorable.

What I remember too Rob is that I always had a good time: In training camp, in practice, and in the games. I enjoyed everything about football even practice.

Even practice?

Yup, even the practice. It was a chance for us to be a bit looser than when we were at game time. We had some fun, incredible years, my wife and I, there in Buffalo. That poor woman, she's put up with me now for forty-eight years. We had fun though, everywhere we went. There were some tough years, of course, but our time in Buffalo was something great.

How much do you think the game has changed?

The money is something else. I never imagined and many others back then, could never have imagined the league would become what it has and good for new guys. There is one thing I remember from my playing days, and my younger days, too, and that's the game seemed much more enjoyable. Everybody seemed to be having a good time, and like I have probably beat into the ground by now, there really seemed to be a different type of bond between the fan and player. Now some players seem and act as untouchables.

I agree. When I was a kid in the 1970s, the game seemed fun and the players seemed to be having a good time, regardless of how much they made.

In its own way, I think it's still fun but many probably play just for the money and that takes something out of it. The game has changed and the players have changed, so everything with football has changed too.

The fans enjoy the game when the players enjoy it and everyone's happy. But, to a large extent, the league has become too business-oriented. I don't know if it's *fan* oriented anymore. Going back to the fans there at Memorial Stadium, the fans, they sat *right* behind the bench, not a hundred yards away or separated by staff and security. They were right behind us. The same season ticket holders were right there year after year and, if someone wasn't at a game, we'd turn and ask, "Where's *Mary,"* or "How's *Sam* doing today?"

Now, the players are here a couple of years and are off to somewhere else. That's not good for the fan and can't be good for team or the game. Do you think free agency has taken that unique bond out of the game?

That's a good question. Free agency is a good thing for many reasons. For the player, it has turned out really well - pensions, salaries, medical, etc. The money is remarkable; I could never have imagined it would have gotten like this. Football is a business, though. The players and the owners should both make as much as the market can pay, but it has changed the game. Free agency makes it hard to keep a player and that *may* have taken some enjoyment out of the game.

Do you think free agency good for the fan?

Probably not. The fan is the one paying the money to go the game and at what point does the fan become unable to pay the price. It's not like ticket prices will ever go down again because the players will never ask for less money. Who loses out? The fan does.

When my brother and I went to games in the '70s, he paid $8.00 or $10.00 for our seats. Now you can't park in someone's yard for $10.00. In my opinion, Billy, free agency has hurt the fan. As a kid I knew what players were going to be there for the Bills from one year *to the next, now you need a flip chart to see who's where.*

I know. When I played, I knew who my center was going to be *every* year. The same with my tackles. We all knew we could count on each other. There wasn't any of the uncertainty as free agency may have brought to the game. Every team has a high turnover now and a guard in today's NFL is fortunate to play next to the same center and tackle for more than a couple of years in a row.

I knew whom the players were going to be in the '70s, but no longer yet I'm expected to pay higher and higher prices for something I'm not familiar with.

I can see how fans would think that, Rob.

Billy, I do think that the camaraderie you spoke of ended when true free agency came to the game. There was no more closeness between the player and the fans. When the player knew he could go to the highest bidder, that bond became an early victim.

I liked the old way better, that's for sure, because there was a mutual respect and friendship that existed between fan and player. I'm not saying that it doesn't exist today but I know it existed *then.*

It's frustrating, but let's move on. Going back to your first year, did you start as a rookie?

Yes, I did. In 1961, we had Johnny Green, who had come over from the Steelers, and M.C Reynolds, who came from the Chicago Cardinals. They split the duties at quarterback. We lost our first game to the Broncos but had our first win the following week when we played the New York Titans at the Polo Grounds. Like I said, for a young kid from Mississippi, going to the Polo Grounds was thrilling.

In 1961, we finished five hundred or close to five hundred. We beat some good teams like Dallas, Houston and Oakland. What I remember most often about that first year was that our last five or six games were on the road. For me it was an okay year. I was more prepared for the following year.

Looking at the first few years for the Bills, September always seemed like it was a hard month.

It was. We had a hard time getting started.

I looked at the month of September for the Bills' first three seasons. Of the eleven games they played in September, the team lost nine of them. What's the old saying, "You have to win in September to play in December?"

You're right. September was a bad month for us early on. We seemed to lose everything we played. In 1962, my second year, we lost our first five games in a season that had only fourteen games. We seemed to be out of it from the very beginning. But the team *was* changing. Lou Saban had replaced "Buster" Ramsey and we had two new quarterbacks, Warren Babb from Detroit and Jack Kemp, who had been picked up off the waiver wire from San Diego. We also now had "Cookie" Gilchrist in our backfield. Many knew that Lou liked running backs and now he had one in "Cookie" Gilchrist.

In 1963, the Bills had another slow start, 0-3-1, but you found your quarterback in Jack Kemp. I saw a big difference in passing yards alone - 1,200 for Rabb in 1962 and 2,900 for Kemp in 1963.

Yes, it was getting better. The experts had picked us to win the division that year. We believed our defense was the best in the league, and both "Cookie" and Jack Kemp were healthy and playing well. On paper it looked good, but we got off to another slow start.

You won seven of the next ten games though, and even with a record of only 7-6-1, you made the playoffs in 1963.

Yes, we made the playoffs with seven wins, and the Bills had their first winning season. We had tied the Patriots in the division, and just after Christmas, we played them there at the War Memorial Stadium in Buffalo. It was pitch and catch, though, for the Patriots.

Babe Parilli had a real good day. We couldn't get much going, but Elbert Dubenion did have a long one.

Though the Bills finished 7-6-1 and lost handily in the playoffs, it was inevitable that the game's experts would start declaring the Bills one of the league's favored teams for 1964. Would you say that the turn-around from a perennial five hundred team arrived at the same time Lou Saban came to Buffalo?

Well, Lou Saban had his first full year with us in 1962. He did a heck of a job turning us into a respectable team *in* '62 and '63 with our seven win seasons. It was his leadership and players of real quality that turned us around. Jack Kemp, of course, but Lou was a running coach, so getting "Cookie" Gilchrist to come to Buffalo may have been the most important move. "Cookie" was with us only a couple of years but they were the good ones.

The experts of the day picked the Bills to win everything and to do that, the team would need a successful September.

September, I know. We *all* knew we were going to have to win in September.

Billy, in looking at 1964, it looks like you solved the September problem.

Yes sir. I guess we did.

You began 3-0 in September, scoring more than thirty points in each game and winning by an average margin of twenty points.

We were winning on the field and our crowds were growing. The team was making more money and we had some of the AFL biggest stars. There were plenty of reasons to be optimistic for the upcoming season or seasons.

Was 1964 the team's best year?

The best? I don't know. We won every game in September that year so that bug-a-boo was gone.

And in October and half of November, as well.

12-2. We had all cylinders moving. Jack and Daryle both had good years, "Cookie" had another thousand yards, our offensive line was good and our defense was *really* good, the best in the league. I sometimes look back and I believe we could have gone undefeated. We were so far ahead in the division and some games didn't matter, so some of us sat out. We didn't stink in September anymore and, when we had the wins under our belt, our motivation grew and we won most everything.

We were about as complete a team in 1964 as one could get. We got Pete Gogolak, out of Cornell, as our kicker so we were better on special teams too. Some folks said that 1964 squad of ours should be listed as one of the all-time great football teams ever assembled. In looking back, it's hard to disagree with what they said.

Did you know the title was possible when you entered the 1964 season?

Well, not necessarily, but when the season moved along and we were 3-0, 5-0, then 9-0, we grew more confident because we had a chemistry. We had the right people doing a good job. Going into the title game, all the writers said the Chargers were going to *run* away with the game and that we had no chance, but we didn't let that get to us because we knew we were good.

The Chargers scored quickly, though.

Yes, they did. Keith Lincoln was running *all* over the place and Tobin Rote hit their tight end for about thirty yards. That touchdown was set up after Lincoln had already run the ball half the field. We could kinda' feel the air go out of the stands.

We were only a couple of minutes into the game. We had to punt and the Chargers were moving down the field again. Rote hit Lincoln on a swing-pass and that's when Mike Stratton knocked the stuffing out of him, breaking his ribs and putting Keith out of the game.

Was that the difference in the game?

Rob, remember that Keith Lincoln was about as versatile a player as anyone could be. He led the Chargers in two or three different categories and he tore the Patriots apart the previous year in the title game. He was a constant threat so when he was put out of the game, it took the air out of their offense and we took charge after that. We would have made a comeback in the game if he *hadn't* been knocked out, but having him gone made it that much easier for us.

The Bills had their first title and were favored to repeat the following year. In 1965, the Bills slipped to 10-3-1, but the Boston Patriots had a large collapse, falling to a 4-8-2 record and finishing in third place in the Eastern Division. The New York Jets were improving behind their new quarterback, Joe Namath, finishing in second place, but still five games behind the Bills. So the divisional title was more easily won in '65 than it had been the previous year.

Jack Kemp was the Bills' starting quarterback in 1965. There was no more shuttling of quarterbacks in and out as in previous years. "Cookie" Gilchrist was gone to Denver and the bulk of the Bills' running game fell upon Wray Carlton, who would finish the season eighth in the league in rushing. The AFL title game would again be between the San Diego Chargers and Buffalo Bills, but this time it would be played in San Diego. The experts again favored the Chargers but, from the kickoff, the game belonged to the Bills. There was only one offensive touchdown, a short pass from Jack Kemp to Ernie Warlick. "Butch" Byrd returned a punt for seventy-four yards and Pete Gogolak added three field goals as the Buffalo Bills shut down and shut out Sid Gilman's Chargers, 23-0.

Back-to-back championships! That was an accomplishment and we all knew it. We knew as a team that we had every right to be looked at like other teams who had done that, the Browns and Packers specifically. We believed we were *as* good as any NFL team of the day.

The 1965 AFL Championship would be the last for the league for beginning in 1966 the AFL would send a team to challenge the NFL in Super Bowl I. I asked Billy Shaw if he felt the talks of the merger had an impact on that 1966 season.

No, I don't think so, Rob. Some of the older guys knew they weren't going to be around when 1970 arrived. We were older, more banged up and as a team; we weren't doing what we needed to replace the losses in personnel. That made a difference.

We made the playoffs in 1966. We won the Eastern Division for the third straight year and had to play the Kansas City Chiefs, who had won the west. The winner of that game would play in Super Bowl I against Vince Lombardi.

It was a bad day.

Yup, we had a bad day. We played them on New Years Day, 1967. We didn't play well and Len Dawson had a great day. They outplayed us and they went to the first Super Bowl.

That would be the last playoff game for the Buffalo Bills during the AFL years, right?

Yes, our run was over after that. Like I said, we were getting older had injuries and, with Lou and "Cookie" gone, we had lost the heart out of our offense. The last three years the team was not good.

A combined 9-32-1.

That's bad. Our finish in 1968 *did* give us the first draft pick in 1969 and every body knows what we did with that.

Billy, did you have any hint that someday you would be in the Hall of Fame?

No, I never had a hint at all.

You were a nine-time Pro-Bowler, an eight-time All-Pro, and a two-time AFL Champion. You were named part of the AFL All-Time team and your name is on the Bills Wall of Fame. You never thought you'd make it?

Honestly, Rob. I never did. The veteran's committee told me once that I was up for consideration. When they announced the inductees, you know they usually name the veteran inductee first but, *that* year, 1999, they were going to name the veteran selection last.

That figures. It just added to the drama.

Oh, yeah. I had to wait that much longer for the announcement to come. I had everybody coming around the house wanting to see me that day, wanting to get my reaction but you know, I just didn't want anybody to see me cry if I got in or if I didn't.

The call came?

The call came. I still get the chills when I think about that day. The Hall of Fame is an incredible, tremendous honor and it brings with it so much, *particularly* a lot of golf. Just ask my poor wife. Sometimes I still can't believe it. I was a small-town Mississippi kid who loved football and who ended up in the Hall of Fame. I got to play the game I loved and I got to make a living at it. As I've said, we made many great friends and there are so many stories I could tell.

Do you have one?

Yes, this is always a good one. There is this one story and it involved an old dog of ours.

I always wanted to go back to small-town life. Having spent years in Georgia, it just seemed right. So when we retired, we settled down in Toccoa, Georgia. It's about ten thousand people, or so, and we had a Boston Bull Terrier.

Now, remember things were a lot different in the south in the '60s. The poor blacks lived in one part of town and us not so poor whites lived in another. Then one day, a very nice, black family purchased a home that some considered being outside of *their* part of town. It's just the way things were then. No body really cared; it was just something new.

I know.

Well, that ol' dog of ours would leave the house first thing in the morning, be gone all day long and would come home when the sun was going down. We'd sit and watch and every day this dog came through the door, his head and back side draggin' like he'd been working in the fields all day.

He wouldn't eat. He wouldn't play and *was* getting fatter. He'd do nothing but sleep. This went on day after day after day. Finally, I just had had enough and decided that I'd follow him. I was going to *spy* on our own dog. I watched as he went out the door, down the walk and hung a left. I was far enough behind him so he wouldn't catch on. He kept walking, took a left, then a *right* and finally, he walked up the steps of *that* new house. It was one of the smallest houses around, too. He just walked right through its door.

I just kinda' stood there not knowing what to do. I finally went up and knocked on the front door. Out came the tiniest woman and she was eyeing me in *no* uncertain terms.

I looked at her and said, "Ma'am you don't know me but my dog just walked right through *your* front door."

That woman kept her eyes on me for a time and then said, "Oh, I know who *you* are Mr. Shaw. You used to park *your* car in *my* front yard every time you played at Memorial Field." We stared at each other. Then she smiled and so did I.

She and her family had moved from Buffalo to Toccoa, and into the house right down the road from us. She had taken it upon herself to feed that ol' Bull Terrier some of the best southern cooking anyone had ever seen.

The dog knew where his bread was being buttered.

Yes sir, and it wasn't too long before that dog and I both began to grow wider. She was one heck of a cook!

There are so many stories. We experienced some great years in

Buffalo with the championships and all that we did. We had begun to have some tough years, though, in '67 and '68 and I remembered the promise that I had made to my wife.

What was that?

I would never abuse football for the sake of a check and I'd never abuse my family for the sake of football. She'd reminded me of that promise as we began the 1969 season. We had another bad year and that's when I called it quits.

It was very hard to leave the game; it really was. At the start of the 1970 season, Bud Adams of the Houston Oilers called me because they had lost both guards during a pre-season game. He offered me a contract that was worth looking at, but we turned it down. I'm glad we did because I couldn't ever have imagined wearing colors other then those of the Buffalo Bills.

Life has been incredible ride for my wife and me. I've been so blessed and, again, I never gave the Hall of Fame much thought until 1998 or 1999 when I was told I was to be on the veterans' list. The problem was that in order to be elected into the Hall a veteran must receive 80% of the vote and I wasn't real sure about getting that.

But we got it.

Rob, I have had tremendous honors in life and being in the Hall of Fame is one of the great ones, but seeing my grandson wear # 66 may just top that.

15
55

Chapter 5
Jack Kemp

"On these winds of victory ride emotions of a year, of work and sweat, guts, glory and fear..."(1)
-John Facenda-

There are many things that made the decade of the '60s unique - the music, the movies, the politics, the moon race and the Viet-Nam war. The Civil Rights Movement changed America for the better and the assassinations made Americans a different people.

What was the city of Buffalo like in the '60s?

What about Jamestown?

Elmira?

South Lima?

What about the kids from *that* time and from *those* towns? I sometimes wonder if all kids are always alike, regardless of where or how they are raised. It's their environment that changes them.

We all daydreamed as kids. As for me, I wanted to be Matt

Dillon riding into town to rescue Miss Kitty from the drunken stranger. I wanted to be a cowboy but came up *just* short.

I was 9 maybe 10 years old when I was riding the range of *my* vast imagination. What did you dream of being when you were that age?

What did you want to be? Did *you* want to be a cowboy? Did you want to be a professional quarterback? Did you want to be a Congressman? How about a Cabinet Secretary or a candidate for Vice-President of the United States? Well, *those* dreams did come true for a young man growing up in southern California in the 1940s.

One of the most fascinating lives of those I've spoken to is that of Jack Kemp. In my story, when I was part of a different time, I played a small role in the 1996 Presidential campaign. It was then that I met Jack Kemp for the first time. In 1996, he was not only traveling with a dozen secret service agents, but his wife, Joanne, his son, Jeff, and Ernie "The Big Cat" Ladd.

Ernie Ladd as you may recall, played with the San Diego Chargers, Houston Oilers and ended his football days with the Kansas City Chiefs. At the time he played, he was one of the biggest to play, - 6'9", 315 pounds and a 52-inch chest. Others of you may recall that after his football days, Ernie Ladd went on to a professional wrestling career where, for a number of years, he had an ongoing *feud* with Andre the Giant.

Rob. Ernie was a great guy, one of my best friends. He passed away just last year. He was someone who was with me on every campaign I was ever in. He was a dear, dear friend and a great man. I miss him a lot some days.

It's good to talk again. It's been a lot of years.

Same here Rob.

You have had quite a life. When you were a kid what did you daydream about Mr. Secretary?

All kids daydream and I was no different. I wanted to be a ball player. I wanted to be great at whatever caught my attention at any given time. All kids are like that. I hope they are. I have been really blessed in life. I have a great family and my *seventeen* grandchildren to love to death, and I had friends like Ernie.

Do you have any thoughts of getting back into politics in a John McCain White House?

Oh, no, not at all. I like this life the way it is. I do plenty with guest appearances on FOX, CNN and the others, giving speeches and writing columns. I stay busy.

I need to ask this question first. When you were in Congress, you had the opportunity to work with Ronald Reagan. What was he like to be around?

Ronald Reagan inspired confidence in everyone he was near. He had a deep love for sports and he loved football. Remember he flipped the coin for the Super Bowl from the Oval Office that one year?

I do remember that.

He had many stories and jokes about the time he had broadcast the Chicago Cubs games back in the late 1930s. He had a tremendous sense of *peace* about him. He was confidant in who he was and that confidence allowed his sense of humor to come through so easily. He was optimistic about America, in his belief in peace through strength and belief in our nation's free enterprise system being able to grow into incredible realities. He was an incredibly optimistic person. As President, you have to be. *As* a quarterback, you have to be too, or your team isn't going anywhere.

Ronald Reagan was the first politician I admired. Prior to him, I had only known Nixon and Carter and, as a young kid in America, neither one of them inspired me.

I can understand that, Rob. Both of them, though, did good things for America during their time in office.

I got President Reagan up to Buffalo one time to meet with Kenny Gleason. Kenny has passed away now, but he was President of the Longshoreman's Union. He was a strong Democrat and a good friend of mine. Kenny and President Reagan hit it off like two old union guys would. Ronald Reagan was from the Screen Actors Guild and Kenny Gleason from the Longshoremen. This certainly ran contrary to what many people were thinking at the time but they did get along great. Again, Ronald Reagan had a tremendous sense of optimism at a time when America needed it, and such optimism was so important to getting us through that period of time. I don't know if the Cold War could have ended if *not* for Ronald Reagan. He *had* to be optimistic about winning the Cold War in order to win it.

Going back a few years, what did your parents do?

A *few* years Rob?

Yes sir, just a couple.

My father was a truck driver in Los Angeles. He had bought a truck and started a delivery company called the California Delivery Service. He ended up with about twenty trucks later on and with that business he put four boys through college. It was a hard working life for my dad. He never went to college himself but he made sure we all did. My mother was a social worker and taught English and Spanish in the public schools for a while but as I got into my teens, she didn't have to work anymore. During the depression years and after the war, however, both my parents had to work.

Which high school did you attend?

Fairfax High School.

Do you remember who your football coach was?

Yes. Frank Schaeffer. He was one of the great high school coaches in Los Angeles.

As a kid, what did you do?

Lots of football. As a kid, I played football 363 days a year. The other two days were Christmas and Easter or Thanksgiving. I was a football fan from the very start, which was unusual at that time because it was such a baseball era. I loved the Los Angeles Rams. I idolized Bob Waterfield, their quarterback from UCLA, and Kenny Washington. They were my favorites so I was a Rams fan immediately.

For those who keep track of such things, Bob Waterfield was born right down the road in Elmira New York.

Oh, sure, the Southern Tier area. I know it very well. I would go to the pro games in the '40s right through the '50s. I loved the game. My brother played for USC, and I wanted to play professional football from the time I was a kid, 7 or 8 years old. For some reason, I loved football whereas many people didn't at that time. I went to as many games as I could because we had no TV.

When did you get your first TV?

Oh, it had to be in the '50s. It was black and white. There was hardly any sports programming - pretty much wrestling and test patterns with various degrees of fuzz.

Football, at least the pro game, had hardly been introduced to the west coast at the time, correct?

Remember, Rob. The Cleveland Rams moved to Los Angeles in the late 1940s, but remained in the Eastern Division. Sid Gilman became their coach in the '50s. Perhaps the NFL placing the Rams in L.A was a response to the Los Angeles Dons of the AAFC, because the Cleveland Rams were having problems competing against the Browns when they were in Cleveland.

In high school, did you have to play both ways?

Oh, yes. It was common. I was quarterback, defensive back and a safety in high school. In college, I was a quarterback and, don't laugh, a linebacker, as well as a safety.

Linebacker? That's hard to see. You were considered small for a quarterback, weren't you?

Yes, I was just a little over 6' and 200 lbs.

How were you recruited?

I wanted to go to Occidental. They played pretty good football and had a good coach in Roy Dennis and because they played the single wing. As a matter of fact, one of my teammates, co-captains and my roommate in college was Jim Mora, who went on to coach in New Orleans and Indianapolis. Anyway, Occidental was close to my family, and they played the type of game I liked. The choice was easy.

You had a couple of tough years at Occidental, 3-6 and 1-7-1, but it looks like you gained experience on both sides of the ball.

I did.

You said that there were several NFL teams that had contacted you prior to the 1957 NFL Draft.

Yes. Green Bay was one of them.

The Lions took you in the 17th round. Did you think you might have gone earlier?

I *was* drafted by the Detroit Lions in 1957 and traded to the Pittsburgh Steelers at the end of the exhibition season. I spent the '57 season playing with Earl Morrall and Lenny Dawson. We were the three quarterbacks for the Steelers that year. Morrall was the starter and Lenny and I were his backups. In 1958, I went back to the Steelers and got cut after the last preseason game. I then was picked up by the New York Giants and spent 1958 as the backup quarterback to Charlie Conerly and Bob Heinrich.

I was then released in 1959 and was signed by the Calgary Stampeders to compete with Joe Kapp for their starting position. In those days, a Canadian team could keep only *one* American player and they kept Joe Kapp, so I was cut and picked up by the San Francisco 49ers. I spent the season behind Y.A. Tittle and John Brodie. There is a story that goes with that, too. In 1959 many had heard that there was to be a new league started and I became the first quarterback for the Chargers.

The Chargers signed you as a free agent. Did they approach you, or vice versa?

Remember, during that time I was hanging on by my fingertips with any number of teams. I ended up on the taxi squad of the 49ers in 1959 and got activated when Y.A. Tittle got hurt and we were playing the Browns in Cleveland. I was dressed and on the field warming up. I was to back up John Brodie that day. Long story short, I go back into the locker room after warming up and our coach, "Red" Hickey, comes up to me and says that Bert Bell, the commissioner, had called him. Bell said that he had just received a call from Art Modell, owner of the Browns, to complain that I had been in Canada for like one quarter of one exhibition game. I didn't even play, but I had been there for the summer playing behind Joe Kapp.

Again, the CFL, at the time, could keep only *one* American quarterback and they kept Kapp. I was cut without even a tryout and ended up on the 49ers taxi squad. Y.A. Tittle was hurt so the 49ers activated me to backup John Brodie for that Cleveland game. I was literally dressed and warming up on the field. That's when I get the news from "Red" Hickey. I had to take off my uniform and sit on the bench in my street clothes *because* we couldn't be part of the CFL and NFL in the same year.

That's a bad day.

I'm not done yet either. The story got some publicity back in

California so Frank Leahy, the General Manager of the Los Angeles Chargers of the new AFL, owned by Baron Hilton, asked Don Klosterman to recruit some players for the team. Don called me on Monday morning in San Francisco and asked me to fly to L.A. the next day. I did and I signed with the Chargers that day with Sid Gilman and Baron Hilton sitting across from me. That would be my first big shot at getting to play.

Those were quite a couple of years. Most of those guys you had a chance to play with were some of the best in the game. Do you happen to know how the phrase taxi squad came into existence?

How did it?

The original owner of the Cleveland Browns in the 1940s, Art McBride, owned several Cleveland taxicab companies. At a time when teams could only have thirty or so players on the roster, the players he had cut became his taxi drivers, so he just replaced the injured player with a cab driver.

Oh, that is a good one Rob.

Those were a couple of hard years, football wise?

Yes it was, but looking back at it, it was a unique opportunity for me to learn and play with some of the greatest quarterbacks to ever play the game.

So you signed with the Chargers as a free agent?

Yes. The Los Angeles Chargers was my first big chance to play.

Your first year was a good one. You had over 3,000 yards passing.

That would be the only time you'd hit that number, though. During your time with the Chargers you didn't have a receiver that had more than 700 yards. Dave Kocourek led the team. It was Kocourek and completions to your halfbacks coming out of the backfield that gave you and the Chargers the good numbers.

Sure, Rob. It was the West Coast offense in 1960, twenty years before Bill Walsh and the 49ers. Sid Gilman was the creator *of* the West Coast offense. Playing for Sid, who was such an offensive genius, was such a treat for me. As a matter of fact, Bill Walsh called Sid Gilman the greatest offensive mind the game ever saw. *My* son, Jeff, played for Bill Walsh, by the way, and loved him and all he did for the game and his players. Sid created the short pass offense. We didn't call it the West Coast offense. We just called it the Sid Gilman offense.

Finishing 10-4 and winning the Western Division gave you the chance to face the Houston Oilers from the Eastern Division.

Yes sir. The Oilers were tough.

On paper, that championship game looked like a good one, but George Blanda kicked a field goal and threw for three touchdowns. He accounted for all their points, one way or another, that day. The 88-yard pass in the 4th quarter to Billy Cannon was the back breaker in the 24-16 loss.

George Blanda did everything. If he had stayed home that day, we, perhaps, could have won.

The Chargers moved from Los Angeles down to San Diego after their first year because, it was said, that the Coliseum was too big and it made any crowd look small. Is that correct?

Yes, the Coliseum *was* too big.

1961 was a good draft year for the Chargers with Keith Lincoln and Ernie Ladd.

It was a good draft Billy Shaw went to Buffalo that year I think, too. In 1962, we got off to another great start, ten or eleven wins in a row, but then I got hurt. We did win the Western Division again. We lost to the Oilers though in the title game for the second year in a row.

Was this time that Sid Gilman placed you on the waiver wire?

Yes, he did. Sid thought that, perhaps, he could slide me by, but Lou Saban had spotted me and off to Buffalo I went.

Was that a hard adjustment going from a two-time divisional champion and a 12-2 record in 1961, to a team that had a 6-8 record that same year? You moved from a first place team to a last place team.

I always saw everything as a challenge and I looked at coming to the Bills like that. Besides, if I hadn't, so much else may not have happened.

What was your first start for the Bills?

Warren Rabb was starting. I did manage a decent amount of playing time though in 1962.

Yes you did, 51 of 94 with a couple of touchdowns. That same off –season, "Cookie" Gilchrist came to the Bills. How would you say that addition changed the Bills?

Easy. "Cookie" was probably the best back ever to play in Canada and to get him in Buffalo for the time we did was what, undoubtedly, helped lead to our championship years.

I looked at the statistics for those early years and it seemed that there was a battle going on at the quarterback spot between you and Daryle Lamonica. In '63 you threw for almost 3,000 yards again. In '64, you had 2,200 and Lamonica had 1,100.

I wouldn't say there was a battle. Daryle was my backup and when I played lousy he came in. There may have been, for a period or two, some rotating in and out. I did start every game that year,

1964, and we won the championship game.

Is that Patriots game of '64, the one where you went up to Lou Saban and said, "Lou, if you want to win, you need to start me."

I think we may have lost a game during the regular season. There was some strong criticism of the team and me, in particular. Whether or not Saban flirted with starting Daryle or not, I don't know. But rumors got back to me and I saw Lou in the hallway one day. I said, "Coach, I feel very good about this and I know I can win it for you. If you *want* to win you need to put me in."

You were right.

Yes, I was, thank God. I have tremendous respect for Daryle. We have become a lot friendlier after our careers were over. I think he was a tremendous quarterback and a tremendous sportsman. He was a good example on and off the field, as well.

You helped begin the American Football League Players Association. Was that primarily your idea?

There was Tommie Addison of the Boston Patriots, Tom Flores from Oakland, and Lance Alworth from San Diego. I'll forget some names, but, anyway, we all got together and formed the first union. Tommy was the first president. The second year, I ran for president and was elected. I held that position for the next five years and succeeded in merging the AFLPA into what is now the National Football League Players Association in 1968. We succeeded in making John Mackey the first black president of an NFL union.

Sid Gilman in, 1965, had some unkind words for you.

'65?

Yeah.

Well, I had beaten Sid's Chargers in 1964 and his words for me in 1964 were far worse than they were in 1965. They were only words, Rob. They should only make you play harder. He was and remained one of my best friends. I spoke at his memorial service.

The Buffalo Bills, in the middle of the decade, were arguably the best team in the AFL, wouldn't you say?

I would, yes. We had some greats: "Cookie", Billy, Mike, Wray, Carlton, and George Byrd. We were a good team.

What caused the downslide of the team in the late '60s?

Well, in 1966, Lou Saban left to return to college and "Cookie" Gilchrist had been traded to Denver. We had never had severe injuries before but some were starting to catch up with us. We did win the Eastern Division in 1966 and met the Kansas City Chiefs to see who would go on to play the Packers in Super Bowl I.

Do you think the Bills could have beaten Green Bay?

I don't know if we would have played better than the Chiefs. We played strong on defense but, offensively, we didn't quite have the firepower that we had when "Cookie" was there. We just didn't do enough rebuilding. I don't think our offense could have kept pace with Vince Lombardi and Bart Starr. I'm not putting the blame on anyone, but with the change of coaches as well as the injuries and losses on offense, by '67 and '68, we were just a shadow of ourselves.

By the last game of 1968, you were 1-12-1 and the fans were apparently rooting for a non-victory in the last game of the season against the Oilers so the O.J. pick in 1969 would be secured.

Well, I was on injured reserve. I had missed the entire season. I didn't play a single game that year, but we did get O.J.

Dan Darragh, out of William and Mary, started that year. He'd be 92 of 215 with three touchdowns and 14 interceptions. Ugly year.

Yes, it was.

What did you do during the off-season?

Early on, I worked for the Chargers my first year in L.A. Then, when we went to San Diego, I worked for the San Diego newspapers, the Copley Press, both the San Diego Union and the San Diego Tribune. I would write speeches and did a lot of their community relations work, and was even part of their editorial training program. I loved politics and economics, even in those days, and I was pretty much a protégé of Herb Klein.

He worked in the Nixon White House, didn't he?

Yes, he did. He was Communications Director for Richard Nixon. He was the one who actually created that position. As a matter of fact, he *just* celebrated his 90th birthday and I was at the celebration for him with Tom Brokaw, Henry Kissinger and Governor Pete Wilson.

That is quite the line up. I usually have my wife, her family and our dog Bubba, at my birthday.

Good, Rob. You love them to death, though.

I do. Not Bubba though. Do you think that growing up in the depression helped? Your family building an entire business from the ground up fueled your interest in conservative politics or economic policies?

No, I don't think the depression did, but my dad was a small business man so I had a proclivity for entrepreneurship and the system that allowed it to happen, or should I say, *encouraged* it to happen. I had studied a lot of the classical economists during the off-season and during the season for that matter. Believe me, I used to take a lot of heat from the coaches who thought I should be spending more time reading my play book than books on economics.

Well, there was probably a good novel out at the time, too. I think Ian Fleming had written Chitty Chitty Bang Bang about that time.

No, I don't think so. I was conservative and, hopefully, progressive in believing that our system should work together for the poor and for the people of color. I was head of the AFL players union, as you know, Rob, when we boycotted the New Orleans AFL All-Star Game. I was captain of the East squad. That is was when all my black teammates from both the East and West came to me and said they were going to boycott the city because of the treatment of blacks. We supported the boycott. It was '63 or '64. Check it out. It was around that time, though.

"Cookie" Gilchrist was active in that boycott, wasn't he?

Yes, he was. So were Abner Haynes, Ernie Warlick and about a dozen others from both the East and West. I think Abner Haynes was the captain of the West squad. He and I met and decided to tell the owners that we wouldn't play under the conditions and gratefully they agreed to move the game to Houston. Houston wasn't that much better but at least it wasn't New Orleans. This was in the south, pre-1964 Civil Rights Act, and it was black and whites uniting behind a common cause.

I was looking through some of your bio and through some of my own personal memories to the relationship between you and Ernie Ladd.

My dearest friend. I spoke at his memorial service. His wife has a foundation and I am on the board. I'm so proud of being on the board with James Harris out of Jacksonville and Doug Williams out of Washington and Tampa Bay.

Did you two play together with the Chargers?

Yes, we were teammates with the Chargers and then against each other, as we went to Buffalo and Houston respectively. We were always friends and when I got into Congress, he campaigned with me in every Congressional race I had, and, of course, during my Vice-Presidential campaign, he was with me everywhere, especially throughout the Southern states.

I was with you guys on three maybe more of those stops.

Yes you were. Those were some fun days. I always wanted to see the economic possibilities of America enjoyed by everyone and during the '60s they weren't. Many of us were in a position to really foster a change in a lot of things. I wasn't marching with Martin Luther King or Andrew Young, but I had sensitivity to making free enterprise work, not just for upper income but for lower income people as well. So that was and *always* has been my desire. That was certainly my social conscience in those days.

Good. You helped broadcast Super Bowl II?

Yes, I did. I was asked by CBS to do the color commentary. So Pat Summerall and I did the color and Ray Scott did the play by play for the Oakland Raider, Green Bay Game from the Orange Bowl.

Do you think of Ralph Wilson moving the team to Toronto?

Rob, I don't think he's going to. I think he will play a game a year there. It's part of the teams marketing plan. A large part of the Bills market is Canada. I think it's a great marketing idea, *for* Ralph is committed to Buffalo, as is the National Football League, as is Jim Kelly and Jack Kemp. I don't think Ralph is doing this for any other reason than to expand his market share in Canada.

His recent comments made many of the Bills fans nervous as to the team's future. It was an ongoing topic on sports radio in Western New York.

Yes, I know. I think it was, perhaps, misconstrued, misplaced but Ralph's heart is in Buffalo and I am totally convinced that he wants to keep the team right there in Buffalo.

That's a wish for so many of us. Mr. Secretary, what is your fondest memory of the City of Buffalo and the people, your fans, your constituents?

The people and the joy they got from winning, the incredible loyalty and the joy on their faces when we won back-to-back championships in the '60s, and the joy on their faces at going to the Super Bowls, despite the losses. I think that was one of the most remarkable streaks in sports history that the Bills could go to four straight Super Bowls.

I don't think that will ever be done again.

I don't think so. That, itself, is a remarkable achievement. I love Buffalo. I learned a lot from the people of Buffalo. I grew up in Southern California and grew up in a very Republican household and community. I find myself in Buffalo, being their quarterback and Congressman. It is such a unique, ethnically diverse, very patriotic, democratic town. Buffalo taught me about ethnicity and having an incredible work ethic, the Buffalo teacher, the mechanic, and the plant worker. They taught me so much and I will always remember and will forever be thankful to them and to the city.

Well, your life has been an American dream. From the time you grew up as a kid with no TV and loving the game, to championship AFL years, to being a candidate for Vice-President of the United States is really something remarkable.

Thank you Rob.

When you left football, did you return to California or did you make Buffalo your home?

Well, I threatened the people of Buffalo. I had retired from the Bills and I said to the city, "Look. Elect me to Congress or I'll come back as your quarterback!"

They took you seriously, didn't they?

They sure did. I was elected to Congress in 1971 and they kept me there until 1989, but I had been getting my feet wet in politics for a long time before I ever ran for office. In 1966, I had worked for Ronald Reagan's Governor's race in California, then as a special assistant to him while he was in office.

I see you had current Bill Brad Butler down there with you for an internship recently.

Yes, I did. What a terrific, articulate, superb young man. He is a solid, young, up-and-coming, intellectual football player and I really like him a lot.

As you know, there is a serious split, right now, between the older retired players and the NFLPA when it comes to benefits.

Yes, there is. Split is the right word. I sit on the NFL Alliance, as you may know along with Jerry Kramer, Merlin Olsen, and a couple former Buffalo Bills, Billy Shaw and Cornelius Bennett. It's a group made up of members of the union, current players and the Hall of Fame and it is designed to help some of the older guys who really need it. There *are* a lot of problems. We know that and we are trying to fix it.

Mr. Kemp, there have been some very vocal positions taken by older players about the situations they have experienced.

I know. Some of it, though, like remarks by Bernie Parrish, is overboard. The NFL will make things right. Just by looking at the alliance and who sits on it, the problems will be addressed. As with most things, it won't happen overnight. I hope that this is understood and that we can all work together on this without the bitterness continuing to go on out there. The NFL is the greatest game in America and we need to make it better for those that have played, are playing and will play.

Catch The Vision
J.D. Hill
Wide Receiver
J. D. Hill

Chapter 6
J.D. Hill

"To everything there is a season and a time for every purpose under heaven." (1)
-The Byrds-

When the decade of the '60s began, there were two professional football leagues. Cynics said that the AFL would soon collapse, as it was nothing but a league of rejects with questionable talent. The AFL did *not* collapse, and it would be the AFL that is remembered as the strongest competition the NFL ever had. The decade began with two leagues and ended with just one, formed by a merger of the two.

The AFL had its stars and it had its great teams and one of the best, if *not* the best was the Buffalo Bills. The question arose; would they be successful in the NFL?

The last couple of years within the AFL, the Bills had terrible seasons: 1967 was 4-10, 1968 1-12-1 and 1969 resulted in a 4-10 record, even with O.J. Simpson in the backfield. The Bills team that took to the field in 1970 for that first game in the NFL was a shadow of what it had been in last AFL game of 1969. There would be 7 new starters on offense and nearly as many on the defensive side of the ball. Two big hits on offense came as both Jack Kemp and Billy Shaw retired.

John Rauch was in his second year as head coach.

O.J. Simpson was entering his second year.

Al Cowlings, a friend of Simpson's from USC was the Bills first selection in the draft of 1970. Dennis Shaw was the second pick and would start as a rookie as the Bills new quarterback.

The Buffalo Bills needed a direction and it seemed, at first, that it would be the running game when O.J. suited up in '69. In his rookie year though he had rushed for only 700 yards. Direction would come but a transition had to take place first.

In 1970 *The Partridge Family* premiered on ABC and as us kids watched *Josie and The Pussycats* on Saturday mornings, George C. Scott won the Academy Award for his portrayal as *Patton.* As Creedence Clearwater Revival wondered about *Who'll Stop The Rain.* 1970 was the year Western New Yorkers had waited for, an NFL team in Buffalo. But that first year was one better forgotten. The first two games at home were losses by a combined 44-10. Their first NFL victory came on October 4th 1970 with a 34-31 against the New York Jets. In 1970 Marlin Briscoe led the team in receiving with over a thousand yards and nearly an eighteen yard average. O.J. had just a little over six hundred yards in *combined* yardage. The Bills ended the 1970 season with 6 consecutive losses and a tie resulting in a 3-10-1 record and a fourth place finish in the division.

There were only three teams that finished statistically worse then the Bills that year. The Houston Oilers 3-10-1, the Boston Patriots were 2-12 and the New Orleans Saints were 2-11-1. The 12 losses gave the Patriots the first pick in the 1971 draft. With it, they selected Jim Plunkett out of Stanford. The Saints took Archie Manning, the Oilers Dan Pastorini and, with the fourth pick, the Bills selected the wide receiver out of Arizona State, J.D. Hill. By selecting one of the nations top five receivers the direction of Bills seemed to be headed to that of a passing team.

Was Johnny Rauch expected to build the Bills into a passing

team? Regardless of what could have been, Johnny Rauch resigned as head coach after a disagreement with Ralph Wilson that centered on a couple of former Bills, Ron McDole and Paul Maguire. Wilson said that he would issue a statement supporting the players and with that Rauch resigned. Harvey Johnson the team's director of personnel replaced him.

The Buffalo Bills, by selecting J.D. Hill seemed to send a clear message as to their direction. Some in Buffalo may have questioned the selection. Why another receiver? The Bills already had Haven Moses, Marlin Briscoe, who had over 1,800 yards receiving between them in 1970. If the Bills were going to be a passing team, J.D. Hill was a logical choice.

The Bills did well in the 1971 draft. As they picked up Jim Braxton, Bobby Chandler and an offensive tackle out of Purdue, Donnie Green. What made J.D. Hill unique though? Why did the Bills take him as their first pick in 1971 and not John Brockington or Jack Youngblood? J.D. Hill was clearly one of the best wide receivers in the nation and had helped to lead the Sun Devils to an undefeated season in 1970, and a 48-26 thumping of UNC in The Peach Bowl.

In 1971, Nelson Rockefeller was Governor of New York and my hometown of Attica was national news as the prison riot took center stage. Jim Morrison had died and the Bills finished their second season with an abysmal 1-13 record under Harvey Johnson. The *one* win came in the eleventh game of the season on November 28th when they defeated the newly named New England Patriots, 27-20. Harvey Johnson was dismissed after the 1-13 season and Lou Saban was brought back to rebuild the Bills. According to some I have spoken with, Lou Saban coming back meant one thing; the Bills would now become a running team. This was not good news for the veteran wide receivers on the Bills, Haven Moses and Marlin Briscoe; they saw the handwriting on the wall and were soon headed elsewhere.

With Lou Saban returning to the Bills, it was expected that the career of O.J. Simpson would be rebuilt. The Bills second pick in the draft of 1972, the 27th, overall was a guard out of the University of Michigan, Reggie McKenzie. The Bills' offensive line in 1972 would consist of Donnie Green at right tackle, Reggie McKenzie at left guard and left tackle Dave Foley whom Saban had acquired from the New York Jets. The Bills were becoming a running team and perhaps the top ranked wide receiver J.D. Hill was being pushed to the side for the sake of rebuilding the career of O.J. Simpson.

J.D. Hill had speed and he had talent but did he come to the Bills at the wrong time?

Hi Rob, I had talent but not much else.

Good to talk to you again J.D. It's always a pleasure.

Good to talk to you again too. God is good and life is good right now.

J.D., before we get started, Paul Seymour wanted me to ask you something.

Paul? Oh my, that's not good!

Paul seems to think that at one time, after returning from a road game, you took a police car for a spin around the Buffalo airport. Is that true?

Wow! That's true. Good old Paul. This is what happened. We were coming back from a game and it was raining at the airport. All the police cars were lined up ready to escort the bus and I decided I was going to ride in something else. I hopped in and took off, and before you know it, I had every police car in the city chasing me around the airport. It was a joke of course, but those guys didn't have much of a sense of humor.

I imagine not. You did have an interesting upbringing.

My family and I had it hard. I didn't have many friends to speak of nor did I get any positive attention until I was twelve or thirteen or so. That's when I found out I could run, jump and throw. When I started to show myself in sports is when I began to get some attention.

You grew up in Stockton, California in the fifties, correct?

I was, born and raised in Stockton, California. I was an adopted child. My grandparents, Judge and Claudia Hill adopted me. My real parents had addiction problems at the time so my grandparents adopted me and they raised me.

They did their best to show me the love and give me the attention a young man needed. They kept me very active in the church. As a kid I *grew up* in the church, so my love, my appreciation as a kid, came mostly from my grandparents and from the church. The area I grew up in was pretty much a country setting. I loved to fish and would bring home dinner most times that way.

I played a lot of baseball, too. That was my main sport when I was a small kid, baseball.

Fishing? What'd you bring home?

At that time, we brought home what ever ended up on the hook. We had bamboo poles with red and white bobbers, and we fished for *whatever* ended up on the hook. There were smaller rivers and creeks where we lived, so we caught carp, perch, catfish and something called suckers. Catching one of those suckers was something. When you caught one, they were so bony they weren't worth the eating at all. They just seemed to eat our worms.

I remember those we called them bloodsuckers. How did you do in school?

School was a struggle. I had some serious struggles with the books. I'll tell you that. I was also burned badly as a kid, too. My arms and chest had been badly burned and I had to wear long sleeve shirts a lot. In Stockton, it was hot, so when I took my shirt off, the other kids didn't want to stand next me. They were afraid of the scars and the way I looked. You know how kids are.

Yes, I do.

I had a lot of issues: abandonment and rejection from my parents who were drug addicts, the teasing because of the scars and bad grades. My childhood was difficult.

I began to play sports as a form of escape. It wasn't until I began to get on the playing field that I found out I could run, jump, throw and catch well. People then didn't notice the scars. For a long time, my love had only come from the church and my grandparents, but when I became an athlete I could show others who I was. I was accepted even the more.

Growing up a baseball fan in northern California, did you follow the San Francisco Giants?

Oh, sure. I liked Willie Mays, Willie McCovey and Orlando Cepeda, and my favorite bat was a Jackie Robinson bat. I took it with me everywhere. I was twelve I think. Baseball was my game at the time and I thought I'd end up playing baseball somewhere.

If it wasn't for sports and some of my coaches, I don't know where I would have ended up.

Your high school coaches?

Yes. College too.

What high school did you go to?

I went to Montezuma and Garfield Elementary School. Next it was Hamilton Junior High School and then, Edison Senior High School. We were the Vikings. My coaches were Charles Washington, Ben Parks and Chuck Chandler. I was one of the few kids who grew up with black coaches, except for Coach Chandler. I did benefit early on from men, *black* men, who were educated and had an idea of what a young black man needed at the time. I'm so blessed that they took an interest in me.

The '60s were a difficult time in America. What was it like for you, at that time, when you were in high school?

It was hard everywhere. I was a teenager in the early '60s in the Oakland area, the bay area. It was a time, I would say, when black power was emerging. Blacks in America were becoming more verbal about change being needed in our society. We had Rosa Parks and Dr. Martin Luther King, but we also had the Black Panthers and the Muslim Movement. It was a time when the blacks wanted to be equal and were making their feelings known like at no other time before. The '60s was a time when the blacks began to come together as a community and to be heard socially and politically. I believe, too, that we affected change in America when we became as united as we were.

J.D paused for a moment.

Rob, it should be remembered that Martin Luther King was our leader in the Civil Rights Movement, but he was a man of God first. People sometimes forget that he was a Reverend. He was a Pastor.

J.D., I was born in 1964 and the Civil Rights Movement did a lot for me too. When I became old enough to know anything, I had no idea that separate drinking fountains or rest rooms existed, and I had no belief that I was entitled to a seat on a bus.

A lot had to happen to get to *that* point, Rob. The racial barriers were being broken down but they went away kicking and screaming at first.

The 1960s. It was a time of the hippies. We had the race riots throughout the country. We had the Haight-Ashbury district out here and back there, Rob, was Woodstock. We had the Viet-Nam War and young black men were leaving our communities and going off to fight for *their* country. It *was* their country now. Just the other day, I was talking to someone from my school, Edison High School. We had one of the fastest relay teams in all of California. Two of my teammates were Darryl Scott and Eugene Dotson went off and served their country. They died for their country.[1] They never had a

---

[1] Eugene Dotson Class of 1966 died in Viet Nam January 18th, 1969; located on panel 34, west line 32, Viet-Nam Memorial.

Darryl Scott Class of 1967 died in Viet-Nam October 19th, 1970; located on panel 06, west line 10, Viet-Nam Memorial.

chance at life.

A number of years ago I went back to see them. Did you hear what I said, Rob? I went back to *see* them. Their names are on The Wall in Washington D.C. too. I was lucky I was really fortunate. I lived. I had a scholarship. I went off to school and did what I did, but Darryl and Eugene never had a chance.

It, the 1960s, was a hard time but one that had to be experienced by all of us. I hope this country learned something from that time. The older we get the more we tend to learn about life. I think *I* did and it started there in the '60s. Anyway, my coaches in school were Ben Parks, Charles Washington and Chuck Chandler. They were and *still are* my friends. They did so much to keep me, as a young man, focused on something as best they could or, Lord knows, where I'd be if not for them. I hated school. I had very few friends because of all I had going on in my life. But my coaches were able to get me focused and *keep* me focused on something. Those guys I mentioned were my football coaches, my baseball coach was Vito Ramirez. Vito always thought I should go on and play professional baseball.

Any regrets about not getting into baseball?

Yes I had regrets, but I still wanted to go to college. If I had known more about the benefits of what baseball could offer I may have taken that route, but I didn't.

When did you first play football?

I didn't start playing football until the tenth grade in high school. Up until then, it was baseball. I was even been drafted by the Houston Astros system later on.

I didn't really excel in football in high school either, until my junior year. The kid ahead of me got in some trouble and I got a chance to play because of that. I sure did take advantage of it too. I guess you can say that football was my second sport up to that point. I played it but didn't *play* all out.

I do.

I am beating a dead horse, I know, but I *really* wanted to go to college. It was probably not so much for the knowledge that I could gain but I wanted to be around the college football game environment. I loved the stadiums and the *big* crowds, and I imagined myself at those football games, playing in front of *those* crowds. I daydreamed like all kids do.

Yeah, I do. Daydreaming, as I have discovered, is the greatest tool of any fiction writer.

Very good, Rob.

How did you end up at Arizona State? Weren't there California schools?

Well, I wanted go to a decent school. Some schools, like Pacific, Cal and New Mexico, were sending me letters but I didn't have the grades to get in. I thought about going to junior college for awhile, then perhaps transferring after I hit the books for a couple of years.

Colleges wanted me. I liked that. I was good on the field and in the 100-yard dash. I had the speed but I didn't have the grades, so a friend of mine, Larry Kentera, had just got a job at Delta Junior College in Stockton. Anyway, one night Larry came to the house and talked up a good game with my grandparents. He was saying oh, we have a spot for J.D. at Delta College. He's going to get a good education and we will make it real good for him there. I was all set to go to Delta and my grandparents were all set to *have* me go there. Then Larry got a job at Arizona State and he rushed back over to my house and told my grandparents, you know Delta's *not* the right place for J.D. We'll get him into Arizona State because *that's* the place he needs to be.

So, I guess you went to Arizona State.

Yes sir. I was off to Tempe. I suppose, too, that if Larry had gotten a job somewhere else, he would have come to the house and talked to my grandparents all over again.

Did you find the college atmosphere to be what you expected?

Yes I did. It overwhelmed me at first. My grades weren't great in college. It was a different world, but I was focused on being an athlete. I knew what it took to be a good athlete and that's what I set out to do. I was committed to being the best I could be on the field.

Your college days included leading Arizona State to that undefeated season in 1970 and a Peach Bowl win. You were named the most valuable player of the 1971 Senior Bowl. You also were named a unanimous 1st team All-American, and you have since been inducted into the Hall of Fame at Arizona State. Good stuff.

Thank you. Not bad for a young man who grew up under the circumstances I did.

The North won that Senior Bowl, 31-13.

We sure did. Rob, do you know who my coach was at that Senior Bowl?

I do believe it was Lou Saban.

It was Lou.

You scored a touchdown on a long punt return, 73 yards still a Senior Bowl record. You also made a touchdown saving tackle on Isiah Robertson, which could have changed the game.

Yes, I did. I had a good day. For me to get to that place though. I have to give the credit to my college coaches. Frank Kush was the best. He went through a lot with me. Take my word. If not for Frank Kush I don't know where I would have ended up. He is a great friend still to this day. My receiver coach was Joe McDonald he taught me *so* much too, they were two incredible men.

Did you think you would have an NFL career?

Rob, I didn't play the game because I wanted to play pro ball. I played because I enjoyed it. If the next step were a possibility, then that would be great.

You were the first receiver selected in the 1971 draft. That says a lot about your ability, don't you think?

I *think* so. When I was drafted, I *was* the first receiver chosen, behind only the quarterbacks of that year. Being drafted that high, I was expecting to be an impact player with the Buffalo Bills or what ever team I ended up with.

Johnny Rauch drafted you?

Yes, I was, and let me share something with you. Johnny wanted a passing team. He liked to throw the ball. He brought me in to be part of a throwing team. I have no doubts in my mind about that.

His career showed that he was a guy who liked to throw the ball, even back to his own playing days at Georgia.

Yes. When he coached Oakland they threw the ball. The year they went to the Super Bowl to play the Green Bay Packers. Lamonica had over 3,000 yards and thirty touchdowns. *They* were a throwing team. Look at their receivers: Billy Cannon, Fred Biletnikoff and Pete Banaszak. He wanted to build a passing team when he came to the Buffalo Bills.

After I got the phone call telling me that I had been drafted, I couldn't help but be happy, knowing that I was going to get a chance to be an impact player, an impact receiver, on a team that seemed like they were going to be a throwing team. Marlin Briscoe was already there, and in the same draft as me, Bobby Chandler came in, as well as Jim Braxton, who could catch out of the backfield as well as anyone.

That's interesting. Rauch wanted a passing team when he had O.J. Simpson in the backfield. Was the plan to eventually trade O.J.?

I don't know about that Rob.

I looked at the numbers O.J.'s rookie year was 1969 and he had 181 carries for 697 yards, a 4-yard average with 2 touchdowns while Jack Kemp had two thousand yards passing.

I will say they threw a lot his rookie year and I came in as a top ranked receiver to be added to an already good receiver corps.

I don't think 1970 was any better for him. O. J. actually did worse. He had 488 yards on 120 carries and Dennis Shaw had over twenty-five hundred yards in the air. Even a casual fan would have to wonder why they kept O.J. with the Bills when he seemed to be under-producing during his first two years in the league.

Looking back, the Bills certainly wanted O.J. to succeed. They wanted him to succeed *in Buffalo*, so they had to build to make that happen.

You never played for Johnny though, Harvey Johnson took over for 1971, and your first season. O.J. still didn't have over a thousand yards.

That's right.

So you were drafted into what you believed was going to be the building of a throwing team but that ended when Rauch left?

Perhaps. Johnny was gone and Harvey lasted only a year. Then Lou Saban came in and he came in for just one reason, which was to resurrect O.J. Simpson. Lou had a history of being a running coach and of *saving* running backs. He did it with "Cookie" Gilchrist and with Floyd Little in Denver, perhaps he came back to Buffalo to save O.J's career.

Bobby Chandler and I get to Buffalo and Haven Moses and Marlin Briscoe were already there. *They* saw what was going on with the Bills and, after that season, they started looking around for other teams.

What was your rookie year like?

I was injured most of my rookie year. We were playing the Detroit Lions in a preseason game. I was on a slant pattern when Dick LeBeau hit me on the left side, up on the left hip, and it knocked my knee out. I had to have an operation and, back then they operated on what they *thought* and not necessarily what they *knew*. Even today, I can't bend my left leg. I didn't come back until late in the season.

I still believe that if I had been allowed to sit out that game against the Lions, I wouldn't have been injured and would have had a good year. I was going to make the team anyway, so I should have sat out.

I had been a tough week anyway. The week before I learned my mother had died, my natural mother. So I went down to Texas, to attend her funeral. I was dealing with all the emotions that come from such a loss and came back a couple of days later. I wasn't prepared physically or emotionally. I hadn't practiced and I had to play in a pre-season game that had no meaning and, bam, I got hurt and was out for ten weeks.

You had 11 receptions for 218 yards and 2 touchdowns that year, though.

Yes, I did, and those two touchdowns came in a game against New England, the only game we won that year.

Your two scores were the difference in the 27-20 win.

We won when I came back from knee surgery, real knee surgery where they opened my knee up. I always wondered why they played me, though. The team was 0-10. What good were a couple of games going to do for the Bills or for me? I wasn't getting the best advice, for if the Bills cared about me and about the future of a passing game, they would have sat me out for the entire season and, in 1972 I could have been the rookie of the year. 1972 was a good year anyway as I went to the Pro-Bowl.

It was a bad rookie year overall, physically and emotionally for you.

It really was.

You were drafted to be part of an emerging passing game but, almost instantly, the Buffalo Bills became a running team. I could see how that would change you.

It changed me Rob. It changed my attitude. I still played hard and played to win but it changed me in many ways and those changes weren't healthy.

We *all* came out of college with a drive to win. I came out of Arizona State where we were undefeated. Reggie came out of Michigan, so did Paul, and O.J. and Bobby Chandler out of USC. We were all winners and we wanted to win. I thought we could win as a passing team.

Listen to this Rob. After a game in Baltimore, Johnny Unitas game into *our* locker room. He said he was looking for J.D. Hill. *Johnny Unitas* was looking for me! Everybody pointed my way and he came up to me. Johnny Unitas, the all-pro-all-star-Super Bowl winner. He came over to me and said, "J.D. you could be one of the greatest receivers of all times. You just went to the *wrong* team. Good luck with your career." I think it was 1972, maybe '73 when that happened.

My attitude was changing. I liked Buffalo, the town and the fans, and so I did my best to become a good team player, doing what I could as a receiver to make the Bills win as a running team.

When folks mention The Electric Company, are you disappointed that your name isn't included on the list?

Yes, sure I am. Sometimes I get disappointed but I don't dwell on it. When O.J. was on a sweep, when he went to the outside who do you think had to take out guys like Jack Tatum or Dick Butkus? I did! Those downfield blocks for O.J. added up to a good number of yards. I was made an honorary member of *The Electric Company* a few years back. O.J. had said that much of what he had done could not have been possible without my downfield blocks.

I think our entire starting offense should be recognized as *The Electric Company*. We all had different roles on the block. Bobby Chandler and I were downfield and Jim Braxton was the lead blocker.

I hadn't thought of it quite that way before. You led the Bills in receiving in 1972, a decent fourteen-yard average. O.J. had twelve hundred plus. To me, that was a good balance.

It was. A balanced approach would have worked better in the long run. With Bobby Chandler and me at the wide-outs and O.J and Jim Braxton in the backfield and with the offensive line we had, we would have been tough. A great two punch team.

I was looking through the game-by-game stats for that 1973 season and came across game two against the Chargers. The Chargers whooped up on the Bills pretty good, 34-7, but you had a great day.

I remember that game clearly. I had 9 catches for well over a hundred yards, but what I remember most was that I was so hungry. I hadn't eaten so I had some guy run out and get me a hot dog.

No way!

Yes sir. In the middle of the game, I had somebody run out to get me lunch!

Well, whatever he brought you back, a hot dog or cheese fries, it worked.

That Chargers game was my best one for the entire year. I had nine catches in that game but only twenty more for the balance of the season and *no* touchdowns at all.

There *is* story that I have to tell you. It's about our wide receiver, John Holland. We were in a close game with Miami. We never ever beat them; so being in a close game was something rare. We had just a few minutes left and we were close to the winning score or tying it up. In those days we shuttled plays in with our receivers. We were all standing in the huddle looking over at Lou, waiting for him to send the play in. Lou was brilliant. We waited and waited. Time was ticking by and he sends the play in with John Holland.

John was a great guy. John had a bad stuttering problem though, so when he gets into the huddle, he sounds like a broken lawn mower trying to start up. The game clock was just ticking away. He was nervous and stuttering like crazy. I said, "John, come on. I've heard you sing. Just *sing* the play, John!" And he did. The play was a success but we still fell short that day. It was always nice to hear John sing though.

It's not that I quit playing hard, I didn't. It was my attitude. I was a disgruntled receiver and undoubtedly it lead up to my trade to the Detroit Lions in 1976. Greg Landry and Lem Barney were there at the time. Lem Barney would actually be part of my wedding. But my first year, my *first* game I caught one ball and got injured again when Doug Plank, of the Bears, took out my left knee. I was out for the rest of the season. I caught a few more in '77 and '78 and the Lions let me go in 1979 because I could no longer run, the pain was so great.

Rob, I a lot of fun in Buffalo, it was a different era. I met my wife Caryl in Buffalo she was a law student at the time. I, *we* I mean to say, so many of us were part of the community. I had my football camps. We went to schools and were on bowling and softball teams. Guys like Tony Greene, Joe Ferguson, Bobby Chandler they always did anything I asked them to do for the youth in Buffalo I was part of.

You had some tough years after football.

I did. Many of us did. As I said, *what* money there was, dried up, I had nothing. There were other guys who became homeless or *so* addicted that they haven't made it back yet. Life was hard on many of us guys. Don't let the NFL, its current leadership or the *money* say any different. I lost houses, furniture, and cars. You name it was all gone after the game ended for me. I ended up with a substance problem; drugs and alcohol, hopeless and without God.

I've heard many stories, J.D., and as a fan, I always thought you guys made tons of money. I also thought the union, the NFLPA, would take care of you once you retired but it's not so.

No, it isn't. The way some of us have been treated is criminal. Guys in the Hall of Fame making a couple hundred bucks a month in pension is shameful. We are the ones who *built* this league and there are those before us that built the game for us. What the NFL is now is because of us the older generation.

So many of us fans understand that now. It's the goal of this book to help educate the fans in what the state of affairs is really like. You're a minister now. Tell me about Catch The Vision Ministry.

Catch The Vision began when I was with the Buffalo Bills. It was football camps then. I didn't know it was going to be a ministry until much later. Even when I left the Bills and the league, I had basketball games with the J.D. Hill All-Stars. It was years later when God began to move more in my life that a ministry was born. I'm sure God had always moved for me but as I got older, I began to pay attention to what *He* was doing and not what J.D. wanted. I had a scripture that I had read in the Bible - Proverbs 29:18 - it says: "*Where there is no vision the people will perish.*"

At a time when I was low, I needed God and I needed that scripture. God began to minister to me through people and I began to *catch* the vision of what God had in mind for me. I had to *catch* the vision to be the man that God had called me to be. The husband, the father, the community leader, the drug *and* alcohol free man. If I had no vision of being *such* a man, how could I set a goal and how could that goal be accomplished?

In order to set a goal, all of us, have to have a vision. Once you *catch* that vision, then we can set that goal and count the costs at achieving it. What is it going to cost you? Remember that the cost doesn't *have* to be money.

You're right. When I was an alcohol and drug counselor, I shared with the active user what was shared with me. Sometimes we must change people, places and things to get sober. For many that was just too high a price.

Yes sir, cost isn't always money.

Life has been good J.D.?

It's been great! In my ministry *Catch The Vision* we work with youth and adults over Phoenix and the nation. We help people to *catch* the vision, *set* the goal, *and count* the cost. We teach that it is belief in God and exercising of faith that will make that goal come to be. What a joy!

Whenever I travel the country, I preach the main ingredient that a person needs is courage. It takes courage to show our faith because of the anti-God world we live in. Temptation surrounds us. I share what God has taught; *be courageous and know that He is always with us*. I am very active with the Dream Center established by my Pastor Tommy Barnett of the 1st Assembly of God in Phoenix. We work with the addict, we feed the hungry and house the homeless. Life has been an incredible ride and now I have been give a special opportunity to be the person God wants me to be. In turn I can help others to catch the vision and be who God wants them to be. Rob, if anyone, anywhere needs help they can reach me through our website www.jdhill.org.

37
12

Chapter 7
Donnie Green

"If you put your hand in mine. We're gonna' leave all our troubles behind. Keep on walkin', don't look back."(1)
-The Temptations-

J.D. is frustrated at how some of the older retired players have been treated by the NFL and by its union, the NFLPA. DeLamielleure and others have said and I'll paraphrase The NFL is a multi-billion dollar monopoly and they are letting us fade away once we are no longer of any use to them. They can't or they *won't,* which is even worse, peel off a few extra bucks a month to make life more comfortable for the older guys in need *right* now.

I have read stories on the late Mike Webster, the old center for the Pittsburgh Steelers, and Willie Wood, a member of those Lombardi Packer teams and in the Hall of Fame, and all they have had to deal with. I have met a number of older players and interviewed many, many more for this and other projects and have

seen what appears to be a growing pattern of neglect by the player's union toward the older retired player. What is the union, any union, supposed to do for its members or former members? Are they supposed to offer proper care? Are those unions, at a minimum, supposed to offer dignity? Of course they are.

Would the fire fighters, the United Auto Workers, the Teamsters, the teachers or any other profession refuse care to their retirees? No, they wouldn't, but the NFL does. Joe DeLamielleure said to me:

"Rob, why does the most lucrative sports league in the United States, if not the world, have the worst pension and disability plan. The answer is because Gene Upshaw runs the show. Upshaw told the Charlotte Observer that the bottom line was simple."

As J.D. Hill and I wrapped up our chat, I couldn't help but think back to those games of the 1970s and wonder how many of those guys I watched now have physical, mental and financial problems as a direct result of playing in the NFL.

When an older fan of the Buffalo Bills is asked to name the members of *The Electric Company*, the first couple of names roll off their tongues pretty easily: the guards, McKenzie and DeLamielleure; then Montler, the center, Seymour the tight end and, if they can name them, the tackles. They are most often named last, Dave Foley and Donnie Green. It was a year or so ago when I was contemplating writing yet another novel that I was reintroduced to Donnie Green.

Donnie came to the Buffalo Bills as part of that 1971 NFL Draft along with J.D. Hill. The other three picks made by the Bills that year ahead of Donnie were Jan White, a tight end, Bruce Jarvis, a center, and Jim Braxton, a well known blocking back out of West Virginia.

Donnie, it's nice to finally talk to you. How are things in Hagerstown?

I've been good, really good, Rob.

Thank you for taking time today. I've been writing this book for about a year now and it wouldn't have been complete without including you in it.

Thanks man, I think. Should I be thankful, Rob?

Oh, sure. Well, except for the picture of you I'm going to use. You might not like that.

Don't do that to me, Rob.

You sure? It's from the 1st grade?

Oh no, man. No!

Okay, no 1st grade picture.

Good. That's sure nice of you, Rob. I was told you're good about stuff like that.

Over the last couple of years I've become familiar with your story, Donnie. To be honest, I lost track of many of you old Bills over the years when I was off doing what I was, and the game had lost me as a fan for a long time too. But I began to read stories about older, retired NFL guys and about the medical problems, about the dementia crisis, about the financial ruin, about the disability claims and about guys like Tom Condon and Gene Upshaw and, in your case, the homelessness. I was surprised to say the least.

A lot of people are. The stories aren't good ones and *we* aren't the millionaires of the NFL. We're just the guys who made everything possible.

The first one I reached out to was Joe DeLamielleure who was all hot, at the time, over the comments made to him by Gene Upshaw. The book snowballed from there.

I'm sure Joe *was* upset. He should have been. He's a great guy he didn't deserve Gene Upshaw.

Again, thank you Donnie for taking this time to talk to me. It has been an incredible privilege to talk with all of you. I can't say that often enough.

Thank you for doing this.

I want to share a little about me so you might will feel a bit more comfortable. I am a recovering alcoholic, 19 years sober this coming August.

Praise God, Rob. Amen! Amen! Drugs and alcohol?

Alcohol. I was a rip-roaring drunk well before I ever started high school. No bones about it. My nineteen years sober would not have been possible if I had not turned my will, my selfish will, over to God all those years ago. He put me in the right place and the right time, and I had to go through all that I did to finally get an open mind.

You're so right, Rob. What got you to that point, though?

I was in Memphis. I had lied and stolen my way for years. I stumbled into a church that I would end up working for, for nearly a decade.

Wow! That's something else there, Rob. Good for you.

You, too. You were born in Washington D.C., just down the road from where you are now?

Yes, I was. There was a hospital there. They changed the name of it since. I can't remember the original name either.

It was like a city hospital?

Something like that.

How many brothers and sisters do you have?

Well, there are nine of us, really. I have a big family.

What did your folks do?

My dad was a career Navy guy and my mom was a store clerk. She ran a small little store.

Your dad was career Navy? Really? When did he retire?

Oh, let's see. He retired…. Well, he'll be 90 in May.

90! Good for him.

Yeah, 90. Dad retired in the early 1980s, I think.

You grew up as a military kid then?

Yea, did all kinds of stuff, kid stuff.

To give you an idea - when I was ten, I was throwing snowballs at you and Costa up at Rich Stadium.

For real? Oh, that's terrible, man! So that's where all those snowballs came from. I see now!

Yeah. I was the little fat kid sitting in the end zone throwing them as quick as I could make them. I was the one with glasses and wool skullcap. Remember?

You know, I think I do remember. That's *terrible,* Rob. You should have been cheering for us, not throwing snowballs at us, man!

Well, that may be so, but I was mad. You guys didn't give me an autograph or mouth guard or nothing.

I tried to sign stuff for everyone. Maybe I didn't like your hat or something, Rob. Funny stuff! I got hit with so many snowballs, though. I probably would have remembered you. You were one of those kids tossing stuff. I see!

Okay. What high school did you go to?

I went to Crestwood High School in Chesapeake Virginia.

That's a great spot in Virginia, from what I remember of Chesapeake, tell me if I'm way off, there is a big old bridge crossing the bay down there.

Oh, yeah, the Chesapeake Bay Tunnel. It's like 20 miles long. It goes from Virginia Beach to Delaware. When it's crossed at the right time of year, it's a beautiful scene.

As a student of the Civil War I have been down there often.

Field stomper?

Yes sir. My first NFL game, Donnie, was in 1974. It was against the Patriots and it was where O.J. ran for over 200 yards. Paul caught two touchdown passes in that game.

Okay. I sort of remember that but it seemed like O.J. was always running for 200.

True. What did you do while growing up?

As a kid, I went to Portsmouth, Virginia schools. We had some little sports teams around town, baseball and basketball, kid stuff. I was the neighborhood grass cutter. Made a couple of dollars doing that.

Lawn mowers really stunk back then too, didn't they?

Oh man, did they. The push and pull ones. Wasn't any riding ones around our neighborhood that is for sure.

When did you start playing football?

I started playing football when I was in the 8th grade. I went out for the team at Crestwood High School. What happened was that my older brother Morris took me to a game and I liked it. At the time, I was going to high school in Portsmouth and coaches started coming around our house talking to my parents. They were hearing a lot about me playing football and they said I would do better at Crestwood. So, I decided to go there. Coach George Quarles came to my house a bunch of times and he finally convinced me that I should go play football for him.

Did you have to play both ways in high school?

Yeah, we did. I played both defensive and offensive tackle.

Did you follow any college or pro teams when you were growing up?

Well, basically we're from Maryland. My family moved from Annapolis when I was 7 or 8 years old. My mom had passed away and Dad got married again, so we moved to Portsmouth, but *I* followed the Baltimore Colts.

The Colts of the '60s? They had one nasty field there in Baltimore.

Yes, it sure was - old Memorial Field. But, they were great - Johnny Unitas, John Mackey, Lenny Moore, Raymond Berry. Man, they were great to watch as a kid. I wanted to know everything I could about them.

That was the time of their Super Bowl teams, too.

Yes, it was. The Colts lost to the Jets in that Joe Namath Super Bowl III, but the Colts beat the Dallas Cowboys in Super Bowl V.

That Super Bowl V was the first Super Bowl after the merger and the AFC teams had been getting the best of it since the merger was announced. John Mackey caught a long ball from Unitas in that one, almost 80 yards.

Yes sir, he sure did. Johnny Unitas had a gun for sure.

How many colleges were looking at you when you were a high school senior?

There were quite a few: University of Virginia and Purdue. I went to visit the University of Minnesota, Tennessee A&I and a lot of other schools. I had a good number of offers for scholarships, thank God.

Good. What made you pick Purdue though?

When I flew up to Purdue for the visit, a friend of mine named John Bullock came with me. He was from the Newport News area and so we played against each other in high school. A guy who had played in the same part of Virginia before us, Leroy Keyes, was already at Purdue. He told the coaches about John and me, so we both flew up the same weekend.

I remember Leroy. He played for the Eagles later on didn't he?

Yes, he did. Coming back after our visit is when we decided that Purdue would be the place to go. We just decided that it was a great place to get an education. The campus was nice and we would have a chance to play some ball.

That would have been 1967?

Yeah.

Who was your coach?

Jack Mollenkopf was my first one, then Bob DeMoss after that. They were really great. They pushed us in every aspect of the game. They had a genuine weight program that my high school *didn't* have so I began real workouts there at Purdue. "Wimp" Hewgley was another coach, my line coach, and he was something else. He would keep me after practice and running drills all the time. I thought he was just being *mean* to me but he must have seen something in me that I didn't see. The Lord must have put him in my life back then. He gets so much of the credit. The Lord gets the glory for all of it. He did His work through Coach Hewgley. I got to love that guy something strong.

They didn't start you guys your freshman year, right?

No you couldn't start as freshman in the Big-Ten then. We could only start when we were sophomores.

Out of all of your college years, what were your most memorable experiences there at Purdue?

Well, it wasn't so much about me as much as it was about Leroy Keyes and Mike Phipps, and our beating Indiana University. IU was our strongest rivalry. I have a hard time remembering what *year* it was but it was getting near the end of the game. IU was leading with about 10 seconds left and we were on the 40-yard line or something like that. Mike Phipps went back and tossed one into the end zone and Leroy went up and caught it between two defenders as the clock ran out and we won the game. That was great! That was one of my best days. There was another time during my sophomore year. We were number 1 in the country and we had beaten up on a couple of schools early that year.

I looked that year up and you whooped up on Virginia 44-6, and beat Notre Dame 37-22 and Northwestern 43-6. That's a pretty good start.

Yeah, it was but then we went into Ohio State and we lost that game in a shut out, and not by that not much. Boy, Rob, I tell you for sure that was one of the *blackest* days in my life. Every paper and every poll in America had rated us number 1, and Ohio State beat us. That was hard. That day really was a hard, ugly, nasty, dark day. That wasn't a *good* highlight.

I guess you mean to say it was painful.

Yea, man. I remember it like it was this morning and it was forty years ago now. We had a great team. We thought we were going to go all the way. For me, the great thing, however, was watching guys like Mike Phipps and Leroy Keyes and just being part of a really good team.

Leroy Keyes was the first person to rush for over a thousand yards in a season for Purdue, wasn't he?

Yes, he was. He did it in that '68 season, I think. It was a great school and great campus, and I wouldn't have gone anywhere else.

When did you have an idea that you were probably going to have a shot at the pros?

Well, I'll tell you. When it got to be my junior year and we had our spring practice and training camp, I began to notice these guys in suits. They were standing around looking at me. My senior year came around and we were going up to Michigan State. Coach Hewgley came back to me and said, Donnie, you need to get ready for the pros because you're getting drafted. I guess those guys in suits were scouts.

You didn't get letters or calls from other teams?

The Dallas Cowboys used to come up and work us out. I was told that Vince Lombardi came up one time to watch us freshman and he had told someone that the Purdue Boilermakers had some of the best freshman he'd ever seen. That's all I remember to be honest.

We did have a big freshman class. Besides me, there were Alex Davis and Paul Baker, 6-5, 6-6, 260, 270 pounds. We were big. The Cowboys used to make us run sprints to check our speed and to do one drill after another. To be honest, Rob, I thought I was going to get drafted *by* the Cowboys. So when draft day came I was sitting with some friends of mine and found out it was the Bills.

5th round.

That's right.

That was a pretty good draft year for Buffalo.

Well, the Lord gets the praise, Brother Rob. There was J.D. Hill, Bobby Chandler, Jim Braxton, good people came to Buffalo in 1971.

Up to that point, O.J. wasn't doing much in his first couple of years and it appeared to me that Johnny Rauch wanted to be a throwing team. Did you think you were being drafted to help O.J. rebuild his career?

I think so and certainly when Lou came in 1972. We all knew that we were going to help get O.J. going.

Had you ever been to Buffalo before coming up for the first day of practice?

No, never. I knew there was going to be snow, though.

Yup. Lots of snow. Always snow. Did you start right away?

No. Paul Costa had gotten hurt and, Harvey Johnson, came up to me and told me, rook you're going to get a start. I did and, after a while, they switched Paul over to left tackle. The Lord blessed me and I did pretty well. The coaches said, "Rook. It's your job."

That 1971 was a pretty ugly season though, 1-13.

Yeah. It was ugly that is for sure.

In 1972, Lou Saban was coach and the first pick was Walt Patulski. Reggie McKenzie came in that year, and the offensive line seemed to be really coming together during the 1972 season. It was apparently for the one reason of salvaging O.J. Simpson's career. Did he know that, too? What was he like to play with on a day-to-

day basis?

I think O.J. knew he was being salvaged. He respected all of us and gave us the credit. O.J. really *was* a great guy. That dude was really fun to be around. When we played in Memorial Stadium and after the Lord gave me a chance to play and to start that first game or two, I'd make these holes for him. He was so smart that he'd be through the hole and seven or eight moves ahead of the defense - quick, smart, precision. He was great.

That's what so many of the guys have said, with the exception of the older ones who played with "Cookie" Gilchrist. They had never seen anyone so quick to the read.

He was smart, quick and there was no one like him.

Does the name, "Bucket head" ring a bell?

No what's bucket head?

That's a nickname that Dwight Harrison gave O.J.

Naw, man! I don't remember that but I knew "Juice" got upset when we talked about the size of his head. I didn't go that way, though. That's funny and that's terrible, too, man! Dwight's probably mad because he could never catch him.

Yeah, I think he was. He told me that there were two he could never catch, O.J and Paul Warfield.

Good old Dwight. Thinking about it, he never *did* catch Paul Warfield.

In the 1973 season, there was you, Dave Foley, Reggie, Seymour, DeLamielleure, and Mike Montler had just come over from the Patriots. You were all together. Did you know early on that you had a shot at a record-breaking season that year?

No, Rob. This is the way I took it. I really took it one game at a time. I was still pretty new to the league and I wanted to do my best to block for my guys in the backfield and to keep the folks off Joe Ferguson. The yards that we were getting were great, of course. I think Reggie came to me when there were about three or four games left in the season and he said, man, we got a shot at getting "Juice' two-thousand yards. All of a sudden, we all went crazy after that.

The numbers sure show that. The last four games of 1973, Baltimore, Atlanta, New England and the Jets, and three of the four were on the road. The numbers show me that O.J. had almost 900 yards in just those four games alone.

We went crazy. Jim Ringo was a great offensive line coach. He put the schemes in there. He said we could be unstoppable with Braxton in the backfield in front of O.J. He told us to get to know one another, go hang out and get to be like a family and we did. When Reggie said that to us about the record, the Lord blessed us and we knocked folks over.

Joe Ferguson and others have said that they had never seen a better lead blocker coming out of the backfield then Jim Braxton.

Dude was great, Rob. We had him *and* Paul Seymour. There were so many times where Paul and I would have to double team the defensive end. I know there had to be plenty of times that the dude needed a lot of toilet paper when he saw us line up against him. Paul was a *big* guy. With Paul and me double-teaming the end, pulling Reggie or DeLamielleure and bringing Braxton as a lead block with "Juice" dancing around it all, it was unbelievable. Man, we were something.

I'm seeing that in my mind and how would anyone stop that? In the game against the New York Jets, the last game of 1973, when O.J. broke Jim Brown's record and went over 2,000 yards, what was the locker room like before and after the game?

I tell you, Rob. It was a zone. It was like everyone was in a zone.

It was something else. I could have played five football games that day. *I'm* serious. I felt sorry for the guy who had to line up against Paul and me because he caught it all for the entire game from both of us. I think it was Mark Lomas or Richard Neal.

Jim Brown's record was broken and O.J. set the record with 2,000 in a season. He paid tribute to you guys in the locker room.

He sure did. He spread the credit and I'm told there is a photo of us at the Hall of Fame.

Moving forward - you lost the division to the Steelers in 1974. Was that the best year for the Bills during the O.J. era?

Well, it was one of the best. I think it was the first time the Bills had made the playoffs in a long time, so it was nice to bring that opportunity to the fans again. But there were so many good times in Buffalo, except for little kids throwing snowballs at us.

Yeah. That sucked, I'm sure. You retired in 1978. Your last year in the league was with the Detroit Lions. Was Greg Landry still there?

No, Gary Danielson was quarterback.

What was it like to go from the Bills of The Electric Company to an all-new offensive line?

To be truthful about it, the Eagles and the Lions both had great offensive lines.

Donnie, what music did you listen to?

Music? I love the Temptations. I love harmony, the oldies but goodies stuff.

I have to ask you Donnie; What do you think of Gene Upshaw?

Man, I don't know what's wrong with him but something's wrong, that's for sure. Gene played the game when we all did. To be truthful about it, I've been praying for him, that the Lord would open up his heart so he could help some of these guys. There are guys out here suffering needlessly. The NFL makes a lot of money and the union is supposed to help its players and former players, but they don't. Any union is supposed to help their former workers. *We* are the NFL's former workers and they have let us drift away. The NFLPA is there to help us be better *and* live better. I don't understand why they have abandoned so many and has instead neglected the guys who paved the way for us, for *him,* Joe D., Reggie and me. Guys like Johnny Unitas. Folks say that he could hardly even lift a coffee cup towards the end. There are a lot of other guys who are suffering but the NFL is just tossing a bone, crumbs, to the folks who need it. It's a shame. It's embarrassing.

I have spoken to so many who have been through numerous surgeries - knee replacements, hip replacements and spinal surgeries. There are many who have degenerative conditions and who have to beat themselves senseless just to get a couple of bucks out of the NFL.

I know, Rob. Previous players built the league for all of *us*, and we did what we could to make the league better for the guys playing right now.

The NFL appears to have set the bar so high in defining disability that very few have qualified. Reports have said that as few as 2% of everyone who have ever played in the NFL actually receive disability. That's an interesting number. At the Congressional hearing last year, it was stated that half of the ball players retire because of injury. Sixty percent suffer a concussion, at least one-quarter of the players suffer multiple concussions and nearly two-thirds have suffered an injury serious enough to sideline them for at least half the season. With the numbers of injuries that high, why does the NFLPA say only 2% qualify for disability?

A good question.

Donnie, I saw that your pension is $600 a month?

Yeah, $600.

That's $7,200 a year. Gene Upshaw makes that in ten hours. Some young guy who has never played a down of pro ball will soon sign a contract with a million dollar signing bonus.

Yup, that's right. I mean I don't blame the new guys for getting as much as they can but if the NFL has the money in the pot to help the older guys, they should. If the good Lord comes between now and tomorrow, I hope everyone is saved, *especially* Gene Upshaw. We won't need the money in heaven. Some guys need it now. Some families need it now. I don't blame the younger guys, but don't forget the older ones.

When your playing days ended, Donnie, what did you do soon afterwards?

I taught school for a while.

Really. Where?

I taught at Kennedy Institute in Washington D.C.

Did you think you were prepared for life after football?

No, I wasn't. I had problems in the league. I started doing some things that I shouldn't have been doing, particularly my last couple of years. Life was good back then, though, so I thought I was making a lot of money for that time. $60,000 a year was great.

For some guys, that's a game check nowadays.

I know. Wow, man. I really didn't know what to do in life. I drifted for years. I drove a truck. Like I said, I taught school for some time. I began to hang out with people I wouldn't have been around before and began to use drugs as a way to get away from everything.

A few years back I was homeless. I had been evicted from my apartment and I was living on the streets. I came to the Hagerstown Rescue Mission and I have been *here* ever since. I always wanted to play more than I wanted to work. My head wasn't on straight for a long time until I turned my life around with the Lord's help.

The Lord is good. He has restored my life and I praise the Lord for giving me a chance to live life again. Sometimes we have to live through experiences to get where we are. Now, I'm not saying I wish what I went through on anyone because I don't. But my circumstances taught me a lot. Admitting my defeat and turning my entire will over to the care of God is what I had to do. He saved my life, no doubt in my mind, or I would have died a drug addict on the streets somewhere if it hadn't been for this shelter.

Did you follow a twelve-step program at the mission?

No, we're a Christian mission. We have classes on Christian living and a different chapel service every night.

As I mentioned, Donnie, the only way I could turn things around in my life. The only way I could stop drinking, was throwing myself completely into A.A.

God gave you A.A. and He gave me the Hagerstown Rescue Mission. I'm going on five years clean now and it took everything I went through, to get where I have, and I am so pleased, so thankful. I praise God each and every day for everything.

Good. What's next for you, Donnie?

I enjoy what I'm doing right now. I let God control everything. I hope that someday I can enter the ministry. I sit in my room some times and I look at the few mementos I have from my playing days. I dream and I remember. The fans of Buffalo were terrific. They have always remembered me and I remember them. I loved playing for them. I hope and I pray every day, Rob that the NFL will help the older retired players in the way that they should. It's the right thing to do.

Chapter 8
Reggie McKenzie

"Hopes that were high in the heat of September can wilt and die in the chill of November. November can be cold and gray, November can be surly with bitter rain upon the world and winter coming early."(1)
-John Facenda-

November crispness. We from the shallow streets of small town Western New York know what that means all to well. When we breathe deep our lungs are refreshed. We pull the collar a bit higher. The skin from the White Birch and the leaves from the Elm crunch in unison as the trees shed their summer wear for a winter coat. The smells! God, I can still smell the South Lima air after all these years, the air that those leaves and trees left behind.

I was still a year or two away from my first game but well advanced at living it in my mind. I was a back yard veteran battered, bruised and triumphant in many belly-jiggling end zone dances. My days after school were filled with dreams of some other place. I would walk the rail line behind my house, in hopes of *finding* that place. I smelled the leaves. I smelled the last cut of grass. I smelled the shore of the lake not so far away and above it all I could smell Mom's home made bread. November was crisp and, all these years later, each and every fall, it still is.

It was the early '70s, 1971 and 1972 to be exact, and the Buffalo Bills were terrible with only five wins in two years to show for their efforts. In 1971, they were 1-13 and in 1972, the Bills were 4-9-1. Nothing seemed to work. Dennis Shaw had 63 interceptions and 35 touchdowns in three years. O.J. hadn't rushed for more than 700 yards in his first several years. They were 35 of 58 in field goals, and they were averaging less than two touchdowns per game, with many lopsided losses, especially in the 1971. A change was needed.

It came with Lou Saban as he returned with one mission, to rejuvenate the career of O.J. Simpson.

As a result of that 1971 finish the Bills would have an opportunity to improve via the draft. They choose first, Walt Patulski, a defensive end out of Notre Dame. It was their second pick though, the first pick of the second round that would cement the team's fate for the next decade. The All-American out of Michigan, Reggie McKenzie, was to be the new left guard.

One of the first things Reggie McKenzie did in our interview was to confirm everything J.D. Hill had told me about John Holland and his ability to *sing* under stressful conditions.

It's true, Rob. It's *all* true man! I don't know how many times John would come in and sing the play to us. John was a great friend and teammate.

Reggie, you are probably one of the all-time fan favorites. Even today, when your name is mentioned, people smile. Nowadays, if I was to mention the names of the current players, fans will shake their head or roll their eyes.

Some players in the league now are terrible role models. We weren't perfect but we didn't act the fool either. One of the things we try to express in our youth football camps is how to be a man of *quality* too. It *is* nice to always be remembered as a good guy by the people in Buffalo. I loved Buffalo. The older I get I really do appreciate my time there so much more. The group of guys we had there over those five or six years was a great group and it was a tremendous period of time to be a football player.

When I was growing up, my brother and I used to go up to Orchard Park and watch you guys' play. We knew who was going to suit up season after season. It's not like today; a fan needs a flip chart to see who is playing from one season to the next.

Yeah, I know Rob. You never know who is going to be there.

As a fan, free agency has killed the game and in many ways sapping much of my own interest in it.

I can understand that. Free agency *was* good for the players but there were a lot of us who fell on the sword in many ways for what these guys have now, and no body cares, no body gives a shit about what *we* did. I think that the pensions are the big thing. There are guys who really helped build the league and now they're just making it on the pennies the league hands out.

I've learned that. What did a little Reggie do? What was your first job?

What did I do as a kid? My first job? I lived in Highland Park and so my job was delivering newspapers and shining shoes. I delivered the Free Press, a morning route, and then I had a small route with the Highland Parker. When I was done with delivering papers, I shined shoes, mostly on the weekends, Thursday, Friday and Saturday. I just did normal kid stuff. I played around the neighborhood, chased girls and sometimes got into a little more trouble than my parents' thought was wise.

Were you expected to go to college? Was it a given. The '60s weren't easy, especially in the Detroit area.

Oh I knew I was going. It *was* expected. I had great examples. Neither my mother nor father went to college they worked. I had an uncle, though, who was a principal down in Georgia and he was a big example for staying in school, working hard, getting the nice things and so on. My mother and father always preached getting a good education and they made sure we all got a quality education because it would be that *and* our hard work that would improve our lot in life.

That's something you express quite a bit in your foundation isn't it?

Yeah, because like I tell people, I didn't get where I am all by myself. God puts blessings on all of us and it's up to us to do something with the blessing or not. I call my foundation my way of putting something back into the community. I'm proud to say that, this June, it will be thirty-five years of what we call the All-Pro Football Clinic and we just finished twenty-three years of our academic program where we teach math and literary skills. Early on I decided that I never wanted to forget where I had come from.

It would seem that thirty-five years operating such a foundation would make you one of the oldest continuous foundations out there. That would put the start date back in 1973?

Yes sir, that's right. We started it in my second or third year with the Bills.

Jerome Bettis had attended your program for a couple of years?

He sure did, particularly when he was in high school. It was at a time when we really began to challenge the kids. I would stand in front of them and say, "Hey man, look. I came out of *this.* So can you." We would ask them at the end of the day, "Who is going to go do what Reggie did?"

It was after one of these talks that Jerome came up to me and said, "Me. *I* am. I am going to go division one and I am going to be big time." Jerome got the big ring.

What high school did you go to?

I went to Highland Park High School in Highland Park, Michigan.

Highland Park. That is completely surrounded by Detroit.

Yes it is.

Let me throw some quick background questions out.

Have at it.

Did you, Joe D. and Paul Seymour know each other as kids?

No. I was from the city, Paul was from Royal Oak and Joe was from Warren. Both were outside the city. We considered those places the suburbs back then. Now it's kinda' all one, big mass.

When did you first start playing ball?

I was in the peewees, seventh or eighth grade. It was something I always liked. When I was growing up it was the time of the Packers and Vince Lombardi. They were tearing it up. The Lions were having some bad years, so there were quiet, secret Packers fans everywhere.

Forrest Gregg and Jerry Kramer. A couple of pretty good guards.

Yeah. They weren't too bad, were they?

Did you play both ways in high school?

Oh, yeah. I had to.

Who was your high school coach?

I had Al Row and Jim Bobbit, a couple of great guys who took a real interest in me developing some skills that they seemed to see in me. Playing football was fun so I did everything - offense, defense, practice, whatever.

What did you play on defense?

Defensive end.

Was that because of speed?

Well, yeah, but I liked knocking the hell out of people too. So when I found out how easy it was to get around the tackle and I could pound some one, I did just that.

During your junior and senior years at Highland Park, how many colleges were trying to recruit you?

There were Nebraska, Brown, Western Michigan and some Big-Ten schools. I probably would've gone to school down south if nothing had happened for me up here. I was lucky that my high school coach explained to me the benefits of going to Michigan versus Western Michigan and everything he said proved to be absolutely correct.

Were you under "Bo" Schembechler?

No. "Bump" Elliott recruited me. I was in his last class. The first year for "Bo" was '69. My first year was '68 but freshmen were ineligible.

"Bump" Elliott goes back to the war years, the Second World War.

Yeah. "Bump" was at Michigan for thirty to forty years, I think.
His first name was Chalmers but he preferred "Bump" though.

I see why. Do you see college athletes declaring early for the pros as a problem? It seems to me that these young guys leave college and are thrust into a world they're just not prepared for.

Not as much football as in basketball. What you have in *both* cases is, at least for some guys, instead of family advisement, it's a *posse*, and the *posse* is nothing but a group of people who blow smoke up your ass. All they do is stand around and tell you how great you are. It really happens in basketball a lot. In football, many of the guys know that physically they're not ready for the next level until maybe their junior year. That's when the *posse* starts in for them. Then it becomes a whole different type of commitment once they declare for the draft. Some of them get their heart broken really easy. They may not get drafted, they may have to sign a free-agent contract and they *may* get cut. They are not prepared for the reality they face.

Back in the late '60s or early '70s, when did you begin to think, "Hey? I have a shot at the pros?" Did "Bo" come out and say, "Reggie, you can make it if you do this, that or the other?"

Shit no! "Bo" wasn't about that. He didn't do the warm and fuzzies with anyone. He wanted you to go out there, do it right and right *every* time. He didn't mention pro ball. He wasn't about that and *we* weren't about that. We were about playing for the University of Michigan, going to class and graduating on time.

The first pick of this years NFL draft, Jake Long, didn't come out early did he?

No, he didn't. He had good people behind him, not the *posse* crap. It's a good thing he didn't come out early because he got the contract he did.

$30 million guaranteed.

I didn't think about pro ball until I was going into my senior year, when I started getting letters and stuff.

How many pro teams were looking at you prior to that draft?

Well, you have to understand that we're talking 1972, Rob. There were only 2, 4 and 7. Cable TV changed football. So there was no recruiting going like there is today. Then there were only 26 teams. I was the twenty-seventh player taken, people used to laugh at how Buffalo used to scout. They had Harvey Johnson, Elbert Dubenion and Bob Salerno and that was it. Bob Salerno was the guy who scouted me. He had come to a couple of games and saw me play and he said to folks who questioned picking me, "If Reggie McKenzie can't play, then *they* can have my job."

Back to Jake Long and the guaranteed $30 million. Matt Ryan, the quarterback out of Boston College, signed a contract with the Atlanta Falcons guaranteeing him $34.75 million, and both these guys have yet to take a professional snap.

I know.

Recently, the NFL owners decided to opt out of extending the CBA because they want to reduce the share of money currently going to the players. These guys are being guaranteed money for doing something not guaranteed. There is no guarantee that they will play or play as well as all the hype has promised. Jim Kelly made less than that his entire career which included four Super Bowls and a bronze bust in Canton. My question, Reggie, is this: the players want more and more money and the only way to get it is to shrink the owners' share or raise the prices that we the fans pay. Do you think ending the enormous guarantees would be good for the game?

To be honest, Rob, it's a long time since I have kept up with all this stuff. I do know that it is harder for smaller market teams to compete. Buffalo is *in* that group, but there is no larger, more loyal group of fans anywhere than in Buffalo, so a happy medium has to be reached.

A 50/50 split?

It's hard to give an opinion, sometimes. You know how that goes.

Yes, I do.

I don't want them to mess with the pensions at all but I do want to see them increase the money for the older guys who need it more. Ultimately, they are going to do what ever they are going to do.

Did it matter to you where you would play professionally?

I wasn't sure if I happy or sad to be drafted. I thought I should have gone in the first round but I was the first pick in the second round so that was okay. I liked knocking the shit out of people so I could do that in Buffalo.

What stands out in your rookie year?

My rookie year?

It was 1972, not a good year.

Well, we were 4-9-1 and the year before they were 1-13, so I was feeling pretty good that we had gotten that much better. Still, *I* had come from Michigan where we went into every game knowing we would win. When I came to Buffalo I laughed. I laughed at the stadium and I laughed at how the guys were playing. At Michigan, we *had* a winning program. What people don't realize about Michigan is that it was always the *other* team's biggest game, so every game was a big game. I got used to that winning mode and when I came to the pros it wasn't that way. As a rookie, that first year, I was the only offensive lineman to stay healthy the entire year.

Getting used to being on a losing team was the hardest part?

Yes. Being in a losing environment was hard.

What did you think of Appalachian State last year?

I'm still sick about it! I'd like for Michigan to play them again and again and again.

In 1973, did you know going into that season that the year could be special?

Sure, even before we started. We had our team photo taken the first day of camp. I looked around at the group we had and I said to the guys, "Now listen. I'm going out on the limb here and say that O.J. is going to gain 2,000 yards this year with our help." With little or no blocking the year before, O.J. had nearly 1,500 yards and in the off year, the Bills picked up Mike Montler, and drafted Joe D. and Paul Seymour so I said, "Hell! We *can* get it." Mike Montler was the first to say, "Fuck it, Mack. Let's do it!"

O.J. had 250 on opening day and had over a thousand at the half- waypoint. Even as the season wound down, O.J. was still going to need 200 yards in the final game against the Jets to get 2,000. At the time of Game 14 against the Jets in '73 was there a change in game plan or a change in routine before that game?

No, none. Everyone was in a zone. Like I mentioned, the Jets were done and their skirts were pulled high. What a lot of people don't realize is that O.J. came out early.

I don't remember that.

Yeah. O.J left the game early. He broke Jim Brown's record on the second or third carry of the game. Then it was sitting back and taking aim at 2,000 and we got that. Then Lou took him off the field. I think he could have gotten 2,100.

One of the biggest debates I've run into is between Joe Ferguson and Joe D. differing as to what the play was that was called when O.J. broke Jim Brown's record. One of them said it was a 27 and the other one said it was a 28. Do you remember what it was?

I think it was…well, let me see. I was to the left and Joe D. was to the right. It might have been a 28 because we went off the right side and that went outside of Joe.

2,000 came over you correct?

Yeah, it did. I tell you what. That *was* a 27 because it went to the left, behind me. 2,000 was a 27. I kicked the guy out. Joe took it upside and O.J. followed him and well…come to think about it, when we broke Jim Brown's record it was a 46.

46? Okay, I think that clears it up.

I'm sure it didn't Rob. It's hard to remember. It was a blur. We have a picture O.J. and me going around the corner to break Jim Brown's record. He came off my block. It was wide-assed open but O.J. slipped and fell.

The game was over before the kickoff so the goal was to win and to get O.J. the records. The Jets had pulled their dress right up in the air and were just running for the bus. We still had a shot at the playoffs though. Other teams had to win and lose and such, but we still had a shot. We were playing with a purpose. The Jets weren't. We needed a miracle to happen. We still had a shot and in the last part of the year, no one was stopping us.

I looked at the last four games of that season. Three of the four were on the road and you won all four by at least ten points.

Yeah. That may have been our best run of the season. But the playoffs didn't happen. After it was all over, we drank beer on the plane and went home. West coast guys just wanted to get home to their families. We enjoyed the fruits that day and I probably enjoy them even more now.

Reggie, I looked at your stats and saw that you had a thirty-yard fumble return?

Oh, God yes. It about killed me. It was in a game against New England. After the snap, I was backing up and saw the ball on the ground. I just picked it and rumbled downfield. No one was near me. Then it was like the Patriots unloaded their bench and everybody was gunning for me.

Any unique memories of O.J., on or off the field?

O.J. *was* a good guy and a consummate team player. He knew the game well and he shared everything with all of us. O.J is the only person I have known that could put on a Frankenstein mask and have it *not* fit. Now you know your head is big if a Frankenstein mask doesn't fit!

J.D said his nickname was "Bucket head."

Yup. "Bucket head" or "*Head*quarters!" His head was too big for the helmets so the Bills had to send back to USC and get one of his old helmets and paint it Buffalo Bills colors.

That's a new one. After you left the league, what did you do?

I finished up in Seattle so I went to work in their front office - sales and marketing, offensive line coach and some work in player personnel, but I slowly drifted back to Michigan.

On the record or off, what is your feeling about the current state of affairs that exists between the NFLPA, NFL and the older retired players?

The union has to come around but they and the owners need to find common ground. Perhaps there is greed on both sides. With all the money out there right now that's being produced by the league, some of it can, and *rightly* should go, to the guys that made this league so great. Conrad Dobler says the real power in America is green and not political and for those who don't have the green, like the crippled former players, they have no power. It will all come home to roost and I believe Gene Upshaw sees the handwriting on the wall.

Chapter 9
Joe Ferguson

"Football incorporates the two worst elements of American society: violence punctuated by committee meetings." (1)
-George Will-

Committee meetings. That *is* a good one. The conservative voice, George Will, was referring to the football huddle and not the suit-and-tie, boring-as-hell, Monday-morning klatches held in boardrooms across the country.

Could you imagine if the huddle was an *actual* board meeting, a true-life committee meeting for some fortune 500 business? How many times would they audible once they saw what their competitors were up to? How many times would a timeout be called to rethink an option?

I think envisioning the football huddle as a committee meeting is well put. The team is a company. The quarterback is the chairman of the board and he gives directives to the various department heads.

The department heads, of course, are the linemen, wide receivers and backfield. The directives are the blocking assignments, the routes for the receivers and the snap signals. The chairman would call for changes if he believed it would help the team be successful.

The attitude of the chairman must be one of confidence. As Jack Kemp said, "One of the most important components of a quarterback is they *must* be optimistic at all times, regardless of what the field looks like in front of them." Always be optimistic was his message.

As a kid in South Lima New York, there was just one player who ever wore the number 12, and that was Joe Ferguson. The *chairman* of the board for the Bills in the 1970s, optimism at its fullest then and, especially, now.

Joe Ferguson was *this* fan's very first quarterback, so Joe Ferguson was one of the first Bills' alumni I reached out to for this project. He most graciously agreed to help in anyway he could. In brief, here is some of Joe Ferguson's biography.

Joe has been recognized as one of the greatest quarterbacks ever to play at the high school level. Joe Ferguson played at Woodlawn High School in Shreveport, Louisiana and he is a member of the National Federation of State High School Associations Hall of Fame.

He had been recruited by some of the finest colleges in the nation but because he wanted his family close, he chose to become an Arkansas Razorback. It was there he lettered from 1970 through 1972. While at Arkansas, he went on to break most of the team's passing records and was named the 1971 Southwest Conference Player of the year.

The Bills 4th pick in 1973 was Joe Ferguson. The Bills badly needed a quarterback for in 1972 Dennis Shaw threw more interceptions then he did touchdowns. As we have previously discussed, 1972 was to be a period of transition for the Bills, a transition that would take the Bills from being a passing team to a running team. Joe Ferguson was coming to Buffalo at a time when *The Electric Company* was being built. Reggie McKenzie was already there, along with Dave Foley and Donnie Green. In *that* 1973 draft, tight end, Paul Seymour, and right guard, Joe DeLamielleure, were also on their way to Buffalo.

Dennis Saw would start the '73 season but Ferguson quickly was moved into that roll. O.J. Simpson and Jim Braxton were in the backfield and Bobby Chandler and J.D. Hill would be the wide-outs. Talent and experience surrounded him when he took to the field as a rookie. What *was* news to me was that 1973 *was* Joe Ferguson's rookie year.

Even before Joe Ferguson came to Buffalo, the Bills were going to be a running team under Lou Saban. They didn't need a thrower at the quarterback spot. They needed a solid leader. They needed stability and someone with a track record of solid college success. The Bills wanted a quarterback with whom they could grow and Joe, when interviewed, told me he wanted a team with whom he could learn and grow. The Buffalo Bills and Joe Ferguson seemed a perfect match.

He had many accomplishments in Buffalo and will always be remembered as one of the all-time favorite Buffalo Bills. When Joe Ferguson was traded in 1985, he held the Bills record in seasons played with 12, total games played with 168, pass attempts with 4,166, completions with 2,188, yards with 27,590 and touchdowns with 181.Thank you to The Greater Buffalo Hall of Fame for these figures. Perhaps, Joe Ferguson can be seen and should be seen as the ultimate selfless player, seeking ways to share the credit and disperse the praise when things went well. He seldom took personal credit for the team's success and often-played hurt, but never said that his poor performance was because of injury.

Van Miller, the longtime voice of the Buffalo Bills, called Joe Ferguson one of his favorites. Van told me there was no one who was more humble and more down-to-earth than Joe Ferguson.

As I mentioned, Joe Ferguson was one of the first alumni I reached out to for The Bills Are Due and he very graciously said yes to the time I would need to tell his story.

Hi, Rob a good time for a chat.

It's always a good time. How are things in Arkansas?

Rob it's beautiful, just a beautiful day.

I have learned about you guys with this first question. What did you do when you were a kid?

Well, as a kid I did what kids do, at least back then. I looked forward to every day like it was a new adventure. We were outside everyday making up games as we went along, and playing until the sun went down. Now, unfortunately, it's the X-Box that entertains our kids.

I know. If you tell a ten year old to go outside and play, they give you a look as if you have a third eye.

True, *I've* seen that look. We kids played every sport we could play in whatever field or yard we could find.

Was football your favorite as a kid?

Sure, Rob. Everyone in Louisiana followed football. Everyone in town looked forward to the game from one week to the next. Sports of all kinds were what my friends and I did. When I played in high school, I don't ever remember our team playing a game in front of less then ten thousand fans, so I was used to big crowds long before I ever played for Arkansas. I was a small-town kid used to showing off in front of large crowds when I was fifteen. I enjoyed it, the high school atmosphere game night and all. It was a lot of fun.

I was just a kid in the early '60s and I did what all other kids do. I played I pretended and I dreamed some and maybe I even daydreamed of playing big-college ball or even possibly in the pros some day. I woke up every day to an all-new adventure. That's what was so great. Every day was something new to me.

Same here. South Lima, New York, was just a couple hundred people with one street located in the heart of potato country. I wouldn't have wanted to grow up anywhere else.

Yes sir. Somewhere along the way things have changed and I don't think it's all for the good. Kids have so much more to do now than when my friends and I were running around. Instead of running around on the football field or baseball fields, kids across the country are sitting in front of Nintendo's. That can't be good.

In my mind, sometimes I'm still that ten-year-old running around the South Lima muck and the world is passing me by at a rapid rate.

Yeah, me too. I have come to see life a bit differently now and wish everything could just slow down for a while and that kids could be kids again.

Let me bring you up to date on what Joe Ferguson has faced the last couple of years. I went years without hearing his name but when I learned of his illness, I was instantly taken back to that first game of mine in 1974.

In 2005, Joe Ferguson was diagnosed with Stage 4 Lymphoma. He successfully won that fight. After seeing him last fall, I, like many believed that he had successfully won the fight. Now in 2008, he is facing more challenges in his fight with Leukemia. According to his wife, Sandy, in late January Joe was diagnosed with Acute Myelogenous Leukemia, a secondary cancer. Patients commonly develop this form of Leukemia after undergoing previous rounds of treatments. Sandy Ferguson said, "Life is not always fair. But because of God's goodness, we have hope! We can't always see God's plan, but we know that He is there. He is at work. He is in charge and He loves us!"

The prayers have certainly been answered far quicker than many may have thought as Joe Ferguson and I was able to pick up where we left off.

How are you feeling? You've been on the minds of many people up here?

I feel as good as can be expected Rob, we go back down to Houston shortly for another round of Chemotherapy, we will be there ten days, so far so good. One thing I have to say is I have been amazed at the responses I've received during this latest period, thousands of emails and hundreds of cards and I would say seventy to eighty percent from western New York. Maybe I was surprised at being remembered.

Joe none of you guys from those teams have ever been forgotten by those of us of my generation, none of us, we were those teams' fans then and we still are.

I've come to see that over the years and I can't tell you how wonderful that makes us feel.

How many children do you have?

I have two kids, my daughter is getting married soon and we are running around getting ready for that and my son is at the University of Arkansas and thank God he's not thinking of getting married no time soon.

Well I waited until I was forty-three.

I was thirty myself and *that* was to soon. Just kidding of course Rob.

Yea. I want to thank you for doing this and we can stop at any time you need to.

No problem when I don't feel up to it I'll let you know, we go back to Houston and you can reach me there if you need to.

Okay let's jump right in. Tell me again what it was like to be a kid in Shreveport.

Well my dad was a painting contractor and I worked for him during the summer learning to paint that was fun, I guess. I played baseball mostly, fished and hunted too. I rode my bike to my buddies house *almost* everyday and there was a big old field in town near his house that we kids kinda' took over. One of the dads used his tractor to make it level and that's where we played football and baseball.

Did you admire any ball player of the time?

When I first started watching football I liked Bart Starr the most I guess. I'll always remember what it was like in small towns though. I grew up and seemingly always lived in small towns and Friday night football was usually the only thing that was happening. Certainly football in high school was more fun than some of the games I was in with the pros.

Small town Louisiana was great, if a kid wanted to find another kid or a parent wanted to find one of their kids they just went to that big old field where we all played because that's where everyone was.

Did you follow any college team?

I'll be up front with you, I had some friends playing at Louisiana Tech, a friend of mine was quarterback there too at the time but I really didn't get into following what was going on. I mean I was to busy outside and I didn't watch much football. I had too much else going on in life to pay attention.

That does seem to be the story for everyone I've spoken to, football was of no interest until high school for many.

Yup when I was fifteen it was girls or fishing or doing something outside.

Joe this I have found this to be a neat part of this book is learning how you guys were recruited. For example, Mike Stratton told me his high school coach dragged him up to Knoxville and strong armed a scholarship for Mike. Since his coach was also a Baptist preacher ever since he has had to ask for redemption. You attended Woodlawn High School, just how big a school was that?

Good, good for Mike. At the time it was the largest school in all of Louisiana and our Friday night football was really something else in Shreveport. It was a community event and our season was nothing but a season of rivalries.

Did you have to play both ways?

No just quarterback. We had enough quality kids that came out so I didn't have to play both ways, as matter of fact I can't remember one kid who had to play both ways. That proved to be good for me as I got a lot of play at the quarterback position and didn't have to worry about learning another spot. At the time I came out of high school I wasn't a running type of quarterback I was a throwing kinda' guy. There was only there were only five or six schools in the country that were throwing the ball, Florida State, Arkansas, SMU, USC and Alabama I think. It was those schools I was interested in going to, well they were my short list anyway, we narrowed it down to one from those five. I went and visited most of those schools and Arkansas was the closest to home and I knew my mom and dad were going to be traveling to see the games so that and combined with liking Frank Broyles helped make my decision.

You visited Alabama?

Yes I did?

Did you talk to Paul Bryant?

Yes "Bear" Bryant talked to me. He even came to *my* house and tried to recruit me, he met with me and my family in our living room and what a *big* time experience that was having "Bear" Bryant in our home. What a different type of person he was, genuinely down to earth and a great person to talk about life with.

That had to be intimidating in a way. I may have signed anything put in front of me if "Bear" Bryant was on the other side of the table holding the pen.

Well it was real hard not to, Alabama *was* my second choice to be honest with you, he was very down to earth and very enjoyable person with many great stories.

So you said no to "Bear" Bryant and went up to Arkansas, when did you start to get some playing time?

I didn't red shirt, we, I played a lot as a sophomore. We had our own freshman team and we played six or seven games ourselves. But the backup on varsity was Bill Montgomery and he got hurt during my sophomore year so that's when I began to get playing time.

Out of your college years what was your memorable game?

We always had a big rivalry of course with the University Texas each year, the so called game of the century in 1969 between Texas who was number one and us, we were number two was something else. I was a freshman but remember the atmosphere around that day. We beat Texas in Little Rock in my junior year that was my highlight, we could go 0-11 in a season but if we beat Texas it was a good year.

How were scouted by the NFL, was it regional? I could see the Oilers, Cowboys or New Orleans but how did you get to Buffalo?

Yea me too, but in my junior year I began to receive letters from San Diego, Dallas and from Miami on a regular basis so I hoped to at least stay in the south. I had never heard a word out of Buffalo until the day of the draft when they called me, they wanted to know if I was going to Canada to play. "Canada!" I said. I had never even *heard* of Canada. *Where's* Canada?

It's not the south.

Then the Bills said they were going to draft me in the next thirty minutes. *Buffalo* has a team? I quickly went and got a map and looked up Buffalo found out where it was at and it was, oh no, snow.

You then discovered that the shore of Lake Erie is not part of the south.

Nope, not the south Rob.

You were the 5th pick of the 3rd round correct?

Yea, Bert Jones was first; Ron Jaworski and Dan Fouts all went that year.

There was a quarterback that went ahead of you in the second round, Gary Keithly out of Texas-El Paso who went to the St. Louis Cardinals. I would think you should have gone in the second round and not the third.

Well my senior year was difficult and Don Brough had left for the Houston Oilers to be their offensive coordinator and we had another coach come in. We had a good team but couldn't get it done offensively. That's what probably hurt me in the draft or I would have gone a bit higher.

Who scouted you?

I have no idea; we didn't have the combine or anything they do today. All we had were folks coming to look at films and some watched us work out but I had no idea who scouted me.

So you come up to Buffalo, how many quarterbacks were there on the first day of training camp?

Let's see, Dennis Shaw was there, myself one other young guy, who ended moving to receiver I think.

Did you anticipate starting that year?

Oh no, not at all. I was one of those naive young kids not a millionaire or nothing and I wanted to do everything I could just to make the team. But because we had such a great running game *and* we had a young offensive line that were coming along it gave me a chance to learn the game and to gain experience. The Bills knew their future was going to be with O.J. and that gave me the chance to get the playing time I needed.

A contented backup?

Yes, I would have been a contented back up.

Mike Stratton told me when he got to camp that Lou had never even remembered talking to him down in Knoxville.

I can see that, I can see that for sure.

Mike also said that there were about a hundred guys trying to make a squad of about thirty-five and there was only equipment enough for fifty, equipment had to be shared. What was your first day like at training camp?

What I remember more than anything else is when I went to my first training camp it was at the Exit 56 Motel there in Blaisdell, that's where the offices were because they were still building the new stadium. We all ran the 40s in the parking lot of the Exit 56 Motel. We had our feet pressed up against the curb and ran our routes in the parking lot that was my first impression of professional football.

The parking lot off Exit 56?

Yup, when I saw that the parking lot was a major part of our practice facility Canada started to look pretty good.

But you knew where Buffalo was now when you got to those new corporate offices at Exit 56.

Yea I sure did.

Good, glad you came. You entered the 1973 season with the other rookies, Joe DeLamielleure and Paul Seymour. You had quite a line already with Reggie, Mike Montler, Dave Foley and Donnie Green. With O.J. in place and the line that you had did you have any idea 1973 would turn out the way it did, at least breaking Jim Brown's record?

No, not really, I was just such a dad gum naive kid. I was a quiet, just listen to everything and keep my mouth shut type of guy just taking it day to day. *These* guys today they all seem to be able to name their tickets, for me, I was just happy to *have* a ticket and be on the airplane to anywhere to be honest with you Rob.

Why do you think Lou Saban brought you to Buffalo if you were going to be a running team?

I really don't know Rob, I would like to think it was ability for what *might* come, nobody knew that O.J. would be around the amount of time he was and perhaps Lou was looking down the road some to a time when O.J. *was* gone.

You're right; your numbers were every year going up when O.J. was there, 2,500 a year, and 3,000 a year.

I was learning the game and it was a great place and time to do that.

It makes a tremendous difference to the quarterback when you have a running game because it helps the passing game and I hope that they drafted me on ability. A nice addition to the running with O.J. once I got the hang of the game a little bit.

How big an asset was it to have Jim Braxton in the backfield with you?

Jim was great; he was tremendous, *just* tremendous. Jim helped me a lot when I was a rookie just in the mental aspect of the game alone he helped O.J. tremendously too. Jim Braxton was a big asset, he was a great blocker, a good runner and everyone respected him for everything he did on the football field.

He's been gone about fifteen years now?

Yes at least that many. Jim was one of the best blocking backs I ever saw I know that.

How much of the '73 season did you start?

What I remember is we were on our way back from a game in San Diego and Lou walks up to me and tells me I was going to be starting quarterback and *he* walked off.

That's it?

Yea that's all. "Well, how 'bout that," I said.

You lost the San Diego game 34-7. It wasn't until the 4th game of the season against Philadelphia that a score came from the quarterback by run or pass and that was you on a one yard run.

Yea a one-yard sprint. Dennis and I weren't playing well that's for sure, O.J. was running all over the place though and that's what kept us going but when Lou told me I was going to get the start I knew I wasn't going to sleep for the next week or two.

Who hit you the hardest that rookie year?

Gosh, I don't have a clue, but we didn't throw it much my rookie year we ran the ball most of the time I don't think I threw it over a hundred times.

You were 73 of 164. Let's put it this way, what defense hit the hardest?

It seems to me that the Baltimore Colts had people that would just knock the *dawg* out of you, guys like Hendricks and Mike Barnes every time I got knocked down it was one of them looking over me.

You were lucky too because you got to play them twice a year.

Oh yea, didn't mind playing them at our place but playing them there at that old stadium that was part baseball, it wasn't a good field. I didn't like playing over there but my buddy Bert Jones and I always got along real well so hanging out with him made the visit a bit better.

How many games do you think you played on artificial turf?

Oh gee wiz, it had just started coming out when I was in college. I played on it at Arkansas and when Rich Stadium was built it had the artificial stuff. I would say I played more than 50-60% of all my games on the artificial stuff.

Any long-standing injuries as a result of that stuff?

Nope. I had a few concussions, several of them that may have come from that, maybe it was the turf. I sure think the artificial turf has a bearing on concussions, the new stuff is a lot better I'm sure, it's made of rubber or old tires or something like that.

Joe let us move a head some. You get to the last game of the '73 season against the Jets, O.J. needed 200 for 2,000 but he needed just a handful to capture Jim Brown. The atmosphere had to be something else surrounding that game.

It was. Surreal in a way. Being in New York City I remember saying to myself that I was going to play just to see what was going to happen. There was a large crowd, all the media and hype set aside I was just going to see what we could do. Our line though was keyed up they wanted to get O.J. the first record, Jim Brown's record first. He needed about fifty yards or so for that.

Do you remember what play you called when O.J. broke Jim Browns record?

Joe D. and I have been back and forth on this a couple of times. If I remember correctly we were running plays called 26 and 27, which was an off tackle play with the guards pulling and Seymour blocking down which was a crushing block for anybody. I believe the play that O.J. broke Jim Brown's record was a toss play, 29 *was* our toss play we ran it that time and when I look back at the film or I look back at the pictures I have it looked like a toss play.

Joe D. said it was a 27.

I know on the pictures I've seen it looked like a toss but the ball in his hands so it could have been a 27 or a 29.

When it came to the play that gave him 2,003 you went over Reggie.

I believe *that* was 27. I don't remember for sure to be honest with you Rob but I'll say 27. We were in the 2nd half and were on the sideline when our public relations guy came over to me and said, look Joe, O.J. only needs this many yards to get 2,000. I went back out into the huddle and told the guys and at that point you could just feel the tightness, guys saying let's get it, let's get it, so we started running the type of plays which we had been doing all day he got it. It was real exciting especially the way O.J. handled it all. O.J. gave everyone credit, he shared openly and often that day and those records.

Where would 1973 rank in your career?

Well it was one of the highlights of course because it gave me an opportunity to learn football and play with that caliber of athletes. I wanted to contribute more; I knew I could but as long as I was contributing to a win that was going to be okay.

Any memories about beating Miami in 1980?

Oh yea, *yea*, that game was such a relief after it was over to finally beat them and get people off our backs about that. It was almost *as* important to get people off our backs, as it was to beat the Dolphins. People in Buffalo were so worked up about beating them we should have a few times before but just didn't.

You had the chance to play with Conrad Dobler for a couple of years, from what I remember he was one of the most aggressive ever to play.

He is still a character too. We knew that Conrad didn't have the physical ability to do what needed to be done. I think he kind of knew it too. But he *did* go out there and he gave it his all and he *did* get the job done. The way he practiced was amazing, *we* watched him practice, his dedication and his routine. His knees were so bad that it would take him hours to get warmed up. The efforts we saw him make on the films, you really had to admire what he did. I don't know how he did it because he could hardly walk his knees were so bad, but he still came out and unselfishly put himself out there.

I remember Conrad mostly from his Cardinal days and he always reminded me of a pro wrestler with a football helmet, he did whatever he had to do to get the guy pinned.

He did what he had to do to get the job done that's for sure and everyone respected him because he gave it is all every time when maybe he shouldn't have been out there.

Joe the goal of the book has been to educate the fan a little on the lives of some of the best players to come through Buffalo. I want to share with the fan some of the problems the older players are having in claiming disability or pensions or getting the medical treatment needed. Have you had any problems in that area?

Well in my situation when I had cancer three years ago, my NFL pension was available at that time and I took it at fifty-five so if anything was to happen to me my wife could get it. I was planning on waiting until later to get it but because of everything going on I had to take it at fifty-five. Now I know there are some older, *retired* players that are having a terrible time and that's a crying shame. Our leadership, the player's union leadership is more attuned to these younger players and *not* to the older players who helped make the NFL what it is. I don't understand that what so ever.

This treatment is very evident and our leadership has *stated* it, Gene Upshaw has said that he is not interested in helping the older players and that he *only* works for the younger players. That's aggravating, *very* aggravating to those of us who played and fought and went on strike for the benefits these guys have.

Fred Smerlas has said the same thing and he retired only a decade or so ago, he made clear to me that the new guys should understand that they are a retired player they just don't know it yet.

That's true Rob. The sad part about the whole deal is, and don't get me wrong I'm happy for the young guys, they are making enough money, and I'll be upfront with you, a lot of those young guys, they don't know what retirement is or what insurance is all about, right now it's the cars and the houses. They haven't thought about all that other stuff yet and now so many of them are signing their name to a big contract they don't have to worry about it either.

So right now when these younger guys have millions and all that money brings there is no urgency by them to improve the situation not only for the older guys but also for them in the long run when football is long over.

You're right. I've looked at the numbers the NFLPA has put out and ten years down the road or sooner maybe in 2011 there seemingly will be a wider gap between what the league has to pay out and what is coming in.

That's right, the league will have to start paying for all the promises they've made and when it gets to *that* point the older guys will have even less of a shot to get the help they need. I do see a lot of lawsuits coming down the road, there is a lot of money out there and so much of this stuff just shouldn't be happening but it is. There is plenty of money to supplement that retirement program for years and to help the older guys who are getting a couple hundred dollars a month in pension.

I have known of Tom Condon for a while but it wasn't until recently that I have learned he is a trustee for the NFL as well as a mega agent representing over 120 NFL players. Now I don't much but to me that sure sounds like a conflict of interest.

You know it is, *he* knows it is Rob, but the NFL is a monopoly. These guys are fortunate to be playing football and these younger guys they don't appreciate that and when their career ends it comes as a shock to them that the real world and another forty, fifty years lies ahead of them. They thought that that money was always going to be there and it's not.

I just hope that something can be done about our leadership, about Gene Upshaw and about how the money is spent. To me the owners, when we had the last big strike, the owners if they had *just* held together they had us right where they wanted us. They could have had standard contracts with base salaries and just load them up with incentive packages and everyone could still be making the good money. Instead they give these guys who have never taken a snap five, six, ten million dollars bonus money, that's ridiculous.

I agree.

Its ridiculous, these guys need to *earn* their money and many of them will don't get me wrong and there were many great athletes who were playing when the owners said they weren't making a dime and lying about it. *Those* great athletes received pennies. If the owners during that strike had *just* held out thirty days or so they could have held out for what *they* wanted, a standard contract loaded with incentives. Players would have to *earn* the money that's what we all have to do and that's what they should do. I have to be completely honest with your Rob, I hardly ever watch the NFL anymore, there are bad role models on the field, it has become a selfish game in many ways and I have lost interest in it.

Thank you, Joe. I want to conclude with something. I have lost two members of my family to cancer and if you want to give some type of encouragement to people as far as your story about the fight that would be great.

Rob thanks, if I was going to say anything from what I've learned about cancer and what causes it, it is to educate people at younger ages say the college level. They need to be educated more as to what cancer is and to what causes it. It is *so* big and affects so many and when you go down to M.D. Anderson in Houston where I have treated you learn just how big it is. There is nobody to teach folks how to head it off or how to prevent it or what type of preventative diets and there isn't anyone really talking about it. I think if anything we should be more on the forefront when it comes education on the prevention and how to head it off. Also and this maybe as important, love what everyday has to offer, love your family and grow in your faith and do like I did when I was a kid, treat every day like a brand new adventure.

76

Chapter 10
Fred Smerlas

"I was a Rebel from the day I left school,
grew my hair long and broke all the rules..."(1)
-George Thorogood-

The year was 1979 Jimmy Carter was in the White House; there was a failure of a cooling system at Three Mile Island, *Kramer vs. Kramer* sold the most seats, The Buggles gave us *Video Killed the Radio Star*, *The Dukes of Hazzard* were on primetime and O.J. Simpson was in San Francisco.

The first decade of the NFL since the merger was nearing an end, the Bills had finished 2-12, 3-11 and 5-11 in 1976,'77 and '78 respectively, 10-44 in three years. In three years there had been three coaches, Lou Saban, Jim Ringo and Chuck Knox. Joe Ferguson was still under center and despite these bad years he had 5,000 yards combined in 1977 and 1978. Age and trades had taken its toll and the Buffalo Bills *still* had not defeated the Miami Dolphins. But there seemed always to be a ray of sunshine lingering around Buffalo and when Chuck Knox left the Los Angeles Rams and signed a six-year contract with the Buffalo Bills it shown through again.

My brother Scott was on the west coast and married now.

My fathers' grave had been blessed the year before and I was *well* into a crush over a new girl on the school bus who today shares my life.

Chuck Knox had a winning record with the Rams; though he'd lost three consecutive NFC Championship games he had the reputation of being a winner. His first year was 1978, the first season with a sixteen game schedule. Reggie McKenzie and Joe DeLamielleure were still at the guard positions but the balance of *The Electric Company* had been gone for a number of years

With such a poor recent history where exactly did the team need improvement? Was it offense? Defense? Special teams? Yes was the answer.

1978 began to look much like the previous years, with a three straight losses to the Steelers, Jets and the Dolphins. It was a season that had blowouts on either side of the ball and in the second game against the Dolphins that year it *was* a loss but by one point 24-25. The Bills would not defeat the Dolphins in 1978 and had but two more chances remaining before the '70s ceased to be. Chuck Knox ended his first year with a 5-11 the best finish in four years and a 4th place finish in the AFC Eastern division.

As part of the trade of O.J. Simpson to the San Francisco 49ers the Bills received their 1st and 4th round pick in 1979. Due to the 49ers 2-14 finish in 1978 the Bills had the 1st overall pick in the 1979 Draft. The Bills selected Tom Cousineau linebacker out of Ohio State number one and wide receiver Jerry Butler out of Clemson was the Bills second pick. In the second round the Bills selected both Jim Haslett out of Indiana and Fred Smerlas out of Boston College.

Keep in mind *trading* O.J. gave the Bills Tom Cousineau.

Those of you who, like me, have followed the Bills all our lives there have been many favorite players; they may have been undersized or oversized. They may have danced, sang or resembled our favorite cave man. But with few reservations one of the Bills all time greatest of characters was Fred Smerlas. Fred came out of Boston College as the Bills 3rd pick in 1979 and he would become one of the greatest nose tackles ever to play the game.

Fred Smerlas was a graduate of Waltham High School and while at Boston College he developed into one of the finest defensive lineman in the nation. Once he was drafted he went on to play in 200 NFL games including 155 straight as a nose tackle, more than any other nose tackle in league history. Among recognitions he was on the 1979 NFL-All-Rookie team, he played in five Pro-Bowls and is a member of the Greater Buffalo Hall of Fame, The Buffalo Bills Wall of Fame and the Boston College Varsity Athletic Club Hall of Fame.

Fred Smerlas once told the New York Times; "The coaches we had before Marv Levy tried to make me a Barbie doll, I'm not a Barbie doll, I've got my craziness and weird ways and you've just got to let me go." (2)

Fred has a *thick* Boston accent and not even close to being politically correct, thank God for that.

Fred, how are things in Massachusetts?

They suck Rob! We have Deval Patrick as Governor the economy has collapsed, the housing market has collapsed, the tolls are going up, unemployment is going up and down here I'm a right wing conspirator against all the liberals. It's all the fault of the Republicans for this mess down here according to these folks. Liberals never get in trouble for over spending or for creating programs that are disasters but Conservatives are monsters for not supporting them.

A conservative in Boston, you must be an endangered species?

Yea. You know Rob it's a funny state, Massachusetts, there is a very hard corps group of individuals that are conservatives. The towns though they are swimming in liberals who are soft on crime and get the judges they want. The judges and the politicians are soft on crime and on the criminals. Boston is very ethnically divided, the Irish, there is Chinatown, and most are supposed to be Catholic but they vote for pro-abortion people and support ultimately anti-catholic people and policies. These special interest groups all start crying for one thing or another and then they get the judges they want and the judges demand laws be passed to support what these groups are whining about. It's a mess, people vote one way but say and worship another, they never seem to vote their convictions, but what do I know I was only born here.

What I've discovered over the years is that the everyday voter is not that educated when it comes to the issues they seemingly vote for the person that says the nicest things.

True, Bill Clinton was great at that but he can't hold a candle to *Obama*. Most politicians are morons anyway. It should be a prerequisite for these idiots who run for office to have held a job in the real world so they can see the implications and restrictions that their laws and taxes place on people. I was watching Hillary a couple of weeks ago, she was asked about how she would deal with the energy situation and without missing a beat she said she would tax the oil companies. What a moron, the oil companies have nothing to do with prices being high and more over what would the government do with the additional revenue? Waste it that's what. Deval never had a real job.

That's what I remember about Deval, he never had a real job he came out of the Clinton Justice Department.

He was hired as someone to solve quota problems and Coke I think was one of those companies, but that's not a *real* job. Now as Governor he has said that he can't lower our taxes or none of his programs he promised during the election will happen.

He said he can't do this and can't do that c'mon Deval you douche bag it's town by town, c'mon Deval yes you can, if you can raise taxes you sure the hell can lower them. He speaks in platitudes and flowery language that makes the liberals feel good, they damn near wet their pants when they hear him speak but there are those of us who have to *pay* to make them to feel good.

What the fuck, doesn't anyone challenge him or any politician anymore?

Why *can't* he lower the taxes, they seem to increase them any time they want and don't seem to have any problem doing that. They create all this crap that is just government within government and no one knows what's going on anymore.

Now that there are no more taxes to take from people, Deval's crying because all of a sudden all these feel good programs of his have failed. He can't understand what has happened, there's no more money to get from anyone to pay for all this shit and like any good liberal politician he will make us feel guilty for not paying *more* taxes for useless programs.

It doesn't stop once it gets started, you know that what they wont call a tax they'll call a *user fee* or rather than referring to something as a tax increase a good liberal will call it an *investment* in hopes of fooling the masses.

Right when a liberal uses the word investment folks better hold onto their wallets.

They're all the same Rob.

With Spitzer of New York slipping it to hookers and Paterson his replacement admitting to affairs and to using cocaine, he's a leach and now the Mayor of Detroit. It's a bad time for Democrat politicians I tell you that, but the press will do their best to shove it all under the table.

Nothing will happen to them because they are Democrats, its like I was in the NFL with San Francisco me another guy heard a player say, I wont mention his name, but he was a black player, he said, I like to rape fat white women to make my ancestors proud. What if I had said that shit?

The press will seldom cover things that ultimately don't serve their own self-interest don't you think?

Oh sure. They'll call us Republican mean spirited for even bringing these things up. It's a mess, maybe we'll wake up sometime before were penniless and gun less.

It's like the NFL they wont do anything that's *not* in their best interest, it's become a gang bang mentality, do you think the league knew about Vick, Lewis and Pacman Jones? Sure they did but *keeping* them is in the best interest of the NFL.

Fred You were born in Waltham?

Born and raised, Waltham Mass., *The Garden City*, home of the Waltham washer!

What did you as a little kid in Waltham?

As a kid?

I ate allot, I was a fat kid, a little fat Greek kid. We grew up in a housing project and we moved to a blue-collar town. We were a bunch of regular rough and tumble kids, fights, screwing around, you know. I never played any sports; there wasn't any huge popularity of any sport around our group. My brother played but I didn't play on the youth level anyways at that time.

Did you watch any sport, the sox?

Nope, nothing.

Others played the sports and I went out with the girls that seemed like a good trade off. I went to schools where you had to fight or die so after being sucker punched a couple of times I started working out, lifting, running, hitting the speed bag and when I hit puberty, ninth grade I went out for football. I was working out just to defend myself but found out I was in shape and could out run and out jump most of the other kids on the field. My friends were still going out and hanging around but I noticed that when I played I saw that cheerleaders were cheering for me so that was it.

You had a mustache when you were in 6th grade or something too, right so you looked older?

I'm Greek! Everyone had mustaches, women, children, everyone had one.

I was shaving in the 7th grade and I could grow a beard in 8th grade. I didn't have a mustache when I wrestled though. I was the first two sport, All-American in Massachusetts's history but as soon as I got out of wrestling in my senior year I grew my mustache and it's been there ever since.

Did you like school?

I graduated let's put it that way. I went on to graduate high school with some bad grades but I was quicker and stronger than anyone else, with a better mustache.

What school was that again?

Waltham Senior High, class of 1975, largest class in history with some 1,200 hundred kids.

What music did you listen when you were growing your mustache?

Music? Shit.

My brother had 5,000 albums, no lie, 5,000 albums; I had two, Suzie Quatro and Billy Joel. I listened to the Stones, The Beatles, Blue Oyster Cult, David Bowie's *Ziggy Stardust* and I loved George Thorogood that type of stuff. I was the brawler and beer drinker, my brother was more of a music, sports kind of kid. He was having to get used to watching videos rather than listening to music, music videos were just coming out.

Suzie Quatro! When I think of Suzie Quatro, I'm taken back to Leather Tuscadero of Happy Days, right?

Leather Tuscadero! She was sweet!

Yes she was.

Rob, remember her sister?

Pinky!

Pinky Tuscadero, she was sweet too.

Yes sir. Did you play both ways in high school?

I played offense, defense, special teams any which way I could.

What did you play on offense?

On offense I played guard and tackle. I wanted to be a running back but I was to big, on defense I played linebacker. Shit when I graduated I could bench press 450 and had twenty inch arms I could play any position.

When you were a senior, did you know you were going to college, was it Boston College all the way?

I was the top tackle in the country. Every school recruited me I think. Every day I was getting a letter from someone at some college. I never really thought about football until high school, then during my junior years folks started coming to my school to talk to me. I'm being recruited by all these people coming to my house all the time, it was getting a little irritating because I didn't know about these places, North Carolina, Notre Dame, Penn State and Maryland.

I had heard of them of course but didn't know anything about them and Maryland wanted me to replace Randy White who was leaving for the Cowboys so they were sending something everyday.

Maryland *was* interesting because I could run, jump and I was strong like Randy White so that intrigued me, but Boston College was right by my house. B.C. I figured had the same type of program I was used to and I could hang out with my buddies.

Did you graduate?

Nope, one semester left. I don't have a lot of memories from my college days either. I was the number one tackle in the country and we were a losing team. I had a personal vendetta against everybody that perpetuated my intensity and probably added to my reputation as a hard-ass. I was on a losing team and playing at a high level and got little national recognition for my efforts. One season I had 144 tackles and got nothing. I enjoyed B.C. because the program wasn't that intense, it wasn't like Ohio State for example where you live the football program. When you're on a losing team you're not recognized much.

Was that 144 tackles in your senior year?

Yup 144 tackles and they'd audible away from me.

You had to run everyone down?

Yes, I had the speed.

One game I had twenty-eight tackles and I didn't even make player of the week. Things like that pissed me off even more and I started to really form a nasty disposition.

My college years are kind of non-existent compared to my high school years where I was top rated in the nation and highly recruited. When I was in the pros I was All-Pro, All-Rookie and All-NFL, nothing like that in college though. In high school it's easy to stand out when you're bigger and stronger than the rest of the kids. But than some of these kids go to college where there are fifty other kids just as quick and just as strong and they disappear into the crowd. You can't be seen by the pros if you can't separate yourself in the college ranks so I didn't think I could separate myself during my college years.

We did have what some called the greatest upset in college football in my sophomore year when we beat Earl Campbell, his Heisman year. We kept him under a hundred yards that day. That was big, that was the only game that year where Earl Campbell was held under a hundred yards rushing.

We were an out of luck team but we had a lot of guys drafted during the time I was there and a lot of them went on to long careers in the NFL. I think we had seventeen guys maybe more drafted from my junior and senior years.

Did you have a football mentor, some one that guided you and helped get you to where you did?

God.

God—He is a good mentor now that you mention it.

I didn't care about sports. I didn't play anything until the ninth grade. I played some little league then my buddy "Tiny" Martin, he was my best friend growing up got me involved in football. I didn't really care about it until he said something.

I don't think I told you this before but he and I went out for football when we were in eighth grade and we quit because they didn't play us, "fuck it," I said it takes up to much time anyway.

In high school it was different, the next year we all went out and we had the psycho coaches I mean they murdered us but we beat the shit out of everybody we played we were 9-0. We easily beat everyone by thirty points or more. I went out for football because a few of my friends did and I had an edge to me you add all that to the cute cheerleaders I was set.

I started in my sophomore year and was All-State in wrestling, it snowballed from there.

So there wasn't anyone I wanted to be like, folks wanted to be like me. I was 6-1 a couple hundred pounds and had the brawler edge to me. I was All-American in two sports and had only started a couple of years before. So all those folks that think you have to start at five years old, I didn't.

Let's move ahead some.

That draft of 1979 was it between you and Mark Gastineau as to who would go first?

I was the number one rated tackle in the country. I was a little to slow in the forty because I had a pulled hamstring at the time but I also had an *uncoachable* label because I got into brawls, shot my mouth of and had that nasty disposition that had been born. So there was a question out there as to whether or not I could be managed.

I slipped to a 2nd round. I thought that I would be a top ten pick that year but found myself hoping to be a top twenty, than a top thirty. I remember I was on the phone with Tampa Bay, they said they had the 4th pick in the 2nd round and they'd pick me. They said it would be great to have me in Tampa. Buffalo had said they were picking Greg Robbins who was already of the board, so Tampa was going to take me. A second later I got a call *back* from Tampa saying the Bills had just taken me.

Right behind them was Chuck Knox, he called me, he said, "I heard you're one bad mother fucker!" I didn't know what to say, yes sir, no sir whatever you say sir. This was nothing like college where there was a suit and tie and the coach was worried about what your mother would think.

Did you think the Bills would take Gastineau?

Yes I did. But I went ahead of him because they thought I was more capable of making an immediate impact on the team than what Gastineau was, so they picked me over him because I was more developed than he was, that's what they said.

I have looked at that draft of 1979 a number of ways and as a result of the O.J. trade to San Francisco and the 49ers crappy finish in 1978 the Bills had the first overall pick and took Tom Cousineau and he was offended by something that happened in Buffalo and never played here.

Well he was gay.

Gay?

Yea he wanted to go somewhere where he would be more comfortable, that's what I thought anyway. Jerry Butler went in that draft too and hc was tremendous but he was limited because of his injuries.

What was your first mini-camp like?

With Chuck, shit Chuck wanted to be the Raiders of the east! We were partying and drinking together it was phenomenal. I wouldn't have wanted be on any other team in a million years.

I came into camp and there was "Big" Ben Williams, Joe D., Reggie McKenzie, Haz (Jim Haslett) was there and shit man what a great, great time we had, fighting, drinking together.

It was phenomenal. I wouldn't have wanted to be on any other team it was the best, it was like being with your buddies Joe Devlin,

Roland Hooks, Will Grant we called him "hooker."

Why did you do that?

He smelled like Hooker Chemical Plant!

Of course.

Yea, we fucked around all week then got to play a game on Sundays.

Fred you had a quote in 1984 the New York Times regarding the Bills coming out with their new helmets, the red ones.

Oh sure, I said they look like shit and I wondered if the Bills would be putting Big Bird on our pants next.

All that helmet did was give you back to back 2-14 seasons and I don't anyone who likes that helmet yet.

It's all about pretty colors now. You know Rob the league is just turning into one big pussy league now, overly concerned about colors and uniforms and helmets. It's not as violent as it was back whenever and what really irritates me is that it *was* about football back then, especially the earlier days, it wasn't about who had the prettiest uniforms or the prettiest ear rings or fancier cars.

I agree with that. As a fan I do see the lack of toughness sometimes. The sight of LaDainian Tomlinson sitting on the bench with his visor down and parka hood up while his team was losing in the playoffs. I didn't understand that. In his own words the MRI revealed only a hyper extended knee. Why couldn't he step up to the plate for his team that day? I remember guys like Youngblood playing with broken legs.

Yup. What irritates the shit out of me is when these young guys say well those old timers couldn't *play* in today's league. Shit! Some of the old-timers could probably play *and* start in today's league and we are beginning to see that some of the college *All-Stars* can't compete when they get to the NFL. I don't have a fear that those old guys couldn't play in *this* era. I have a fear that some of these guys couldn't play in *that* era because they're just not tough enough.

Here's a quick story we were in Cleveland to play the Browns and we had this loud mouth young guy who had been watching films of Doug Dieken. This guy of ours ran a 4.5 or 4.4 and played defensive end and he was chuckling over what he was going to do to Dieken. Us older guys shook our heads and said man you need to be careful because he *will* get into your head.

This young guy laughed.

On the first play Dieken fucking clubs the guy.

The next play leg whips him in the stomach.

The next play he drops on him, backs up and leg whips him in the balls, the kid comes back into the huddle, his eyes rolled back in his head. He wasn't worth a shit after that. Doug Dieken just stood over him after each play blowing snot bubbles at him. That kid never recovered, never; don't ever underestimate these guys I told him they'd play more mental games than physical ones.

What about Conrad Dobler?

Conrad was a rotten, *psychotic*, bastard but he sure the fuck taught me a lot about getting into peoples head. Thumbs to the throat, knees to the balls, that's what Conrad did. He was a monster but that's how the game was played and Conrad did whatever he had to do to get the job done.

What do you think about the possibility of the Bills moving to Toronto?

Canada?

Fuck them. Go up there with a cap pistol and take them back. When America flushes Canada gets water. Let's face it New York City has killed Upstate, Buffalo and Rochester. New York City has killed homeowners and businesses in Upstate. The city has made Upstate what it is and when the corporations leave because they are overwhelmed with the regulations and the homeowners leave because of the tax burden having to finance that shit hole in New York City, there is nothing left to keep an NFL franchise going. When the Bills leave, or *if* they leave, blame should be handed right over to New York City.

Do you think that Michael Vick should be given another chance once he gets out?

Why Not? Bill Clinton got to stay in office.

Ted Kennedy is still in office he murdered people, my God Michael Vick would have paid his penance why not let him back in? First of all the NFL knew what was going on. They took pictures of everyone going in and out of Vicks house, they knew what was going on, c'mon give me a break. They knew about Pacman Jones. If you pay your dues, your penance and go through the suspension then you should be able to make a living again. Do one of two things either shoot the kid or when he serves his time and comes out, welcome back into society.

He *has* to earn his way back in, like everyone. It's like the IRS if you pay your taxes they leave you alone if you don't pay your taxes they pick you clean. Look we all love dogs but he broke the law and when he pays his dues he can do and should be allowed to do whatever he wants. I think Clint Eastwood said once, those who beg for mercy the most will be the ones who give it the least.

The same people that are saying kill' em, kill 'em, kill 'em will be the same people who piss their pants when they get a traffic ticket.

Clint Eastwood, one of the all-time great philosophers.

I love Clint, he had a couple great lines„ but in one of his spaghetti westerns I think he said to some guy before he killed him, *those who beg for mercy show it least*. He was my idle, I love Clint. I watched him when I was a kid. I grew up outside, building motorbikes and go-carts and watching these guys on TV. I didn't give a shit about sports back then. I played chess with my neighbors and still can put anyone in checkmate in three-moves. I lived in a tough neighborhood fifty punks who were in a fight everyday. I lived next to this brainy kid from Italy who played chess and *Stratego* everyday. I was a pro-wrestling type of guy learning to play chess from him, what a disaster.

So in between fights you learned chess?

That's it!

Okay, your coaches, was Chuck Knox your favorite?

He was, Chuck was an innovator, he was tough he said don't talk a lot of trash just be tougher than the other guy, we only had an hour fifteen minute practices and we were tough. Kay Stephenson was a nice guy but a terrible football coach, he copied a little bit of what Dallas was doing and a little bit of what Washington was doing, with Kay it was three hour practices and no real identity when it was over.
Then they brought that brain dead jellyfish in Hank Bullough.

Brain dead jellyfish?

Yes sir.

There were some tough seasons, back-to-back 2-14.

Well it all boiled down to this, it's all about coaching. You have to put a coach in there, look at the Raiders why do they keep getting high first round draft picks, well they suck, they don't have a coach and their ownership sucks. Herm Edwards he ruins teams wherever he goes and look at the teams who are perpetual winners, the Colts, the Patriots. In us we had Chuck Knox, a winner but then we had the dumbest of them all, the brain cell, the piece of shit. Rob I played in the NFL all my life and during that time you run into some real *granite* heads, Hank Bullough made anyone of those granite heads look like Einstein. He was the dumbest man God had ever put together!

Don't hold back Fred.

It was like God had a few drinks to many and made Hank.

Unbelievable. That was just before Marv Levy came in.

Yup, Marv came in and he was anything but Hank and we just loved him.

You wrote a book By A Nose, have you thought of writing another?

I don't know I might run for something, but you never know with the insight I have about all that went on during my playing days, some of that shit pisses me off still. Some of those guys were just so bad and it has progressed to the point where the league and the union are today. A player's honest insight would be new and nice.

I wrote By A Nose because I ran into people with my head and I got into the game because I enjoyed the competition. The older I got I got involved in politics because it's still competition but of ideas. I grew up a bleeding heart liberal but I began to read and to understand concepts. People need to understand the concepts of this country and not just accept blindly what the politicians and judges tell us.

Whether it's the 2nd amendment or trickle down economics. I am dumbfounded that people don't even have a grasp of basic capitalist ideas.

They don't, simply, government kills economic growth by taxation.

Right the biggest tax cut in history before Ronald Reagan was from John Kennedy. The world blames America for everything well I got news for the world when Americas breathes they get air, most of the world is nothing but a pimple on our ass so they need to be careful we don't pop it.

Fred the goal behind this book has been to educate as many people as possible on what the older, a retired players is having to deal with when it comes to disability, retirement and medical benefits and why the NFLPA is making life hard for the guys who built the league.

You know what current players are?

Current players are nothing but retired players, they just don't know it yet.

They are retired players in waiting and this piece of garbage Gene Upshaw when he said he doesn't represent retired players, all these players now are just retired and they don't know it. They are all going to be retired players Gene you *fraud*, you *crook*!

That shit is unreal, that's another thing, these current players can't be that stupid to think that they're never going to be retired so when they hear that shit Gene Upshaw saying he doesn't represent retired players that means at some point he will not represent them either. Can these current players be so stupid that they never think they're going to be retired?

I'm getting paid, or I will get a pension, I'm not getting it yet but I played more games at nose-tackle then anyone else in history and my pension is going to blow. Why does Gene get $2.4 million from properties alone when *I* get nothing? Why does the league send out all this information to players asking how they would like their pensions structured? What the fuck? Don't they know what's in the player's best interest? Isn't that why we elected them again and again and again? Why does Gene get properties while the rest of us don't?

You get nothing from licensing?

Not a fucking thing! Why is that?

You had mentioned earlier that sixty percent of the revenue going to the players will inevitably hurt the smaller market teams, am I stating that right?

Well let's compare the luxury boxes in Los Angeles, New York or Dallas. They can be sold let's say for $2 million dollars; the team gets 40% that's $800,000. Meanwhile teams like Buffalo can only sell their boxes for $500,000 and the team gets $200,000, a big difference. Who the hell is the brainchild that gave that up? Gene is responsible for that shit.

I think Gene is corrupt and I think the NFL owners back him. He uses the race card if outside forces push him to far, but let's face it the race card is diminishing some, fairly critiquing a black man now is okay, as long as its fairly. Barak Obama has given us *that* chance when the world met Jeremy Wright.

A segue Fred. Tell me about Birth of a Child King your movie?

Birth of a Child King was a movie about a handicap child and his brother who wanted to go on a journey to find the truth about Christmas and as they go on their journey they see that Santa exits anywhere and everywhere they are. The tollbooth, the restaurants, the stores, Santa is everywhere, it's a nice little story. I just played the big dummy for the bike gang.

Are you ever going to be on Rescue Me with Denis Leary you're your buddy Lenny Clarke?

Denis Leary is a dumb ass liberal. He gets on the radio down here in Boston and starts shooting his mouth off and I call up just to bust his balls. He doesn't know what tough is. I'm tough because I had to be, I don't know many tough liberals. Gene Upshaw thinks he still a hard ass, he is a shit head and clueless to what the real world is for the guys from twenty to thirty years ago.

But Fred my wife says Denis is cute.

Shit Rob tell Kendra *I'm* cute Denis is a dink.

3 8
BILLS
KELSO

Chapter 11

Mark Kelso

"Make every moment be your best moment and every day your best day."

I'm returning again, briefly, to my days as a snot-nosed little kid sitting in front of our black and white Zenith in South Lima, New York. As I prepared myself for that Sunday's game of the week, the Fluffernutter sandwiches and bags of Lay's Chips encircled cans of R.C. Cola. Something took place in front of me - the NFL pre-game show.

In the early seventies the show was pre-recorded with a host talking about a player or a specific team. It wasn't very informative or as entertaining, as today's pre-and post- game shows are. There was nothing live or up to date about the show what so ever until, in 1975, CBS opened the season with *The NFL Today* with Brent Musburger, Irv Cross, Phyllis George and Jimmy "The Greek" Snyder.

I wondered, "Who were these guys?" "How come Jimmy "The Greek" never picked the Bills to win a game?" What I *did* know was that as soon as these guys came on, the games themselves were close behind and after the pre-game team came the broadcast team.

As I grew older the pre-game show became more of a *real* show, a warm up act. I began to see that former NFL players were part of not only those pre-game shows but also part of the broadcast team. There would be a professional broadcaster like a Gary Bender or Jim Nance, and then there was a former ball player like a Johnny Unitas or Ken Stabler. Even Jack Kemp was a *color commentator* for Super Bowl II; by the way at that time he was the first current player to help broadcast a game. The loose job description of the *color commentator* is to provide expert analysis and overview of strategy of the teams. Their unique knowledge would aid in doing that.

Do *you* remember the *Monday Night Football* crew of Frank Gifford, Howard Cosell and "Dandy" Don Meredith? The game was sometimes just as good as the warbling going on between Don Meredith and Howard Cosell.

Why did the game need *more* then one voice?

What did the second voice offer the audience that the play-by-play could not?

As mentioned, the play-by-play guy is usually a professional broadcaster. Most times this was true but not always as Frank Gifford and Pat Summerall were former NFL players and held play-by-play roles for a number of years. The professional broadcasters were the guys who had toiled in minor league parks and had nurtured their talents to where they also were called professionals. The second voice in the press box had a more intricate knowledge of the game, a former ball player.

From my early days, the second guy in the booth was Roger Staubach, Irv Cross, Johnny Unitas or Bart Starr, and today there is any number from Troy Aikman to Mike Golic to Steve Tasker to Mark Kelso. I have wondered as I've gotten older and seen some less than quality performances from the color commentators - did any of these guys have training before they assumed their new color commentator roles? If not then why were they hired? Were they hired not so much for their skills but because of their reputations as ball players?

How did these professional athletes make the transition into the broadcast booth? Did they have extensive training in mock studios while hoping to get the call that they had been drafted into the broadcast league? Or, as in most things now, they waited for the network with the largest check to knock at the door?

I took a look at the former Buffalo Bills who have remained in this area and saw that Steve Tasker has been doing some national work with CBS, and Alex Van Pelt worked in the radio booth calling games alongside John Murphy for a couple of years. Whether it is on the national level or at a regional home game, the color analyst has to be knowledgeable of the game because the die-hard fan will read through the smoke. They must be knowledgeable but *not* judgmental.

When doing color analysis on the radio, for the most part the audience is a regional audience and they probably already know everything about the team that there is to know. Bringing in a former player from that team to help with the broadcast is a logical move. Local voices are a must to bring familiarity for the fan. That's why there was always Van Miller and why there is John Murphy and why there is former Buffalo Bill, Mark Kelso. It is a local game called by local people and just for us. It's fundamental but it works.

I believe that for a radio broadcast to be successful it has to have *that* local flavor. Ideally that person in a color analyst's role should not be controversial. For example, I couldn't imagine Dan Marino or Don Shula being a color analyst for the Bills radio network, could you?

After nearly forty years in the radio booth for the Buffalo Bills, Van Miller retired in 2003. There was some shuffling around while looking for a broadcast team that could fill that airwave void. John Murphy, a longtime fixture in local television, had been color analyst alongside Miller from 1984 to 1989 and again from 1994 to 2004, was selected to fill the big chair. In 2006, after Alex Van Pelt took a position with the Bills, former free safety Mark Kelso was selected as the new color commentator for the Bills broadcast.

I can tell you that there was no one involved in the making of this book that I found to be egotistical or who was unwelcoming, and without question, none were kinder to my wife and me than Mark Kelso.

In Steve Tasker's book, Tales from the Buffalo Bills, he recalls one incident.

"One time when we were flying back from a Monday night game, we went through some pretty rough turbulence. I mean, the plane was bouncing around so much that even some of the big, tough guys were getting nervous and sick. In the middle of all this, the late Mitch Frerotte, a big offensive lineman and one of our crazier dudes, got up and started running frantically up and down the aisle. He finally found where our safety Mark Kelso was sitting and plopped himself down right next to him."

"We asked him why he did that, and he said, "If this plane goes down, I know one guy God is going to save, and I want to be sitting next to him," (1).

Mark came out of North Hills High School in Pittsburgh and was scouted as a free safety by Danny Smith of the College of William and Mary, now a Special Teams coach with the Washington Redskins. In talking with the schools longtime head coach, Jimmy Laycock, who coached Mark in the '80s, he said this;

"I have never, I mean *never* in all my years of coaching, and it's some thirty years now, ever seen someone so strong and competitive on the field while being so unassuming and off the field."

"Danny and I saw that Mark was so good that he could start for any number of schools, much *bigger* schools, but we told him that he could start here and that's what he did. He started here as a freshman. He chose William and Mary when he could have gone to any number of schools."

So Mark started from day one?

"Yes, he did. Well, a couple of games into the season. We saw him as a strong, levelheaded young man who could do what he did on the field and still be a decent, kind young man off the field. That's a great mix for any coach and team. I mean he could separate the game from the real world like no one I had seen."

"If there is such a thing as being *too* nice, Mark could be too nice at times. I'm not saying that's bad, because in this world, we need more people like Mark Kelso. Everyone liked him - teammates, coaches, students, the administration. Everyone liked him."

"Here's an example of how he could separate what he did on the field from what he did off. It may have been Mark's first game, or maybe *one* of his first games, and we were playing up at Dartmouth, in New Hampshire. In that game, Mark got three interceptions and we got the win. I looked for him after the game but couldn't find him because Mark was the first off the field, first into the locker room, first showered and was the first one back on the bus. He was studying Spanish."

"Many guys who had a game like that, they might have searched out every television camera and newspaperman who would tell them how great they were. Mark was never like that. He was so unassuming and so great at the same time. I knew that Mark would do well in Buffalo because of Marv Levy. Marv spent years down here at William and Mary himself."

Mark, why did you choose William and Mary?

Rob, I wanted a good education and I believed I could use football as a mechanism to achieve that. William and Mary had what I wanted in the classroom and on the field. Coach Laycock is a great guy. He was probably right about Spanish. Long bus rides were good for studying that, though for that game at Dartmouth, I think we flew into Boston.

It's important to understand that football is only a game. If I was good enough to play at the next level, I believed *they* would find me, regardless of what school I went to.

In other words whatever happened, happened?

It had to be. I didn't play football in order to get to the next level. If I did get to the NFL, great, but I played football to get a good education.

Did you play football right from the start, peewee on up?

I played pretty early. My mom would know better, I think it was around 5th grade or so, when I began to show interest in wanting to play. I begged Mom and Dad to let me. They really didn't want me to because I was still a pretty small guy. They were always concerned about injuries. I want to say it was in the 5th grade when I played on a ninety-five pound team. Everyone would climb on the scales in his shorts and t-shirt to get to ninety-five pounds. I'd have to climb on with all my pads and still didn't get close to ninety-five pounds. That year was a lot of fun and I built some friendships in the league with the other kids.

You grew up in a strong football area. The University of Pittsburgh and Penn State weren't to far away.

Yes it is, two hours or so, as far as producing quality football players it does have a great reputation.

Did you know Jim?

No, Jim is from East Brady, which is like saying Jamestown is part of Buffalo when it comes to Pittsburgh. The guy I knew and played against in high school, was Dan Marino. That area, the Pittsburgh area, was and is a blue collar town, and when you have a blue collar town, people look for cheap entertainment, whether it's football games or volunteer work or their church that becomes a big part of their social life.

So everything was well-attended football, basketball games everything. My parents *still* attend the football games there. I think those communities were pretty close-knit and the communities put a lot of emphasis on sports and community. I don't think there are necessarily better athletes or better football players in eastern Pennsylvania than anywhere else. It seems like there is just more of a focus on football in western P.A. or Ohio than other places.

Texas too?

I think they eventually got to that point. If I'm not mistaken, I think they rank the success of a states high school football program by the number of division one players they produce. I believe

Pennsylvania was third last year. Alabama and Texas are always high on that list. Of course, Florida, Ohio, and California are too.

You attended North Hills High School in Pittsburgh?

Yes, I did.

Did you play both ways in high school?

Yes. As a junior, I was defensive back and I split time at running back. I would shuffle the plays in and out. As a senior, I played both safety and running back.

What did your parents do?

Mom was a stay at home mom and my father was an accountant and worked as a Chief Financial Officer for a highway company out of Latrobe, Pennsylvania. Dad did tax work on the side and Mom kept the books for a lot of the small businesses around town. That *is* exactly why I am *not* an accountant.

I do understand that. The Eagles in the 10th round drafted you in 1985.

Yes, they did.

That seemed a good draft year for both the Bills and Eagles, with Bruce Smith and Randall Cunningham going to those respective teams.

Yes, it was. I *was* waived by the Eagles, though, and came to the Bills to work out as a free agent in October of that year. In February, I signed a free agent contract with them. I moved up here and for the first five months, I lived in the Sheraton while working out at the stadium.

So your first year in Buffalo was getting preparing for training camp?

More or less, I had said that I'd give it two tries to catch on with an NFL team and it did take two. I played in the first three games of my Bills career and, after a minor knee injury; I spent the balance of the year on injured reserve. This was a blessing in disguise, though, as they signed Dwight Drane in the USFL supplemental draft. I believe he played for the Los Angeles Express. If not for my being on injured reserve, I believe I would've been cut to make place for him. Dwight and I did become good friends. He played for a number of years for us and on a couple of our Super Bowl teams.

I remember you wearing that double helmet. What was that about?

Folks called it a gazoo helmet, you remember, after that character from The Flintstones.

Yes, sadly I do remember that.

I had had so many concussions that I needed something that provided extra protection and Bert Straus; an engineer from Erie, Pennsylvania designed it for me. I remember the first game I wore it. *Everyone* was picking on me - my teammates, the other team. *Everyone* laughed at it, so, after the game, I took my wife and daughter down to the stadium so they could see it and they laughed too. I couldn't believe it.

You had a couple of seasons with 7 interceptions. You had a long return in 1988. What was that?

We were in the middle of a good winning streak in 1988.

A seven game streak.

The Packers were in Buffalo and their quarterback was Don Majkowski, a Lackawanna product.

"Magic Man."

Yeah. There was a lot of pressure from Bruce and Fred up the middle. The pass was tipped but came near the target anyway. I was able to get there and gather the ball in. Because I was moving forward, I headed downfield right away. I remember I cut back across the field and saw Fred throw a block on a lineman just as they were catching me. The sidelines were empty. I didn't look back and just pressed toward the goal line until I crossed. I knelt down to say a prayer. Our linebacker, Scott Radecic, was the first to congratulate me.

You beat the Packers that day 28-0.

We did.

I can remember where I was when O.J went over 2,000 and when you guys came back to beat the Oilers, and I remember where I was when Scott Norwood missed that kick. What were you doing when Scott was lining up?

I was on the sideline, saying a prayer and *no*t looking at the kick. I judged what happened by the crowd's reaction. We were concerned about Scott though. He was my roommate and he didn't show up after the game until late in the morning, feeling like he let everyone down. The kick was a bit out of his range but we would have never been in the Super Bowl if not for his foot. Scott won plenty of games for us and everyone knew it.

For professional athletes, getting to their game's championship is what they dream of. As kids, we all fantasize about making the game winning catch in the Super Bowl. Football is the only sport where the championship is sudden death. One game, it's over.

How did it feel to win that AFC championship in a blowout against the Raiders and be the first Bills team to play in a Super Bowl?

It had been quite a run already for us by the time we got to the Super Bowl. We were just coming together as a team. Everything had gelled. Still, so many didn't expect us to be there.

Some folks called those Bills, "The Bad-luck Bills" but those teams won four straight titles and were the best football team ever to represent Buffalo.

That we did, winning four consecutive AFC titles. I don't think many understand just how difficult that is. It probably will never be done again in this age of free agency and for that I am awfully proud. My four conference championship rings will go to my children.

Just a few more short questions Mark. In Steve Tasker's book, he cites a quote from Mitch Frerotte. Have you heard that one?

Yes, I have.

He said if the plane was going down, he wanted to be sitting next to the guy God was going to save and that was you. I would like to think I'm a good Christian. It's hard some days to be a decent person. In the NFL, it has to be very difficult, what with the money, fame and all the peripheral things that go with it.

Well, money brings with it so many distractions there's no doubt about it. I don't want to say it wasn't hard. My wife is *my* best friend though and I *love* her dearly. I don't want to spend time with anyone else *but* her. So, when practice or a game was over, I went home to my family. I think it comes down to not putting yourself in bad situations. If you're out at the bar and it's after midnight, you're probably going to find yourself in a bad situation. I'm not going to say that there aren't a lot of temptations because there are. Sometimes *they* find you and sometimes *you* find them. It's important as a believer to do the right things and it matters what your priorities are.

Now I participated in *The Big Tree Friday Afternoon Club* where the guys went out to drink beer and have lunch. It gave me the opportunity to get into conversations with them, some *great* ones about life. It was after practice so we just talked about what was going on - marriage, taxes, social issues, and etcetera. In our situation, many of us had played together for *so* long that we had some real friendships. Rob, one of the opportunities I had to talk to my teammates about faith and the Lord was by going to the bar with them after practice on Fridays.

I think what my teammates respected was that I was consistent. I wouldn't preach one thing or talk one thing and act in an entirely different way. I was consistent. You don't have to wear it on your sleeve or preach it to be consistent with your behavior.

I had this Christian rap song that I used to sing. Remember guys had to sing at training camp, especially rookies?

Sure. Like in the movie, "Brian's Song" where James Caan had to stand up and sing his al-mater song in the cafeteria.

Right. They still do that stuff, but Marv didn't like it saying it was disruptive. What would happen is that the young guys would go in, eat as quickly as possible and get out, because they didn't want to sing. What Marv did do is have a rookie night, which was a talent night for rookies. Technically, I was still a rookie when I came to the Bills, even though it was my second camp. So when I got up I sang a Christian rap song. I was quiet and unassuming and I think that was the first time I exposed my Christianity to the team.

Good stuff Mark. Was it difficult to make the transition from player to broadcaster?

I didn't find it too difficult of a transition. Remember that I was out of the game for nearly ten years before I went into the radio booth. I was in the high school game and youth game but not the professional game for ten years before I went into the broadcasting side of it. That time lag created a situation where I could approach the game differently. I took the analytical approach and not the critical approach. I think guys who jump right into broadcasting after they play tend to compare it to every play and everyone they played against, and, perhaps, without knowing it, are more critical of the person or play. Some of the guys who do that seem to have a difficult time in separating themselves from the game.

When I went to interview for the position, I said I would be analytical and *not* critical in my approach. I would describe the play and let the fans make up their own minds as to whether or not it was a good play. I wouldn't say that a play was terrible or a particular player screwed up. I might say that they, the team *or* player, might have liked to do it differently but I wouldn't bring it to the personal level. I told them that if I was not good at it, tell me and I wouldn't do it because I don't want to go out there and sound like an idiot. I do think there are some guys who do this and sound real bad when they do.

That's why I asked the question. As a fan, I watch games all the time and I know what I like in a broadcast team and what I don't. I don't like to be told that one team has a bad game plan or one player is performing at a sub par level. Let me decide that.

Exactly.

I guess I'm trying though poorly to compare broadcast styles. I don't like Michael Irvin's approach.

It's not rocket science. I think that you need a good approach. There are some guys who are really good at it and then there are some guys that I honestly don't know what they're thinking. It also takes some preparation. If a person takes the time and invests in it, they will be good at it. What I think is important is that some of these guys should critique themselves or listen to other people and see where they can improve. That's what I've done and it has helped.

Michael Irvin is certainly a very flamboyant personality. I think he might be more effective as a talk show host than a broadcaster. Television is much different than radio because with television it comes down to filler. People have already seen the play so they don't need to be told what just happened. What needs to happen there is describing what a team has done leading up to a play or what they should do now. I think some guys are really good at this. Troy Aikman does it real well. He also took a couple of years off before going to the booth. I think he is analytical and does his job with a calm demeanor.

Mark, I'd describe what I prefer as a flamboyance-free style of broadcasting.

Yeah sure. My goal is just to paint a picture for the listening audience. That's why I like radio because the vision that people have of the game is the one John Murphy and I put in their minds, and the better we are at our jobs, the more they enjoy the game. Generally, my job is to analyze what has just happened. Murph makes it easy. He creates the excitement. I can than take what Murph says and analyze it.

It wasn't until a few years ago, after listening to years of games on the radio, that I understood the importance of one phrase, and that's going right to left or left to right. If not for that, I'd have no way of knowing what direction the play was headed.

Murph does that well. He is always giving updates on players, injuries and other games. I don't know how many people actually listen to all of the game. They are doing something around the house or they may just listen to three-quarters of the game. That's why we update the way we do. Some outlets will *never* tell the score of another game. Perhaps that's a way of keeping you tuned in. If a broadcast team is not giving you the scores of other games, it may be because in their game, a team is up by fifteen or down by fifteen. That's why they do it. They don't want to lose a listener or viewer.

Kendra and I know many people who will have a Bills game on the television with the volume turned down but have the radio turned on to your broadcast. They will listen to the game while watching it at the same time.

Sure. That's because Murph and I are hometown guys and they identify with us.

We did that a couple of times last year and noticed an obvious delay in what has happened on television and what is called on the radio. Why the delay?

Well, there are some serious financial repercussions for certain words and generally there *is* a delay for that but the transmissions sometimes have to go via a satellite.

After you left the Bills you went into teaching, young ones, too. Why teaching?

I put my education to work. I love to teach. Two of *my* role models were my coaches in school and I'm aware of how very important positive influences can come from teachers. I hope I can be and *have been* a role model and positive influence for respectful behavior as a teacher, coach and administrator. My first teaching job was in 1996. I substituted a lot, as I was finishing up my education degree. I had a business degree but went back to get one in education. I know the influence that can be given to children on the elementary side. I like building a strong foundation. Teaching a child to read is *so* important. If they don't learn to read well early, a child will suffer in everything and that frustration will continue all throughout life.

It's a blessing to me because I see my kids here. I drive them to school every day. They drop into my office all the time and I have watched them grow and mature. It's fantastic.

As a young man whom did you most admire?

That's easy. Even as a youngster, I most admired men of faith and growing up in the Pittsburgh area there were plenty of good role models. There were some Pittsburgh Steeler players that I looked up to. Rocky Blier was one because, having known what he went through, Viet-Nam and all, and showing his grit and determination, was something that was really admirable. There were other Steelers too who were men of faith. I don't remember hearing a lot about that aspect of an athlete's life back then but, undoubtedly, they had strong religious beliefs. Most notable were Mel Blount and Donnie Shell. The other was not a football player. He played with the Pittsburgh Pirates - Roberto Clemente. He had an incredible sense of community and philanthropy that I admired and still *do admire* in anyone a great deal.

My high school coaches were important to me, too. John Wiley and Hank Marziale did a great deal to keep me focused when I could have drifted. I'll never forget them and we are great friends still today.

Where do you see yourself in twenty years, when Kendra, you and I are all in our sixties?

If I can afford it, I will be sitting right here at this desk with one of the best co-ed Catholic schools in the country.

With a second window?

No I don't think I need a second window. I need a new auditorium though. I *love* it here. If the Lord blesses me, I will be *right* here. I love Catholic education and certainly I want to see it improve. I love it here. I love giving a kid a safe place for a good quality education, where they are free to grow and express themselves.

Many of us were concerned when Ralph Wilson visited Toronto and as we saw an eight game deal reached for the Bills to play up there. Any fears the Bills may head north?

I hope not. Buffalo has the best sports fans in the world and there is no place my family and I would rather live.

You stayed in the area after you retired?

My wife and I love the Buffalo area. We bought a home here and established ourselves in the community and in our church when I was still playing. We had our family and it was important to us that we not move around with young children. That's why after I retired we stayed in Western New York and didn't return to Pittsburgh.

Mark. You had a number of good years with the Bills. Among the highlights is one heck of a trivia question.

You can say that. It's something I'm proud of. I am the only player in the history of the Bills to have returned an interception, a fumble recovery and a blocked field goal for a touchdown. I did that against the Packers, Browns and Oilers respectively.

Mark, if you had one thing to pass onto any young football player what would it be?

Football is *just* a game. What they do after the game is going to be far more beneficial to their community, and to them. All the work Jim Kelly has done for Krabbes disease is remarkable. He is just a different person now than when he played. He is a different man now. There are a lot of guys who have done better things once the spotlight is turned off. Time is a continuum, as Einstein said. Time is just a continuum of time and space, and we just never know what part of our lives will affect the most people. I think we go through each day doing the best that we can. I hate it when I hear people talk about college being the best time of their lives or their NFL days or that day or another day. What does that say about the next fifty years? We never know when the best time will be. Make every moment be your best moment and every day your best day.

Chapter 12
Kent Hull

"Like sand through an hourglass, so are the days of our lives."(1)

When most casual fans think of the Buffalo Bills during their Super Bowl years, they tend to think of Jim Kelly, Andre Reed, Darryl Talley or Cornelius Bennett. We need to remember, however, that during those years, the Buffalo Bills had one of the greatest offensive lines of all times: tackles, Will Wolford and Howard Ballard; and guards, Jim Richter and John Davis. With few exceptions, they were always there. There was *only* one who was *always* there, center, Kent Hull. He would start eleven consecutive years at center and would be the only one ever to snap the ball to Jim Kelly.

Kent grew up in Greenwood, Mississippi, a small town in the western part of the state. As a kid he had little interest in football, basketball was his game. It wasn't until his high school years, when he grew up *and* out, that he excelled in both sports. There were several colleges he considered but chose the Mississippi State Bulldogs. The rest is, as they say, a happy history. Kendra and I sat down with Kent a few weeks ago to listen to the *rest* of the story and what a story it is.

I pulled out a picture of Marv Levy. On one side of Marv was Kent Hull and on the other was Jim Kelly. They were towering over Marv Levy. Kendra wanted to know how such a small guy kept all of you big, huge guys under control?

Let me tell ya all this. Marv Levy was the best I'd ever seen at managing players. When I first got here, Hank Bullough was the coach and he was a *bit* confrontational. As a matter fact, I saw him at a team meeting one time, Bruce Smith had come late. Right in front of eighty-five football players, Hank said, "Where you been, Bruce!" Bruce just looked at Hank. Being called out put Bruce on the defensive right away. Bruce said that his grandmother had died. Then Hank asked him how many grandmothers he had. "Bruce, that's about the fourth one this month."

Fred didn't like Hank either, did he?

Oh No. Fred didn't like Hank at all! I remember one time Fred told a story about an airplane flight. Fred was flying up to camp. There was this guy on the plane wearing white shoes and being rude to a woman and so Fred gets up, goes up and calls him out, and said, "Look man. You don't talk like that to any woman." The guy turns around and it was Hank Bullough. Fred said, "He ain't ever liked me since and I ain't much liked him since."

We got off to a bad start in 1986. Marv takes over and Bruce comes in late again and walks in the opposite direction of Marv. Marv just looks at his watch. Bruce heads to the back of the room and grabs a seat. Well, after that meeting, Marv forms a players committee and he puts Bruce on it. I was on it, Andre was on it, Jim and a couple of others too. *We* had to levy fines on the players and the first player we had to fine was Bruce, and Bruce was *on* the committee. We fined Bruce five grand and told him next time it would be ten. Marv didn't do it. We did it.

I love Mississippi, by the way. I've been all over down there - Oxford, Yazoo City, Vicksburg. It's a great part of the country.

Really. I live in Greenwood.

Isn't Fort Pemberton close to that?

Yes, it is.

A nice visit for Civil War buffs.

Oxford, though. I call that the lawyer school.

Ol' Miss?

Yeah, the lawyer school. I went to Mississippi State.

Why not Ol' Miss?

Well my father played basketball at Mississippi State, to be honest with you Rob I just wanted a good education. I had no idea I'd end up playing somewhere. It just happened to work out. I really got a break everywhere I went. I've been the luckiest man when it comes to about everything. When I went to college, I was 6'5 and weighed 220-230 pounds or something. I was standing on the sideline. I had the helmet with only the strap on it 'cause I knew I wasn't going to play. Two starters get hurt and they yell, "Hull!" I yelled back, "Man, what do you want?" I wasn't paying attention to the game. I was talking to some other guy and when the coaches called me in.

Were you wearing a uniform at least?

Oh, yeah. It wasn't a pretty one but I had one.

Back to Mississippi for a minute, I went to Oxford for couple of days, William Faulkner Days.

Oh, sure Rob. Did you ever read any of his stuff?

No, man. Not on purpose, anyway.

Real hard to read. You have to read each sentence like three times. It's all that southern lingo.

We're not that far apart in age. You grew up in the '70s, more or less?

That's right. I was born in 1961. I graduated high school in 1979, Greenwood High School.

Did you play ball in high school?

I played my junior and senior years. I quit my sophomore year because I wanted to be an NBA basketball player. I had my eyes set on that.

The NBA in the '70s.

Oh, man. I was a Julius Irving fanatic. The NBA had just merged with the ABA and I was following Willis Reed and Wilt Chamberlain. That's when the big men really meant something. They've kinda' taken that away with all the three-point shooters.

Basketball was one and football two?

You bet. I'd stay up 'til midnight. I saved my money and bought an outdoor light and hooked it to the house. I'd shoot all night and my folks would have to come get me. I'd say if I could make *ten* in a row from a big ol' rock than I'd go inside. Well, I'd never quite make that tenth shot.

What did you do as a kid, other than miss the tenth shot? Your family had cows?

Yes sir. Dad had cows all his life but it was just a weekend thing for him. He had a job during the week. When Saturday came and I heard those feet coming down the hallway at 5 A..M., I knew what was up.

I was just a normal kid. I was active in every sport. I didn't know any different. We didn't grow up with a lot of money. We weren't poor but we weren't rich by any means, lower middle class. Anyway, I learned a lot about life long before I was supposed to, I guess.

I have interviewed three generations of Bills players: Billy Shaw from Natchez, Jack Kemp, all the way through to you guys. With one or two small exceptions, I can't say the stories have been that much different.

No, I wouldn't think so. The game *is* different. I saw changes that were subtle changes. When I came into the league, it was the steroid era. Everyone was jumping on steroids. I saw people like Tony Mandarich come in and bench 315 thirty times. Take him off steroids and a year later he loses thirty-five pounds, and he can't bench the same amount fifteen times.

There has been a big transition in the game. It went from fast, strong 280 pound offensive linemen, to big guys who aren't as strong or fast and they weigh 350. They don't even block. They just seem to stand up shielding people. *Our* job was to move them. Now they don't move them.

Like Siragusa?

Right. The "Goose."

Did you play both ways in high school?

Aagh! I tried to, but I wasn't too good on the other side. I was a tight end in my junior year. This is what happened Rob. I was a *quarterback* in ninth grade maybe it was tenth grade. I guess I wasn't fast enough so they moved me to tight end. So I quit. If I couldn't be the superstar, then I was quittin'. Then coach challenged me. He said, "If you really want to be an athlete, you're going to have to play football, and right now, you're *not* an athlete."

He called you out?

Yes sir he did. I said, "Hold on now. I can play anything out there on the football field." So, I went out for tight end. Then someone gets hurt. I get thrown in there. I'm only 155 pounds and I get crushed, but I was fightin' as hard as I could. That attitude stuck with me.

Who was your high school coach?

Hollis Rutter.

That's a good name, Hollis Rutter.

Good guy. Down in Brookhaven, now. He could get my fire going that *is* for sure.

You got a scholarship to Mississippi State. Did you start in your freshman year?

By accident, I did. There were two centers in front of me. They were both red shirt. They were 6'2 and 270, prototype centers, both of them. By now I was 6'4 or so, 210, and had a new nickname, *Ichabod Crane*, because I was tall and skinny. So *they* get hurt and they send me in against Tennessee. My offensive line coach said, "Ichabod, you know leverage?" I said, "Yes sir." He said, "Then you make sure you're lower than the other guys and you'll be alright." I never once got off the ground that day. I was crabbin' around the whole day. We were running the wishbone so I was on all fours.

I didn't get my first start until Maryland. We had a week off so I had two weeks to sweat. We *all* went up to Maryland. My whole family took a train to Maryland and that's a long train ride. The first play of the game, I was nervous. I didn't know what to do. On the first play, I was over the ball and just took off and started blocking people. I had forgotten to *snap* the ball! I left it right where *it* was. I embarrassed everyone, especially ol' Ichabod. My family wasn't real happy, I tell ya. I knew I was supposed to do something but just forgot to. God and country, were watching me be stupid.

Here's a story. The freshmen came in two weeks before the veteran offense. We had two-a-days, one in the morning and one in the afternoon. Man, I tell you, it is *hot* down there, you know that Rob. I thought they were trying to kill me. Well, we had this red headed boy; I can't remember his name now. He goes down on the field with something he faints. They went and got a sheet and covered him up. I'm standing there with a dumb look on my face as they covered him up with this white sheet, and I said, "Man, this guy *is* dead!" "This guy is dead and *I'm* goin' home!" They started throwin' buckets of water on him but I had my mind made up. If guys were dyin', I was goin' home! He got out of that spasm stuff and got up.

After that practice, all of the freshmen, about thirty of us, go over to these bench presses. The coach said, "Even yourself out." I couldn't bench a hundred thirty-five pounds even once. So the strength coach said, "Hull! Get over here. You and I are going to work afterwards." He worked with me and I got stronger every day.

How did you end up at center?

Well, after my junior year, a guy gets hurt and the coaches asked who wants to play center. Everybody was looking around and coach said, "Hull, *you* can't do it." I said, "Man, give me the ball." That was the end of that. I've been a center ever since.

Was Henry Bellard your coach?

Yeah. I think Henry was actually the father of the wishbone. Folks think it was "Bear" Bryant but it was Henry.

Any other colleges look to you at the time?

I had scholarship offers from everywhere for basketball and football. I'd have gone to LSU and played basketball but my coach, the same one who told me I wasn't an athlete, said to me, "Hull, it takes 22 to start on football and only 5 to start on basketball. You'd have a better chance at playing football somewhere." So I went to

Mississippi and enrolled in engineering school *Ichabod* was going to be an engineer!

That's what you took in college?

Well, it lasted one semester. I got hooked on *Days of Our Lives.*

"Days of Our Lives with Bo and Hope?" Kendra asked.

Yup, Hun. Shane and Kimberly too.

Are you done?

Yup. Anyhow, I was always watching it. After that first semester, I had a .58 GPA so I changed majors right away. Coach called me in and said, "Hull, w*e* got a problem. You have to pass 16 hours in order to play next year!"

"Well, I better get out of engineering then, Coach." He asked me what I wanted to do. "*Not* engineering!" So I took every elective I could take: First-Aid, Golf, Drivers' Ed., even ROTC. I was marching around campus with a wooden gun.

I feel safe now. Two bowl games, the Sun Bowl and the Hall of Fame Bowl. What happened in the Sun Bowl, 1980?

It was the first bowl game Mississippi State had been to in a while. We had to go over there and play Nebraska. We were all thinking about taking a day trips over into Mexico though. Nebraska pulls up with tractor-trailers full of weight equipment. They're liftin' weights while we're stealin' cars and goin' to Tijuana.

That would explain the outcome. You played in the Blue-Gray game too?

Yeah. That was a fluke too. I was a fill-in in that one. I was still only about 240 or 250. I'll never forget our quarterback, Reggie Collier. He comes up to the line of scrimmage and puts his hands on the *guard.* "What are you doin', man. I'm the one with the ball!" I said. Reggie had never seen such a skinny center as me.

Did you have any thoughts at all that you'd be able to make a pro team? The NFL didn't draft you did they?

No, I was drafted by the USFL and signed with them. They told me back then, that NFL wouldn't draft you if you signed with the USFL. Some teams would spend a draft pick to hold a player's rights but no team was going to waste a draft pick on Ichabod.

I'm curious, why Ichabod?

I was tall and skinny I guess.

The name Ichabod Crane comes from "The Legend of Sleepy Hollow." He was the main character; Washington Irving wrote it was from New York.

Really? I never even read it. I figured it was just another put-together nickname.

You had three years with the New Jersey Generals of the USFL Were you signed by Donald Trump?

No. The owner then was a guy, an oilman, out of Oklahoma somewhere. Chuck Fairbanks was the coach and he said they had drafted me in the seventh round, I think. He asks if I had an agent. I said, "No." "Well, you want one?" he asked. I said, "I don't know." Anyway, I get an agent and one day he calls me up and tells me that they're going to sign me for *forty* thousand dollars for the first two years and, *and,* a ten thousand dollar signing bonus!

Well, I told my girlfriend I was rich, *absolutely* rich, that we could get married now, and if I came home the second day, I was rich. I'd never have to work again. Man, I had to *borrow* money to get home from New Jersey after the first season.

I was spending $1,200 a month for an apartment that had nothing in it and, of course, I had to go out and buy a car, a Cutlass Supreme with T-tops. It was *nice* - black with mag wheels. I went over to New

York City with it and they threw me out of there. They said, "Man. Folks here take those mags off it when your still doin' forty. Go ahead and go back where you came from."

Amazing it really is. Doug Flutie was quarterback in New Jersey?

The first year it was Brian Sipe from the Browns. Then they signed Flutie, Herschel Walker and Maurice Carthon all around all the same time. Those guys complemented each other real well but I knew nothin' about pass blocking. At Mississippi State, it was the wishbone. So they bring Doug Flutie in and I learned how to pass block in the USFL. If it hadn't been for those days in the USFL, I'd have never made it to Buffalo, I promise you.

We do one on one drills the first day and folks were just zoomin' by me. I wasn't touching any of them. Fairbanks comes over to me and helped me out. He said that my *left* hand was all that I had to hold on with. I became a pretty good pass blocker after that. Chuck Fairbanks really helped me out. Look at these fingers here.

Kent held up his hand.

Those things are pointing east and north at the same time.

Yup. I remember I broke an index finger; it was just a swingin' loose. I said, "Jim, we got a problem." We were running the no-huddle and he was saying, "Get on the line! Get on the line!" I said, "Jim, *we* got a problem." Jim said, "Man, bro. just wait till after the series." I showed him my finger and he said, "Push it back."

I looked at him funny and go over to the sidelines. They shove a Popsicle stick underneath it and, for seven or eight weeks, they'd shove a needle in it and I'd pass *plumb* out. I can't *stand* needles. The team sends me to Montreal, Canada to one of the best hand specialists in the world. He said, "Son, I can fix that but I'd rather not. But I know a guy who probably could." He sends me to Mississippi of all places to get it fixed.

I get down home and that doctor said he couldn't do it quickly and that it would take eight months to heal and that I couldn't play football in the mean time. I said, "Doc. Then cut it off right there at the knuckle." He wouldn't do that, insurance reasons I think.

You only missed one start and that was in 1993. What was that?

Knee. I've had four surgeries and every one of them came from my own players throwing somebody into me or rolling up on me. It was just a freak thing. We had a week off. I went and had surgery during the time off and made it back. I wasn't 100% but I played. That was the only time I missed a game.

The USFL sued the NFL, which was the beginning of the end.

We won the suit now, Rob!

Yes, you did. $3.00!

$3.00!

At the end of that season, what were you thinking? Did you think it was over?

Probably, but I had played with some guys who were ex-NFL guys trying to extend it a couple of more years. They said, "Hull. You can play over there." Dave Lapham, a guard for the Bengals for years, said, "Look. You can play in the NFL." The next thing I knew, I had eleven teams calling me. I was a free agent because I hadn't been drafted by anybody. Forrest Gregg had me up in Green Bay showing me a farm house with a bunch of cows and that was *right* up my alley. Then I talked to my wife and said, "If we're going to do this, I need to go somewhere where I'm going to do somethin', and not just because of the money or farm." Buffalo had just lost their starting center.

Tim Vogler?

Yeah, Tim went out. Hank Bullough called me at 1:00 o'clock in the morning and asked, "Son, what's your problem?" "*My* problem?"

I asked. He said, "We need you. Is it money?" I had a pulled hamstring so I was buying time anyway. I said, "Yeah, its money."

They'd offered a $10,000 signing bonus if I signed with them right then but they already had offered a $25,000 bonus if I spent the summer with them Well, I knew I was goin' home to them cows so I said, "If you put that 25 on top of that 10 and make it 35, then you got a deal." Hank said, "Get on a plane first thing in the morning."

I arrived and was headed to Fredonia. I ain't had no sleep and I'm in the back of this painters van with no windows. It's full of jocks, pads and football helmets. That van stunk! I was sitting on my luggage and I was looking out the front window and I kept seeing all these signs hanging from the overpasses. Signs said, "*Welcome to Buffalo!*" "Oh man, this is great!" I said.

That made you feel real good, didn't it?

Sure it did. People were waving and there were helicopters. I said, "Man, th*ey* love me!" "They can't see me but *they* love me!" I looked closer and saw that there was a limo ahead of me carrying Jim Kelly, who'd signed the same day. I was following him to Fredonia. Jim came to Buffalo in a limo and I came to town in a painter's van filled with stinky jock straps. I told folks when I retired; I wanted to go out the same way a van ride to the airport. I didn't want any party, just a van ride.

This is what's really sick to me. You signed as a free agent for a $35,000 signing bonus and you had three years USFL experience behind you. These guys who were just drafted will sign a contract with a signing bonus in the six if not seven figures.

I know. My last year, the guy behind me made a million more than I did. You know what Rob. It's all relative it doesn't matter to me. I could have left Buffalo in 1993 for more money. I said no. I wanted to be *here*. I love Buffalo city and I'm going to in Buffalo. I signed a three-year deal in 1993 and my son cried like a baby. He was about seven. He wanted a dog real bad, and I told him that he couldn't get a dog until I retired. I told everyone that I was retiring in '93 so the kids were looking forward to their puppy. Then Jim,

Thurman, and everyone talked me into hanging around. We were in the back seat of a car. I had my wife, my son and daughter with me when it came over the radio: "Kent Hull re-signs for three years." Oh man, they cried. No puppy!. But, in '96, they couldn't talk me out of it.

You were the only center Jim Kelly ever had?

Yup, we still hold the record for the longest streak for quarterback and center starting combination.

170 games?

That sounds about right. I know Peyton Manning and his center are getting close. In another couple of years, they should have it. Jim and I are pretty *intimate*.

"*Oh,* that's sweet!" my wife, Kendra said.

More so than my wife and me. Let me tell you this story - Jim likes this one. We were playing a Sunday night game, national audience. Well Jim gets his hand all ripped up, the knuckles, the skin, everything. It was a bloody, nasty mess and he was bleeding like a hog. Well, Jim put his hands under me, so what starts to happen to those white britches of mine? By half time, my whole butt was covered in red and everyone was saying you got to change those pants, dude. I didn't have time, not at all. I said, "Jim. You got to put something on those cuts." He put some band-aids on them and they lasted about two plays. He was bleeding again and, by this time, it was starting to come down my pant legs. It was really embarrassing. After the game, my *mother* called me. She said, "Kent, you really need to do something about those *hemorrhoids*, son." She thought I had hemorrhoids! If I had hemorrhoids like that, it would have been the worse case in history.

That is a good one especially visually. Moving ahead a bit - after that, you guys won the AFC for the first time.

Giants?

Giants. I know where I was when Scott lined up for that kick. What were you doing?

I was the guard. On field goals, the defense is going to make a good surge and if they can't get there, they'll quit. Every kick that Scott Norwood kicked would start out right and hook. I stood up and I was saying, "It ain't hookin'!" "*It* ain't hookin'!" We went into the locker room and he was still dressed. Kickers are usually the first ones out of a locker room but Scott was still dressed when I got in there. I knew it was killing him, I said, "Scott, if I had done my job better we would have gotten you a few yards closer." He was kicking a long one on grass when he was used to kicking on the artificial stuff. They never sweated. Scott was great.

The four Super Bowl losses?

Yeah, it's tough. You know I haven't watched the Super Bowl since I retired. If I write a book, it's going to be called Horse Shoes and Hand Grenades. Those are the only things that matter when it's close.

"You mean to say that you aren't proud of what you accomplished, in doing what you did?" Kendra asked.

Let me tell you. The first time, we *were* proud of what we did.

"Every fan was so proud of you," she added.

The next time, when we played the Redskins, Superman and Spiderman couldn't have helped us win. Then it was the Cowboys in Pasadena and we turned the ball over nine times. I think a high school team could have beaten. The last one we should have won. That hurt worse than the first Super Bowl.

You could see the age creeping up on the team. We were a family, so it made it different. Many of us had been together for so long and we knew *that* game was probably the last shot. It'll never happen again because of free agency, I assure you.

Now, the fan loyalty is to the logo because they never know who's going to be there and who isn't. Loyalty is not to the player but to the logo.

I agree. So many of the older guys I have spoken to feel the same way, like Joe Ferguson. He hardly ever watches the NFL anymore.

I don't watch it, either. I check the scores in the Monday paper.

It's so different now. We knew who the Bills were going to have on their line one season to the next. We didn't need a Rolodex. Billy Shaw said that there was a unique bond that existed between the fan and the players. That bond ended with you guys.

It did. These guys who sign now won't be around in a couple of years. Now, you don't have time to develop people any more. Just as they are getting good, they are gone to the highest bidder.

Buffalo is unique when it comes to this though, because I've never been to a city where we are accepted *not* because you played football, but just because you're here. I remember going out into those parking lots in the late '80s when we were terrible, and the folks knew who I was. They'd feed me and send me home with a six. I never saw a place that was so full of love, friendship and good-hearted people like Buffalo. When I say I was the luckiest person around, I *really* was.

Do you think the team will be moved to Toronto?

I hope not. I really hope not. This city needs a champion so bad after those Super Bowls. It wasn't about Ichabod or Thurman or Jim. It was about the city of Buffalo. It was about the people who supported us. We wanted to bring something home and we couldn't do it. Boy, that just crushes you, man.

We lost that first one and this city went crazy when we got home. I was in Hawaii and watching it on TV. Scott Norwood was getting embraced like no one else. We got close, but that only counts in *horseshoes and hand grenades.*

You're on the short list for the Hall of Fame.

I don't know. They had to call me and tell me I was. The way I look at it, I'm in there five times. Jim *wasn't* going without me. Marv *didn't* go without me. Thurman, Lofton and Ralph Wilson *didn't* go without me.

Looking at your numbers, when you throw in the USFL you played fourteen years in pro ball, all of it as a center. Probably started over 200 games and you started 19 playoff games.

I guess, I don't keep up with that stuff. I didn't know until recently that guys are spending thousands on the Hall of Fame voters - dinners here, flying them other places. I say if I can't get in on my merits, then don't put me in.

When I was growing up watching ball players I had a good number I could choose from to emulate they were good role models. In today's NFL there are guys like Pacman Jones, Chad Johnson, T.O. and Michael Vick.

There are people who play in this league that literally *embarrass* me because *I* played in the league. I'm an alumni and they *embarrass* me by their behavior. I tried to emulate one person and that's Dwight Stevenson of the Miami Dolphins.

I'm telling you he whipped people so bad they didn't know what happened, just ask Fred Smerlas.

Who was the toughest nose tackle?

Joe Klecko, no hesitation on that one Rob.

He was an animal, my very first game was against the Jets, and it was a sell out. The Bills had a big ol' picture in the lobby of that, I took it home by the way. I told them *I* took it, it's down in Greenwood Mississippi hangin' on my wall. Anyway my first game I'm facing Joe Klecko he cocked and rocked and he had hit Jim about ten times without me snapping the ball. So Will Wolford and me tag up. I stick my hand out and it gets up under his facemask and the next thing I know my feet aren't touching the ground. He had me by my shoulder pads with *one* hand. "Hull if you ever do that again I'll kill you," he said. Now if I said yes sir he'd be all over me so I crashed down on his arm and I was still swinging in the air, so I said, "Okay Joe *I* promise I'll never do that again."

What is your opinion, on the record or off of Gene Upshaw?

You can print it. Gene, let me tell you this, Gene turned this union around, let's get that straight right now and it took him not getting paid for a few years, I can't take anything away from him but *now* he's making up for all the salary he didn't get I can promise you that.

$6.5 million a year.

Yup. He's going around now telling folks what he's doing for all the retired players; I sat on the executive council with Gene. I've been in those meetings and I can tell you that the retired players *are* a big part of those meetings for about a ½ a day and we're there for *six* days. It has to be stressed that it is us that signed that Collective Bargaining Agreement that gives everyone this money. I think it's the worse thing ever made, at least what came from it, I didn't see it then but I see it now.

Free agency?

Free agency, it's *killed* the game! It's killed the loyalty of the players; it's *not* killed the logo. If you went out there to the stadium and seen 32 get the ball you knew who it was or if 34 got the ball you knew who it was, you have no idea now.

Gene he knows his money is only coming from current players and these *retired* people aren't paying any part of that salary of his so he has to keep things good for the current player because it's the new guy that will keep him in his job or get him fired. He knows where his toast is getting its jam.

This world is full of leaders and followers and if you're in a room with fifty-three football players and you can get the right *ten* you'll have *all* of them, you'll have what ever numbers you will need and Gene knows how to do that.

Thank you. What did you do after football?

I went back to them cows.

Life's been good?

It has. A cattle farm is a lot of work, more hours than football probably, not quite as strenuous as football but its tough. My grandfather who is ninety-two told me this when I borrowed two-thousand dollars to buy my first cow, he said, "Kent if you can't take care of those cows just cut the wire they'll take care of themselves." I can't wait to get out there in the mornings and I know they want to see me, they know my white Ford and when they see it and they come a runnin'.

This wouldn't be complete with a comment on the comeback game against the Houston Oilers.

Hmmm, yea, that was the strangest game. I tell you I played in four Super Bowls and I can't remember ten plays from all four you get tunnel vision and you don't remember nothin'. But in *that* one we're down at half time like 28-3 and it was the playoffs, so if we lose we're going home there ain't a next week. Guys are startin' to think about where they're going to go on vacation. I remember Darryl Talley going through the locker room slappin' the stink out of people, saying get that milk out of your eyes we can win this game! Well, we go back out Frank throws an interception for a touchdown and now were down 35-3. I look over and see a guy who was motioning to his wife to start making reservations I grab him by the throat and said this game ain't over. He gave me a look.

I'm sure.

Next thing you know we score, we get an onside kick and score again and this same guy is now motioning to his wife to cancel the reservations. We had 10,000 people leave before we made the comeback and 400,000 people have told me they were there that day a great, great day that was, folks went nuts.

Kent if you had one thing to say to the fans of Buffalo what would it be?

Well, like I said Rob I have to be the luckiest man on earth to end up playing football in Buffalo. I've never felt more at home anywhere, other than Greenwood than here in Buffalo from the first day I got here to the day I left. There is no more loyal fans anywhere in the league than here and it's not just us who say it it's the other teams. Western New York is probably the best-hidden treasure in all the United States; people don't even know where this is but Ichabod does.

BIKE
56

Chapter 13

Darryl Talley

Get the milk out of your eyes!

There are few players in the history of the Buffalo Bills that bring with them the aura that a smallish linebacker out of Shaw High School in Cleveland did. He called himself a midget and began to play football in the big city just so he could hold onto his milk-money and not be called a "sissy."

Darryl, how is it going in Florida?

Things are great down here, nice and sunny, light wind, a chance of some rain but overall, real nice down here.

Thanks for that. We have rain with chances of increasing slush here in Western New York.

Oh, *I* know. I remember the weather all right.

Just some back ground to start. You were born and raised in Cleveland?

Yes, I was.

What did your parents do?

My dad was a saw master. He worked at a foundry cutting pieces for engines for companies like Boeing. It was a typical childhood, I did what kids are supposed to do and sometime what we weren't supposed to do.

What did you do?

I was always a midget. I was *really* short, a lot shorter than most of the other kids. I looked a little different than everybody else too so I had to fight a harder than everyone else just to make it through each day. *The* girls in the neighborhood were bigger than me. That wasn't fun, I can tell you.

Where I grew up. We only had a few girls in town I married one of them.

I've known *my* wife since we were young, too. There's a story about that which I'll tell in a bit Rob. When I was a kid, I had long, stringy, wavy hair, and that sure looked a lot different than everyone else in the neighborhood.

Fred Smerlas told me that the only reason he began to play football, was that he was in such good shape from fighting all the time that he was stronger than everyone else.

Us too! *Me* too! In my neighborhood, either you fought or they would do to you whatever they could if you didn't defend yourself. It was survival man.

Did you start in the peewees?

I started playing football on a challenge from my dad. He had asked me if I wanted to play. I said I would play if he did. I was a smart aleck so if I was asked something stupid, I'd give it right back to folks. So Dad went out and bought me an old jersey somewhere.

I'll never forget the first game I played in. First of all, my uniform was different from everyone else's because I had come onto the team late. It was even a different color, too. In that first game, the field was muddy. It was raining a little and so I went onto the field. After awhile, everyone was a muddy mess but my uniform was *still* spotless. It was clean the *entire* first half, so as we were getting ready for halftime, the coach came over to me and started in. He asked, "Darryl, why aren't you playing football?" "I am playing," I said. He said, "Look at you. Your uniform's not even dirty." I said right back at him, "It's because I'm not being knocked down!"

Nobody was blocking you?

No, and here's the thing. I was defensive tackle and no one could knock me down. No one was even touching me.

The first half of the game I *was* nice and clean but the second half of that first game, I was the nastiest thing crawling around, mud comin' from everywhere. My mom wouldn't let me get into the car. I had to strip in the parking lot and ride home in my underwear.

Yup. I've done that – "get dressed in the garage and we'll hose you down out there."

You got it!

Again, the town I grew up in was small. In my backyard-football-glory days, we played all the back yard stuff, football, baseball, you know, where the sewer was out of bounds.

Oh, sure. We played the same thing in the streets of Cleveland, where every three cars was a first down. We played tackle on the asphalt and I can tell you that there were a lot of people who were getting their side-view mirrors knocked off. Like you guys, we would have to wait for the cars to go up and down the streets.

Yup. When the tractors went by, those were our TV time outs.

If I ever decided to tell people how I really started out playing football, they'd look at me like I was crazy. But that's how I did it and man did I grew up around some *real* characters.

With all the players I have spoken to, very few had a structured football upbringing. Instead, most of the stories stem from playing the game for the sake of neighborhood survival or doing it just because there wasn't much else to do. I think that unstructured playing ended with you guys, if that makes sense.

Sure it does. Everybody now has a tendency to play organized football. But still today, in the area where I grew up, there are kids playing tackle football in the streets of Cleveland. When we played, a lot of times it was out at the city dump, too. We took the rocks off the ground and we used them to mark the sidelines for football and bases for baseball. Sometimes we would scoop up the rock salt from the streets to burn the grass so we'd have yard lines.

There aren't a lot of kids playing outside the way we did when we were growing up.

No they don't. It's a video-game generation, not a healthy one either.

You grew up in the late '60s and early '70s in Cleveland. Did you follow anyone at that time?

I didn't follow anyone, really.

I was little but I don't remember the Browns being that good back then. Were they?

Oh, yes, they were Rob. They had Gene Hickerson, Leroy Kelly,

Paul Warfield, Bo Scott and Walter Johnson. There was a bunch of guys who played some really good ball during those years.

The pre-merger days. Sure, I remember Gene at the Hall of Fame last year. What made you go out for high school ball? Was it because everyone else was doing it or survival or what?

Here's the thing. I was little, *so* small that I couldn't play high school football until my junior year. I was smaller than everybody else so what I had to do was to play peewee and bantamweight football through my tenth grade year. I lived in the suburbs and we played in the city some times. *Those* guys naturally said, "Well, those guys in the suburbs, their football isn't any good. They can't tackle, run, and hit, whatever." We had a reputation of being weak when we played them so I had to prove myself.

The peewees gave you a chance to develop the skills you already had, while giving you time to grow up, for lack of better words.

Yeah. My body needed time to catch up with the skills I had. Anyway, I'd say back to those city kids, "C'mon, man. Suit up and let's play. Let's see who is the best. We'll beat your butt." When we did get a chance to play them, we did beat them and when I finally got to play high school ball, I had a reputation, a strong one. The other guys said, "Hey! Darryl can hit; he can tackle; he can run!"

I saw that you played running back in high school?

I *tried* to. I tried that for one year and I said, *no* way. Again, I played bantamweight football through my sophomore year. It was a lighter weight class. Then went out for the varsity team in my junior year but all those guys had played together since they were little kids. I was the new guy in the group, coming out for varsity in the 10th grade, I had to prove myself. I was still a little small. That's why they tried me at running back but it didn't work.

I'll move ahead just a little Darryl. When did you first start getting letters from colleges that were interested in you? How were colleges approaching you?

To be honest with you, Rob. I wasn't very highly recruited out of high school at all. I'd only played in ten varsity games in two years.

Ten varsity games? That's not many at all.

No it isn't, seven in my junior year and three in my senior year that was it. Four schools, mostly from the Mid-American Conference, recruited me. There were Iowa, Iowa State, Syracuse and West Virginia. They were the only four big schools that were looking to recruit me. I wasn't going to Iowa. I came real close to going to Syracuse but decided at the last moment to go to West Virginia because I thought I would have a chance to play there.

That would be 1978 or 1979.

I went to West Virginia in 1978. I was red-shirted my freshman year. That was the first year freshman *could* red shirt.

Who was your college coach?

After my red-shirt year, they hired Don Nehlen to replace Frank Cignetti.

Don Nehlen turned things around pretty well at West Virginia didn't he?

He sure did. We became a winning program there. He would be coach there for twenty years, at least, I think.

I looked at the West Virginia schedule for the '81 season. It's not like you had a powder puff schedule. You played some good schools and started out 4-0.

Yes we did. People sometimes are amazed when I tell them whom I played against in college. I played against Dan Marino. I played against members of two or three All-Pro teams between guys who went to Penn State, Rutgers, and Virginia. A lot of the guys I played against in college, have made the trip to Canton, or are well on their way there.

You left quite a legacy at West Virginia, quoting Wickipedia here: five tackles for a loss against Penn State, fifteen tackles against Boston College, "Sports Illustrated" Player of the Week, Hula Bowl, 282 solo tackles for your career, 19 sacks, you were on the short list for the College Football Hall of Fame, and played in an upset win in the Peach Bowl. That's a lot to be proud of Darryl.

Thank you. Not bad for a midget, is it?

No it isn't. Now, there was that 1981 Peach Bowl victory over the University of Florida and the 1982 Gator Bowl. Tell me about the Peach Bowl.

In the Peach Bowl nobody expected us to do anything at all against the Gators. West Virginia was still an unknown program and we were going to play Florida in that game. They were expected just to run all over us. They were the big favorites. Nobody, the experts anyway, said we stood a chance against the big, bad Florida Gators and Charlie Pell.

It was a slop day.

Yeah, it was. It was cold and it was raining like hell that day. They wouldn't even let us warm up because the field was covered. When the game started, we turned Mickey Walczak loose on them. They had never seen a *mud turtle* before. Mickey wasn't that big but he was a hell of a running back in the mud, and there was some nasty shit that day.

I see he scored both of the touchdowns for the Mountaineers. You said in the "Mountaineer Magazine," and I'll paraphrase: football is made to be played outside in the weather and in the elements so you can throw mud in the guy's face and when he is on the ground you can push his face in it.

That's true, isn't it?

Yes sir it is. Despite the expert opinions, you guys whooped up on the mighty Gators pretty good.

Yes we did. We confused them all day long with changing schemes and running Mickey Walczak at them every which way. They were frazzled and never got under control.

In an excerpt from the Mountaineers website, Don Nehlen said that that 1981 Peach Bowl team was probably his strongest team ever.

We *were* a good team, one of the best to play in Morgantown in many, many years.

In 1982, it was the Gator Bowl against Florida State.

Yeah, in Jacksonville. Essentially a home game for the Seminoles.

Bobby Bowden was the coach at Florida State. He had coached West Virginia in the '70s but left for Florida State, pissing a lot of people off because he seemed to do it without notice. Florida State had all the best runners from Ohio to. There were a bunch of guys from around my area and they had speed. They beat us good.

I'll skip another step or two ahead. I spoke with Kent Hull a couple of weeks ago when he was up here. We were at a restaurant and he walks up to the table with a big ol' mouth of chew. I said, "Kent, the first thing I'm interested in is the 1993 comeback game against Houston."

At this point Darryl Talley let out a prolonged, guttural laugh.

So you know in what direction I'm heading?

Uh huh. Yes sir, I do.

Kent said to my wife and I, "You know what Darryl did during halftime of that game, don't you?" I said, "No, I don't. Why don't you tell us Kent?" What did you do that day, Mr. Talley?

Man, I'm not goin' to tell you Rob! Let's put it this way, I threatened everybody. I said if they quit, I was going to beat them up, and that's putting it mildly.

Did you clean that up a little for the sake of our younger readers?

Yeah, I did man. I pitched a literal bitch. It was a nice little tirade.

Now many of those guys have told me, "Darryl may or may not have done this. He was going around the locker room slapping everyone, saying, "Get the goddamn milk out of your eyes!"

Well, *yea*! We had guys getting ready to take their vacations and it was *only* halftime. I cussed everybody out and *threatened* everybody. Then we go back out onto the field. *This* was a funny part of it. Our offense gets the ball and were moving, when Bubba McDowell intercepts the ball and runs it back all the way for a touch down. Now we were down 35-3! I turned to Mark Pike and Eddie Abramoski who were standing next to me and I said, "Fuck it. That's all right. We got them *right* where we want them now! We got them right where we want them!" They looked at me, then at each other, and then shook their heads. Mark looked at me like I was crazy. I had told everyone before we came out that if they *do* beat us they would *not* be able to play the next week. The Oilers would *not* be able to play the following week if they beat us! I said, "Hit them! If they're out of bounds five yards, hit them! I want them hit and I want them beaten!" We went out and got into a street fight.

In that year, 1993, there was quite a group at linebackers. How did you manage to fall behind in the first place?

What happened is that we were playing nickel and dime coverage so Warren Moon had his way with us. He had a half that was something for the history books. He could do absolutely nothing wrong. He hit everyone in stride and all the Oilers made great plays, offense and defense that day. It seemed early on that we were in for one hell of an ass whoopin', and we sure got it that first half.

So it was nasty from the start?

Nasty is a good word for it. We couldn't find our way out the tunnel, it was so bad.

Do you remember Van Miller?

Oh hell, yes! How can anyone forget Van Miller?

He tells a story about that game. He said he went nuts with his pandemonium, fandemonium echo.

Oh no! That was me that said that! I said it and then Van *borrowed* it in his own special way. I had never seen fans act like that on the field. It was insane. Van is taking credit for that, is he? That's okay. Let him. I'll see him soon enough.

There is a story I'll never forget about Van. I used to wear a fur coat. I wore a coyote-collared fur coat. Van came up to me one time after a game and said, "Darryl, c'mon over here. Have *I* got a coat for you." He had a black bear coat fifteen sizes to big for him with *Van* in big letters on it. He had it stuffed in a bag and he wanted me to *buy* it. "No, Van. I don't think I want that black bear coat." I never will forget that. Van figured I was the only one that would wear something like that.

Speaking of Van Miller, he told me this story once. He said, "Rob, never leave home without an empty beer cup." He goes on to tell me this story. When he first began to broadcast Bills games, it was 1960 and he did everything, the pre-game, game, and the post-game. He did it all. He was in the booth at the start of one game when in walks this woman wearing the biggest, gaudiest of fur coats asking if she could sit and watch for a while. He said take a seat. She stayed for the first quarter and then, the second quarter. Van had to go to the bathroom but couldn't leave the booth because he was the only one there. She stayed for all of halftime and the third quarter. Van was having issues. It wasn't until late in the fourth quarter that she left, at which point Van was grateful for the empty beer cup.

Oh shit, no!

Yup. I was looking at the 1983 NFL Draft. The USFL was on the stage at the time. Did you get any bites from USFL teams?

Oh yeah. They told me they were going to draft me. I told them not to *even* bother. Don't waste picks on me because I'm not going. They said that they would draft me the first day and I told them again to *not* draft me. They did it anyway, though, in the second round.

New Jersey Generals?

Yup. New Jersey. I told them again that I wasn't going there, that I'd be going over to the *real* league.

They had some good players in the USFL. I've tried to learn about the lawsuits and all the antitrust mess that was going on and frankly, it's mind blurring. But they did have some good ball players in that league.

They did, but a lot of them didn't make it in the NFL, though.

Jim Kelly did okay.

Yeah. Jim *did* do all right. Kent Hull. John Corker. Anthony Carter. Bobby Hebert, the "Crazy Cajun." Some good players did start out there in the USFL.

You get drafted in '83. Did you expect to go in the first round?

Yes, I did, because I was told that I *would* go in the first round. I was told that I would go early in the first round, too, but the only linebacker taken in that round was Billy Joe Smith from Arkansas who went to the San Diego Chargers. I looked at that and said, "Okay. If that's the way you're going to be, I'll show you and everyone else just how good I can play in this league."

That year was the quarterback draft, Elway, Kelly and Marino, but as far as on the defensive side of the ball, no one ahead of you had a bigger impact in the NFL than you, even those players selected in the next few rounds after you.

Thank you Rob. The Bills picked Tony Hunter and then they selected Jim. They held his rights anyway because he went off to the USFL. Tony Hunter was a great basketball player and a big tight end but he never panned out at the next level. Then they took me as the eleventh pick in the second round.

I'll be jumping around with some of my questions. Kay Stephenson's staff drafted you. How was he as a coach?

I think Kay was a good guy. He was an okay coach, a better line coach perhaps than head coach. My opinion is that Hank Bullough stabbed him in the back.

Okay. That'll be my segue.

Kay had brought Hank Bullough in as the defensive line coach and to shore up the defensive side of things. It seemed that Hank came in just to stab Kay Stephenson right from the start. Perhaps you can tell I have no love lost for Hank Bullough.

I can tell.

I thought he was the most worthless piece of shit that I had ever laid eyes on.

Feel free to be honest Darryl. Fred Smerlas said that God got drunk one day and made Hank Bullough.

Yeah. I'll take it a step further, with all due respect. God got drunk one day, took a big shit and out plopped Hank Bullough. Let's put it this way - anytime a man keeps a ledger of what he gave his kids to go to college and then expects them to pay him back after they graduate, he is no man at all. It says a lot about him.

That is low.

Yeah. That came *directly* from his son. Hank *did* stuff like that. The guy essentially tried to get me out of football, too. He and I? There isn't a lot of love there. Bruce Smith wanted to whoop his ass for calling him out in a team meeting. Hank was just a nasty guy. Stories came from Cincinnati where guys knew him. He would take a head of lettuce and keep it in his lunch box until it turned brown. That's how damn cheap he was.

This is what he did to me. He called my dad one time. He called him and told him that I needed to concentrate on my football and that I was up here running around with this white girl instead of concentrating on football. Hank told my dad that I needed to *leave* her and concentrate on football. *That's* what he called my dad about!

My dad said, "Man, *you're* his coach. You tell him. I've never told him what to do since he was fifteen. I always asked him. You're his coach. *You* tell him that." The woman happened to be my wife. We met in my junior year in college and we've been married ever since. It's not like I was messing with a floozy or something. I'd known her all these years. I thought, "Man. This dude's out of his fucking mind."

The stories are consistent when it comes to Hank Bullough.

Here is another one, I think Fred put it in his book. It was 1986 and we were in Tampa playing the Bucs. We were 2-6 up to that point and we knew if we went into Tampa and lost, then Hank would get fired. I made a play in the backfield and when I got back to the huddle Fred was frothing at the mouth. He said, "What the fuck you doin' man. Don't you know if we lose, Hank's gone? So stop it, you cock sucker. We want Hank out of here!"

Bruce Smith *said* this and Fred Smerlas *said* this on the field.

Fred was slobbering and snotting everywhere. "We want this mother fucker out of here. Don't you dare make another tackle like that!"

You guys did lose, 34-28!

Freddie was looking all kind of crazy and I wasn't about to let him beat me up. So I did what he said.

Makes sense.

Well, we lost the game. Hank was fired and Marv came in. Hank was one true, genuine ass-hole, that is for sure, but Marv *came* to the rescue.

Okay. When I put his name in the glossary, he'll be defined as a genuine ass-hole.

Yup! Everything turned around when Marv came to town. We went from 4-12 and within a couple of years, we were in the AFC Championship. At the end of Marv's first year, we were 7-8. We were in the last game of the season on the road in Philadelphia. You can ask Cornelius this one. I told "Biscuit" in '87 that if we stuck together, we were going to be pretty damn good. We just had to stick together because we had everything we needed *right* there!

You dropped that Philly game but, for the most part, you did all stick together. In '88 you were 12-4. 1987 was strike year though.

Yes it was and I think that really drew us closer together. That strike did a lot for us because there were guys who didn't have a lot of money that stayed out because the rest of us were out. Guys who couldn't afford to be out went out because the rest of us were out. That meant a lot. We said that no one was going to cross the line.

A couple of them did, though.

Yes, they did. Carl Byrum and Keith McKeller crossed

Really! K-Gun Keith?

Yup. Cornelius and I took it out on him everyday in practice for a long time.

Looking at your stats, you had two touchdowns and they were both long returns, both over sixty-yards. Do you remember what games?

I took one back against the Raiders, Browns and *Jets* too, I think. New York was great because I would argue with the fans behind the bench. That was the best part about ever going to New York.

I have to ask about Super Bowl XXV, of course. I remember where I was and, being a Bills fan from the time I was six or seven, it was a big day for the team and me. The goal in the '70s was to beat the Dolphins bit it didn't happen until the '80s. The goal in the '90s was to win the ring.

At home, maybe. I don't think it was until '83 that the Bills beat the Dolphins at the Orange Bowl because I sacked Dan to send it into overtime.

Yup, okay, 38-35 in October of '83 at the Orange Bowl. What about Super Bowl XXV?

What did I *think* of it? Let me put it this way - Super Bowl XXV was the best thing to happen to me other than the birth of my children. That's the way I looked at it. We were at war at the time, the Gulf War. *Our* country was at war. Men and women were fighting for us overseas.

That was Whitney Houston's day too. That was the best yet.

When Whitney Houston sang the national anthem, the hair stood up on the back of your neck if you're an American. If you're not, you need to leave the country. That's what I said to everyone, too. If you're not American, you need to leave the country. *That* moment, *those* moments, were some of the most spine-tingling moments I ever had.

As far as the game goes?

You know I get pissed when people say, “If Scott had made the kick.” Well, bullshit. If somebody else had made a block, a catch or if I had made a tackle, we would have been ten yards closer or we may not have been in that position at all. I don’t buy into the fact that it was the kick. I don’t buy into the fact that everyone was putting the entire loss on Scott’s shoulders. I told Scott, *right* after the game, not to worry about it, that he had won a lot of games for us. Another thing that really irritates me is why Scott Norwood isn’t on the Wall of Fame? We won a lot of games early on because of him and people get on him because he missed the kick in the Super Bowl. *I* missed tackles in that Super Bowl. It seems like Scott just vanished and that’s a shame. Let me ask you this, Rob; how much money did *you* get for Super Bowl XXV?

Me? I actually lost $50.00.

Well, I made money for that game and I made a hell of lot more because of the foot of Scott Norwood.

Darryl, the die-hard Bills fans up here don’t think that of Scott and we will never forget not only what he did for Western New York, but you, Jim, Thurman and everyone on those teams did. You became a member of many an extended family up here. We will always be proud of all of you.

A big thank you to everyone Rob. Darryl Talley will never forget you either.

One of the goals of <u>The Bills Are Due</u> is to raise money for the older guys. There has been a lot of bickering back and forth, a lot of name-calling, a lot of Gene Upshaw, a lot of this that and the other. I know, too, that it’s probably a little more difficult for you younger, modern-era guys but, on the record or off the record, however you *want to go, what do you think of Gene Upshaw?*

Okay. I'm thinking about how I want to start this. Here's my thinking. Gene Upshaw has done a lot for the players' union. He saw some of the inadequacies and he's adjusted *some* of them. *But* my thing is this: if it were not for the older guys who came before *us*, and for all they did and sacrificed, we wouldn't have what we do today. What I think Gene is forgetting is that he was once a foot soldier and was once in their shoes. He was one of them and he was one of us. He seems to have forgotten. What's happening now is that he knew of the inadequacies that existed. He made some improvements and, on others, he did nothing. It should be remembered that I went through two strikes. A lot of guys went through two strikes to give these new guys what they have now.

Exactly. It was you guys, Fred, Shane, Cornelius and everyone else who were the founding fathers of what these new guys just signed their names to. There were the players of 1983 that gave it to you and the players of the '60s and '70s gave it to them.

Right, because we weren't going to get anything. My dad always told me, "Son, whatever you do, make it a better place than when you got here." If I do that then I did my damned job. I agree with some of the things Gene has done and disagree with some others. There is one comment that he's made that has really irritated me. That was when he said that he doesn't work for the former player but just the current player. "Gene, did you forget where you came from?"

It's a funny thing that some of the players who are playing today don't even know there was *ever* a strike. They think that it was always this way. It wasn't always this way.

That's right. Some of them may not have even been born in 1987 or they may have been one or two years old. They have no clue as to what you guys did for them.

That's right. I met a kid who had been playing in the league for five years or so. He was at a convention I attended last year and he said, "Strike? You guys didn't go on strike!"

"Are you kidding me?" I asked. This guy had no clue. Younger and older players alike don't have a clue as to what the older guys did for them. I'm really torn about Gene. He's done some good but some of the good doesn't always outweigh what should have been done long ago and hasn't been done. You had the best quarterback of all time die an angry man, die a broken man.

Johnny Unitas?

Johnny Unitas. He was the face of this league for how many years?

I remember him playing at the tail end of his career as well as doing broadcasts.

He was treated like dirt. It was uncalled for. The other guy I used to watch was Mike Webster, the old Pittsburgh Steeler. He gave his everything on the field. This guy laid the groundwork for the modern era centers.

I see a big change in the players as well, do you?

The big change that I see is that it doesn't seem like there is the love of the game, like it was for us, and those before us. Now there is a love of the *check*. They play for the money they don't play it for the love of it. There seems to be a cavalier attitude about how they play. Some, *not* all, play like we did, but there are some you see, who shit, just don't care. They don't even teach guys to tackle anymore. They try to shoulder knock you down. Everyone is going for an ESPN highlight. They want one big hit rather than five good wrap-around tackles.

Kent Hull said that no one is taught to run block anymore. They just stand up and let their blubber get in the way.

That's right. There is no technique anymore, none. The basics of the game are disappearing. Now players would rather out-scheme the other person than outplay them. This is a simple game - running, passing and tackling. If guys have been taught technique, they will win. Guys now won't use their hands because they don't want to get hurt. In our days, it was the *Run and Shoot* or the *K-Gun*, which everyone looked at as odd, but we still had to tackle people. No one tackles anyone any more.

Hit someone and do it with your face up!

You bet. Tackling is a dying art in the NFL. These guys want the big ESPN hit, to get the big contract. No one wants to make the good clean tackle. I have scars from four elbow surgeries to prove that I never let go of someone when I wrapped them.

Did you come out of the game physically okay?

I had thirteen surgeries in all so nothing is where it's supposed to be. It's all pointed in different directions.

Life has been good for you?

Life has been interesting. I bought a business and it is a completely different environment than that I was raised in. I could count on my teammates with the Bills to do something when they said they were going to do it. In the business world, it's not that way at all.

Darryl, this has been great. You are one of the best to have ever played here, and you're never forgotten by folks of my generation, I assure you.

Thanks Rob. I promise you I'll never forget Western New York.

Chapter 14
Frank Reich

"It is pandemonium. It is fandemonium."
-Van Miller-

We all have unforgettable moments in our lives. Moments so ingrained in our memory that they become part of our lexicon.

"Here we go, 32 yards from the center of the field, it's 38 all, the Bills can win it..."

Those moments become part of a question such as where were you when?

"Reich puts the ball down, the kick is on the way, and it is good..."

Mom always remembered where she was when Pearl Harbor was bombed, my older siblings could tell me where they were when those shots rang out in Dallas.

In our lifetime; Where were you when Pope John Paul was shot?

Where were you when Elvis died?

When John Lennon died?

9/11?

In a whole different light and one far less meaningful in the overall scheme of things, there is *the* comeback.

"...The Bills have won it! The Bills have won it!"

"They win 41-38...incredible...what a comeback by the Bills!"

Where were you when the Bills had the greatest comeback in the history of the NFL?

"It is pandemonium. It is fandemonium!" said Darryl and Van.

Darryl Talley may have been the first to say it but Van Miller immortalized it.

Kent Hull said, "Rob, eight people have told me they sat in section 331 row ten, seat 6, at half-time ten thousand people left the game and yet 400,000 people have said they were there that day against the Oilers."

January 3rd, 1993 found me living in Memphis in a small apartment near the University and way too close to the railroad tracks. I was a social worker for the homeless and found myself more of a baseball fan than a football fan during those years. The NFL no longer interested me in the way it had when I was a kid. The emergence of the Buffalo Bills as the preeminent team in the AFC brought me back as a fan be it just a little bit. Even in the south, Bills' games began to be televised more and more often.

Life had changed for me. I'd been through bad and good, and was aging more quickly than my three-decade old frame could keep pace with. Things were changing in the NFL too, as all the players I remembered were retired. I couldn't really identify with the new age, new style of flamboyant player. In that year of 1993, the play clock was reduced to 40 seconds, Drew Bledsoe and Jerome Bettis would be among the 1st round selections and, for me, seeing Joe Montana wear the color of the Kansas City Chiefs just wasn't natural.

The Buffalo Bills had lost the two previous Super Bowls and their record had slipped from 13-3 to 11-5 in 1993, losing the division title to the Miami Dolphins. In order to return to the Super Bowl, the Bills would have to do so as a Wild Card Team. They would have to win three games to go to Pasadena. The Bills would host a Wild Card game on January 3, 1993, squaring off against the Houston Oilers.

The Houston Oilers had finished in second place behind the Pittsburgh Steelers in the AFC Central. Jack Pardee was their head coach, Warren Moon, their quarterback, Ray Childress, their defensive end, Webster Slaughter, their wide receiver, and Al Del Greco, their place kicker. They had good players who had put together a good season.

The Bills, Andre Reed, Don Beebe and Pete Metzelaars, would be catching the ball, Thurman Thomas would be running it, Steve Christie would be kicking it, but Frank Reich would be throwing it that day instead of Jim Kelly.

Frank, good morning.

Hi, Rob. Good to finally catch up.

Good to talk to you, too.

That playoff game was one of those moments where football fans, certainly Buffalo Bills fans, could tell you where they were when it was played.

Oh sure. I played many years in the league on four different teams. It was my most memorable moment, as you could imagine.

Let's back up a little though. What did you think of the recent draft?

I didn't look real close at what the Bills did in the draft this year.

I become interested when they get to the field. You know then, or soon after, if they are they going to live up to the hype and earn the salary. I don't get too excited by the draft. I want to see how they fit in with the team.

I understand that, a number of top picks who had the hype, crashed on the field.

Exactly.

Frank. I'm writing The Bills Are Due for a couple of reasons. It is primarily to help raise funds for former Buffalo Bills who are having some tough times in life right now. There are a number of them, more than many could imagine.

Yes, there are. I'm aware of a few but I know there are far more.

I was taken aback a couple of years ago when I began to read stories about the guys I'd watched playing when I was a kid. As I've come to find out, stories similar to Donnie Green's are not that unique.

No, they're not, and I appreciate your support of those guys. I don't even know all the horror stories but I'm sure there are a lot.

You were born on Long Island?

Yes, I was. We were only there for a couple of years. My dad was a schoolteacher and football coach in Freeport.

Your family headed to Pennsylvania after that?

Yes. My mother and father were there in Freeport for six years. Then I was born at the tail end of those six years. Dad took a head-coaching job at a school in Lebanon, Pennsylvania and that's pretty much where I was raised.

Is Lebanon in the middle of Amish country? It seems to me that we visited there when I was growing up?

Well, yeah, it is. Yes, I'd say that's a fair characterization.

It's a beautiful part of the country.

Yes, it is.

When did you first get interested in playing football?

Peewee, actually. I'll never forget. We were on a family vacation at the beach somewhere. When we got back, I found out that all my buddies had gone out for the peewee team and that I had missed try-outs. I went home and was real mad at my dad because every other boy's dad had told them when tryouts were going to be. When I got back, I asked, "Dad, how come you didn't tell me when football tryouts were?" He said, "Well, I figured if you were interested in playing, you would have told me."

So he knew but just didn't fill you in?

That's right. My dad was the captain of the team at Penn State. He was a good player and a good coach. You'd think he would have pressured me to play but he never did. Dad left it up to me to decide if I wanted to play or not. So when we got back from our trip, I had to go straight down and beg the coach to let me try out. He did. I made the team and I've played ever since then. I was nine when I started.

Frank, when I was nine or so, the guys I imitated were either Joe D. or Reggie. I'd write number 63 or 66 on a ratty t-shirt. Was there a particular player that you emulated from the time you were that age?

In my earliest days, I was a New York Jets fan so I followed Joe Namath all the time. Because of my mom's ties to the Pittsburgh area, I eventually became a Steelers and a Pirates fan in the early seventies.

That was a good time to be a fan of both of them, wasn't it?

Yes. It sure was. Even though we lived closer to Philadelphia, I drifted toward the Steelers and Pirates.

What high school did you go to?

Cedar Crest High School.

Did you have to play both ways in high school?

Yes, I did.

What did you play on defense?

I played safety on defense. As a matter of fact, not a lot of people know this, and there *really* isn't any reason to know this, but in the *Big 33* game, which is the high school all-star game for Pennsylvania, I actually played safety. Another coach from my area said that I deserved a chance to play in the *Big 33*, so he put me in at safety.

Did colleges recruit you as a safety?

No. The only reason I played safety then was because of that one coach. He was from a school near mine and he thought that I should be playing in the game as quarterback. Because I didn't get picked, he squeezed me in on the team anyway, but on defense.

Was your dad your high school coach?

No. My dad was actually coaching at what would've been the archrival of my high school. When I got into high school, he didn't want to have to coach against me. He retired from coaching so he could come watch me play.

He wasn't forced into a position of taking notes and scouting for the other team?

Yeah, exactly. Plus, dad had a younger son coming up behind me, so he wanted to watch us.

How many colleges were looking at you to play for them when you were in high school?

Let's see: the University of Virginia, Purdue, Rutgers, Penn State and, of course, Maryland. There were other smaller schools too, but these were the main ones.

Why did you pick Maryland?

Maryland had a great business school that interested me and they did have a good football program, too. Jerry Claiborne was the coach there. He had come and really turned the Maryland program around. He seemed like a great coach and person, and I put a high value on the education I was going to receive. So combining the them made Maryland an easy pick.

Did you start in college right away?

No, actually. Back then, you couldn't red shirt your freshman year, so I red shirted my sophomore year.

Football-wise Frank, you are probably known for three accomplishments, all of them comebacks. In college, it was the game against Miami and the 1984 Sun Bowl and of course the Houston Oilers. Tell me about the Sun Bowl. You were down by 21-0 to Tennessee at halftime, but scored 21 points in the third quarter.

Yes, we did, and another 7 in the 4th quarter. We won 28 to 27. That is honestly what I remember. Frankly, Rob, I don't remember a lot about that game. It was the greatest comeback in the history of the Sun Bowl, though. However, going back to our Miami Hurricanes game earlier that year, we had the greatest *college* comeback. In the rest of the games, the 3 or 4 that remained that year, we had to come from behind to win *every* single one of them.

I looked through my research I had collected and saw that 1984 was an odd year for the Maryland Terrapins. You had lost the first two games of that season and then were hurt, and replaced by Stan Gelbaugh.

That's right.

In a story posted by Heather Dinch on the website of the Baltimore Sun, it says that after you were injured, the Terps went on to win five of the next six games under Gelbaugh. Head coach Ralph Friedgen walked up to your father after a game, and your father said he didn't think you could lose your job because of injury. Coach Friedgen told him that he was talking like a father and not a football coach. The following week, when Maryland was trailing Bernie Kosar and the Miami Hurricanes down in Miami, 31-0 at half time, Gelbaugh was pulled and Frank Reich went in to what was expected just to be mop-up duty. In the 3rd quarter, however, Frank led Maryland on three scoring drives, and a fourth one just as the 4th quarter began. With Maryland now trailing only 34-28, Frank would drive for two more scores, ultimately giving the Terps a 42-40 win and the greatest comeback in NCAA history up to that point.

Yea, it was something. We just went out and took it one play at a time. You can't score more than once a series, so we couldn't take it any other way.

Frank many fans of the Buffalo Bills know that you have pursued the ministry. How difficult is it or was it for you to maintain a dedicated Christian life while being in the NFL? Let's face it, the league offers plenty of opportunities but an incredible world of temptation too.

Well, in some respects, yes, it was difficult but in some other ways, it really wasn't. One of the great things about playing for the Bills in the years I played was that there was a very strong core group of guys who were committed Christians. We were all seeking to grow and mature not only as football players but as Christians.

Part of that was understanding that our faith in God wasn't

something that we only had when we went to church. It was something that we had every day. There was a strong group of guys who could encourage one another when times became hard. It just can't be said enough that *that* team was a very close-knit team. Even those guys who weren't necessarily excited about spiritual things had a respect for it, and for those of us who did. There really was a brotherly love among us then. I think it was, and *is,* important for those of us with strong spiritual lives not to look down our noses at those who aren't there yet. They were my friends, my teammates, and I was proud of them.

Yes, there were challenges when it came to the fame and fortune. Let me say this, and I have seen it unique to football players, in particular; when a football player is committed to something, he is usually pretty strongly committed, and he's not afraid to stand up for what he believes in. The guys on the Bills who were Christians weren't afraid to stand up for their positions. We stood our ground when we had to, and that encouraged us that much more.

I found this article online from "The Goal." It does cite the Bills-Oilers game a little, but it applies more to your career. It's about a song, "In Christ Alone."

That's right. I've been asked many times if I think God was on my side at certain times and I said yes, of course, but God was also on the side of the other person or the other team. He's not selective.

No, He's not selective. He is on everyone's side but not everyone is on His side.

That's correct Rob.

I looked at that draft of 1985. The first round seemed to me to be one of defense and wide receivers, with Bruce Smith being the first pick and Jerry Rice going to the 49ers. There wasn't a quarterback selected until Randall Cunningham in the second round. You were the 2nd quarterback selected that year, the first selection of the third round. When you got drafted, Vince Ferragamo was wrapping up his last year or two. Did you anticipate being a starter, perhaps in 1986?

Well, honestly, Rob, I thought I could start in my rookie year because I did well during mini camp. I'd really did do well, so I thought I could start. But I ended up pulling out of camp and didn't get back in until late in the year. I had lost that opportunity. I did get some playing time after coming off injured reserve, suiting up for the last three games of the year. I did think they would bring someone else in 1986. Vince was going to leave leaving Bruce Mathison and me to compete for the starting position. I just didn't know they would bring in Jim Kelly, is all.

Yeah. Jim had a couple of good years.

Yeah. Jim did okay. This is a true story. I was good friends with "Boomer" Esiason. We were best men at each other's weddings. It was after my rookie year and "Boomer" had a gold tournament for charity. There was a bunch of us there and Jim was there, too. Jim and I had met at a Penn State football camp when we were in high school. Anyway, that night after the tournament, we were all at dinner and Jim and I were reminding each other *of* that first meeting. I was with the Bills then and Jim was still with the Houston Gamblers of the USFL. Jim looked me right in the eyes and said, "Frank, I promise you, there is absolutely no way I will *ever* end up in Buffalo."

He did seem to play a few years up here, didn't he?

Yeah, a couple, come to think about it.

Regardless of how many years I watched the Bills in the 1990s, you were Jim's backup. From what I have seen, you and Jim had the longest-standing backup quarterback relationship I can remember.

Yes. We still hold the record. We were together nine years.

Kent Hull was Jim's center for just as long, too.

Longer, I believe. I think they still hold the NFL record for the same quarterback and center teaming.

Statistically, your best season was with the New York Jets?

Best? I don't know if it was my best. It was where I played the most. I think I threw for over 2,000 yards in 1996.

Yes, you did, and averaged two hundred yards a game, too. Frank, you are best known for that one game, January 3, 1993.

Yes, that's okay for me.

I had begun my mid-South afternoon watching the game but quickly gave up. I missed so much of it, could you take a few minutes and tell me what happened the rest of the way? All I remember is you being down 28-3 at half time. What were you thinking during that half time?

It was simple. Marv Levy's comments to us at halftime were to go out and play hard, and he said if we go out and played like men, no one could ever say that we had quit. He told us to take it one play, one series and one first down at a time. I don't think anyone was thinking that we were going to come back and win the ball game but everybody knew we could go out, play hard and do as Marv had said, take it one play at a time. Our nose tackle Jeff Wright said, and I'll paraphrase, we were embarrassing our Defensive Coordinator Walt Corey, we were embarrassing ourselves and we were really embarrassing the fans of the Buffalo Bills.

We had to go out and execute in the second half, but my first pass of the half was intercepted and returned all the way for a touchdown, giving the Oilers a 32-point lead.

A 32-point lead with about twenty-eight minutes to go in the game. You needed more than a point a minute and they, certainly, would have to be held to three and out for the rest of the game?

Sounds right.

In after the interception return the ensuing kickoff was a squib kick that gave the Bills good starting field position. Frank took the

Bills on a fifty-yard drive and their first touchdown, a short run by Kenneth Davis.

On this kickoff, Bills' kicker, Steve Christie, recovered his own on-side kick and a couple of plays later, Frank hit Don Beebe with a forty yard pass for a score. It was now 35-17. Perhaps the Oilers had begun to look ahead a bit and, as some have told me, the stands at Rich Stadium were still emptying out halfway through the third quarter.

A few moments later, after Houston's first punt, Frank connected with Andre Reed and narrowed the deficit to 35-24. On the following possession, Henry Jones intercepted Houston's quarterback, Warren Moon, and on fourth down, Frank connected with Andre Reed for the Bills fourth touchdown in a little more than five minutes in the third quarter. It was 35-31.

Time was running out in the fourth, Frank drove the Bills down to Oilers' red zone and threw his third touchdown of the day to Andre Reed, giving the Bills their first lead. Warren Moon responded driving the Oilers down to the Bills' twenty-yard line. Al Del Greco tied the game at 38, sending it into over time.

The Oilers won the coin toss. Moon's attempt to Ernest Givens was tipped and intercepted by Nate Odoms. A fifteen-yard facemask penalty was tacked on, giving the Bills the ball on the Oilers' twenty-yard line. Steve Christie kicked a 32-yard field goal, marking the greatest comeback in NFL history. Steve Christie's kicking shoe is now enshrined in the Hall of Fame in Canton and the Houston Oilers are a footnote to league history.

Rob it was unbelievable, an incredible, remarkable day.

That was the NFL memory for you?

Oh, most definitely.

You did play most of that Super Bowl that year, Super Bowl XXVII. I remember that being rather forgettable though.

Sure. In a lot of ways it was, but it *was* a record-setting performance for me. I ended up tying the record for most fumbles in a Super Bowl. Even though it was difficult and we lost 52-17 and turned the ball over nine times, I have moved on in life. I have learned to take the bad along with the good. The comeback game was the good and that Super Bowl was the bad.

In that song I quoted earlier, "In Christ Alone," the final verse states, "Now I know no greater honor than to know Him more."

That's right. Life lessons come from the good and the bad.

I read that paragraph as - it didn't matter if we, you, won or lost, just accepting the outcome.

Well, I would say it this way. *It* did matter if we won or lost. I wanted to win the game bad. Don't get me wrong when you're a football player, you're playing to win the game. It's very important to you, but at the same time you understand that once the game is over, there are lessons to be learned. No one knows God's intentions for *that* game or *that* day. I knew when I went into *every* football game that it was going to be an opportunity for me to grow and to learn, as both a football player and a person.

I have seen a big change in the players over the last twenty years, going from the days of Joe Ferguson through to you. Guys, who are known more for off the field stuff, like Pacman Jones, Chad Johnson and Michael Vick. What do you think of these young guys who, in my opinion, may not be ready for the NFL but who are in the league because of the potential for the amount of money they can make?

You know Rob, I'm not sure what to say. There is no doubt that things in the league have changed but I also know there are still good people in it. I still think there are good, quality football players who are coming out, who are also strong morally. Are there more downsides now then there were a while back? Yes, maybe so. I know there are problems but I try to focus on the solutions and not the bickering. My attitude is not to judge anyone or any team. A team can sign whomever they wish and, as a fan, I can have my choice of teams. I will do my best to focus on the positive of the organization and if I don't like a team, or there are a number of players on that team that don't represent what I believe is best, then there are other teams to choose from. To be a fan means supporting what a team does on and off the field.

The city of Buffalo and the team have been through a great deal and now we don't know if the team is going to be around many more years.

Rob, I know every player thinks the fans in his city are the best. I know many, if not all, of our players believed that the fans in Buffalo were a very special, a *very* unique, loyal group. There was just a tremendous sense of the twelfth man being ever so real. We did respect the fans that paid their hard-earned money and came out to watch us play, good or bad. We felt there was a connection between the fans and us. I don't want to put my head in the sand and ignore the negative, but the NFL has impacted lives personally, not only the players, but the cities and the countless charities. Losing a team will have an incredible impact on Buffalo.

Are the players perfect? Are there organizations that are not ideal? We know the answer to that but I do think the NFL has worked hard to build a positive image. I played on four NFL teams. Buffalo was the most special, of course, but each team, in its own way, worked hard to build a positive community. I have no reason to believe that the future of the league will be nothing but positive. There were probably more negative stories back twenty years ago that we didn't know about because there just wasn't the coverage that there is now. People are people, and I believe there are far more good ones than bad out there. I believe that the NFL will continue to have a positive influence on our culture.

69

Conclusion

Conrad Dobler

Gone, but not forgiven.

This book began with the forward written by the Bills' Hall of Fame Guard, Joe DeLamielleure. I thought it only natural to conclude the book with the man who replaced him on the offensive line. The Bills, after losing Joe to the Cleveland Browns were in need of an experienced starting guard. Chuck Knox found one.

Now there are names of NFL players which, when mentioned to a true football fan of my generation, will always bring a smile or, perhaps, even a quiver or shake of the head. One such name is Conrad Dobler.

The Buffalo Bills acquired Conrad Dobler from the New Orleans Saints in 1980 for an undisclosed draft pick. But, for me, he will always be a St. Louis Cardinal. Those Cardinal teams of the mid-'70s were something to watch; Tom Banks, Bob Young, Dan Dierdorf and Conrad Dobler.

In 1977, the cover of *Sports Illustrated* labeled Conrad Francis Dobler as the dirtiest player in the National Football League. Drafted out of Wyoming by the St. Louis Cardinals in the fifth round of 1972, Dobler once said that he punched "Mean" Joe Greene and kicked Merlin Olsen. He always said, "*You* play the game to win it, not to make friends." On the field, he exhibited what has been discussed again and again in this book, *courage, toughness and self-denial*. Especially now, these traits have never been more evident. He has remained one of the toughest ever to play the game.

Hey Rob. I'm chewing Nicorette so if I slobber some please excuse me.

Alright. No problem. Slobbering's fine. Just don't bite me!

Funny, real fucking funny! I only bit that *one* guy and he still bitches about today.

Doug Sutherland?

Yeah, I bit him. He kept stickin' his fuckin' finger in my facemask. It's not like he was looking to tickle me.

Have you two talked in the last thirty years?

No, and I don't give a fuck, either! Some folks just hold grudges forever. *He's* one of them, and Merlin Olsen is another. Fuck him, too. I hit Merlin Olsen so hard one time that he's still whining about it today. I never forgot that Olsen went on to play *Father Murphy* on NBC. He was doing a graveyard scene in an episode and shit, one of the tombstones read, "CONRAD DOBLER, GONE BUT NOT FORGIVEN." It's nice to see I'm still on his fucking mind, though. He goes on to selling flowers and I get nothing, *almost* nothing. That beer commercial was pretty cool, though.

That was cool.

Olsen doesn't talk to me and I don't give a shit. It's funny that after all these years, though, that he is still pissed off about whatever he's pissed off about. So let him be pissed off, I say.

Do you... I tried to interject, but to no avail.

Merlin Olsen goes on to the flower bit and broadcasting, but what's cool is that when *I* go somewhere, it's nice to still have someone shout out, "*Tastes great!*" and to see them laugh when I yell back, "*Less filling.*" That commercial did more for my career than ten years on the field did.

Miller Lite, my favorite long ago, one of many favorites.

It's someone's favorite. After ten years in the league, being labeled as a famous troublemaker by Miller Lite changed my life almost instantly.

Okay. So far we have Nicorette, slobbering, Doug Southerland, Father Murphy and Miller Lite.

Don't imagine any of that shit was on your list of questions, huh, Rob?

No, but this is wonderful stuff for a creative non-fiction mind.

Did I tell you we lost my dad in Canada one time? It's a true story.

Canada? What happened to your father in Canada?

Well, the sign said, "Drink Canada Dry." We haven't seen dad since! Ha!

Okay. Great. A big swing and a miss from me. Shit. In 2,000 you had a great quote that applies to every over-forty-want-to-be, I will mess it up, but it goes, that under all this flab I have washboard abs.

That's true! I was coaching my son and others in football at the time. I think they were fifth and sixth graders. My son's a senior now, and it was before my knees went bad. Well, so many of the kids had fat guts, they couldn't even touch their toes. I could do a full split *with* my shitty knees and being fifty-five or so, and I was still touching my elbows to the ground. Those kids I was coaching couldn't even touch their toes. I'm wondering what the hell is wrong with these kids. They just didn't exercise or play. They *never* went outside, hardly worked a job *or* worked out. It's all video game shit now. They may have the strongest, most agile thumbs in the world, but they have fat, flabby guts and, unfortunately, their minds are headed that way. As a country, we should be ashamed for letting this happen to our kids.

This generation of kids I have to worry about. It's become such a *me* generation. When I was a kid, I worked my ass off. What does this generation do? They sit in front of the fucking TV, play video games and then they cry for stuff for doing nothing. I'm starting to wonder if they even know how to carry on a conversation with anyone because they just text or email. Communication skills are shot to hell.

You're right. I don't think there is a kid under sixteen that doesn't have a cell phone. I don't think many of them could even write a letter in today's world.

C'mon kids. Get your goddamn fingers off the remotes and get outside. That's *my* motivational speech.

Good one. Of course, in today's overly sensitive world someone would sue you for the emotional damage to his or her child. I have a simple question; what did you do as a kid?

Worked my ass off!

Simple.

That's what I did, - my family, we all did. I was born in Chicago but my family moved to 29 Palms, California. My brother had asthma so we headed to California for cleaner air. My dad bought a home delivery milk business there and, shit, I worked all the fucking time, unloading and loading the trucks that came in *all* the time. It was tough working ourselves through L.A. the way we did, but we did it. He worked us hard but it taught us a lot. These kids, *not all*, certainly, but many, haven't a clue what it's like to work their asses into the ground.

I was lucky. I made a dollar an hour picking potatoes by hand.

You were lucky.

What high school did you go to?

Easy to remember; 29 Palms High School.

I grew up watching you. Of course, I remember you primarily as a Cardinal. In the sixties, when you were ten or twelve, who did you follow, the Chargers, the Rams?

No one. I worked. A lot of us had it real hard. I can still remember when we got our first television set, a Zenith black and white with just two channels of snow. Later on we put this piece of paper over the top of it so that would make it color. I was green on the bottom and blue on the top. That was our colored TV.

Older, then. When you were in high school did you...

In high school? *Yes*, I *did* get laid, which is important.

Well... yes. Getting laid in high school does take precedence over math class.

Your wife is there? Oh, shit. I meant to say the first time I got laid I was alone. No the first time I had sex I was by myself. Is that better, Rob?

That's better, I suppose. I think she's heard the word somewhere else before. Thanks for cleaning it up and for providing a better picture of your youth for everyone. In high school, did you play both ways?

Yes, both ways. I was a linebacker on defense and I was a running back on offense.

Running back? Really?

Well, yeah. I was huge for those days. I was two hundred and twenty pounds, man, and I just rolled over those small high school guys. I went to a Catholic grade school early on and there were no organized sports teams, so I didn't try out for football until I went to 29 Palms High School.

When I graduated from that Catholic Grade School, my entire class was only eight students. Everyone else in town went to the public schools. When I get up to 29 Palms, *my* freshman class was a hundred and twenty or thirty. I was the outsider right from my first day there.

When I got home from school, I had to unload these milk trucks from all these drivers. That was getting old real quick so, to separate myself, I went out and played sports. Because I worked hard all those years, I was strong and agile when others weren't. Actually, I started playing football to get away from having to load and unload all those fuckin' trucks. So by the time I got home from practice, the drivers were already done and gone home. I went out for football because I wouldn't have to go home right away.

So you liked the two-a-days in the summer time then?

Well, even during the summer when we had two-a-days, I still had to go home and work with my dad on his trucks and then go back to practice. Anyway, I got into football because I knew if I didn't, that after I got out of school, I would have to go home and work on all those trucks. I became the new kid in school who could do real well on the football field.

I used to hitchhike back and forth everyday to practice, twenty-five miles, or so, back to Yucca Valley where my family was. This shit that Gene Upshaw shoots out about how hard *he* had it growing up and his rough and tumble childhood - he ain't the only one.

I know. In other words, you didn't play guard until you got up to Wyoming then?

Well, yeah. I was a 220-pound running back. When I get up to the University of Wyoming, their running backs were speedy and were like 170 or 180. They were forty pounds smaller then I was at the time, so I played guard at Wyoming.

What other schools were looking at you at the time?

Quite a few. I had quite a few other schools looking at me - University of the Pacific, Cal. Arizona, Utah, Utah State - but I wanted to go to Wyoming. Remember, at the time Wyoming had won the WAC and had just lost the Sugar Bowl to LSU in the last couple of seconds of the game. So Wyoming had a good couple of years.

That would've been '68, with high school being in the mid-sixties. Correct?

Yeah, and I believe 1969 was the one hundredth anniversary of college football. That also is when all the blacks at the University decided to wear black armbands and our coach kicked them off the team.

That's new to me.

That year we won *one* game and it was against Colorado State. Of course, later on I played with or against many Colorado State guys and they would say, "Oh. You played on that Wyoming team that was so lousy?" I'd say, "Lousy, yes, but we beat your ass."

Life as a kid to that point wasn't easy. It wasn't easy to get where I did in life. It was hard on a lot of us. Many of us had it harder than Gene Upshaw *ever* did.

What is your opinion of Gene Upshaw?

I don't talk to him and *he* ignores me. Well, shit. Gene Upshaw, is the Pope and as a Catholic, I know how hard it is to get an audience with the Pope. He is the Pope and there is no way anyone can take on the Pope and win.

I have nothing to do with someone who forgets where he came from and forgets who helped get him there. I have no respect for him and if a bus hit him, I wouldn't care.

Well, so many agree with you, basically, saying they wouldn't piss on him if he were on fire in front of them.

Well, neither would I. With Gene, it's not about money anymore. He's got tons of money. It's about the *power* that goes along with him in his role. Gene Upshaw is one of the most powerful black leaders in America today if you can believe that, but he is dumber than a box of goddamn grapefruits. He, well, his brain is somewhere between a head of lettuce and a head of cabbage, but it's the power that goes with it all that he doesn't want to let go of.

Gene Upshaw is living the high life and he doesn't want to give that up. He has twenty, thirty million dollars stashed away so he could go away and live on an island somewhere, he doesn't need the job, he doesn't need the money he wants the power. It's seeing how many people will lick your boots that keeps him going.

Lord Acton said it best, Power corrupts and absolute power corrupts absolutely. It means that absolute power will mold the brains or corrupt the brains of those who have absolute power. And Gene Upshaw has absolute power! He doesn't give a shit what he does or how it impacts others.

Gene Upshaw has become a virtual dictator and hell, how do you get him out of there? You get him out the same way we got Saddam Hussein out. We drag their ass out by the back of their neck. That is the only way they will ever give up the power. Throughout the history of any government or any organization, that's how dictators are removed.

So you're saying that the only way he's leaving the gig he has is by being dragged out?

Absolutely. I'm not condoning anything like that but I am saying the only way to get him out is to forcibly remove him. In Upshaw's case, the *union* will have to act to toss him out and that means the players or the owners with balls need to do it. They will have to say they are no longer recognizing the union if Gene Upshaw is the head of it. The situation is bad right now and it will not change. The current attitude is to screw everyone, except those who are here right now, enjoying the absolute power they have. Screw everyone to keep *our* millions coming in. It's the current players who will have to step up to the plate and do something.

Do you think that Gene Upshaw has made the owners and players so cowardly that they are afraid to do anything? Andre Collins, the NFLPA's Director of Retired Players, is, for lack of a better word, his handpicked successor, isn't he?

Well, yea, and Andre Collins is in his position illegally because I believe you have to be an active player to have his position and he is not active.

In 2007, I saw that Andre Collins issued a statement that was interpreted as a threat. He said he would close any retired players' chapters and remove their leadership for actions that were deemed detrimental to the players union as a whole.

That's right.

I used to be able to go into the NFLPA web site and get links to the various retired players' chapters around the nation. I can't do that any more.

Nope.

I can only believe that the detrimental actions that Andre Collins spoke of were the increased activities by retired players toward the union, not only blogs, but also litigation. The NFLPA doesn't like any of that do they?

No, they don't. They fear change. Why would Gene Upshaw *or* the league for that matter want to change things if making those changes impacts their power? They don't. We all know that the real power in America right now is not political power. The power is *green*. Getting anything done or changed depends on how much *green* is involved.

Now many of us know that Gene Upshaw is dumber than a box of sand but, man, he sure doesn't want to let go of all the perks he has right now and he doesn't really care either from what I've seen. He doesn't give a shit what Conrad Dobler or Joe DeLamielleure has to say. If he can fly on the corporate jet to Hawaii or is invited to all the best parties in town, all while making millions a year in salary, he doesn't give a shit at all!

In an interview I did with *Sports Illustrated* just before the Super Bowl this year, I said that there is a cultural difference in the league right now. I was called politically incorrect for saying something like that. There *is* a cultural difference right now in the league. That *is* a fact. It is about values and beliefs. It has little to do with race, because race is just race. The league now is a *me* generation. What are we supposed to do when 70 to 80% of the league is black and 70 to 80% of the retired players are white? That *is* a fact. Why or how can someone be called politically incorrect when the statement is based on fact?

Even if you look at the steering committee on our retirement board, 80-90% of that board is again black while 70-80% of retired players are white. I don't have a problem with that just as long as they do *their* job. But they haven't done their job. The problem I have is that I don't believe they are doing an honest job for everyone involved. Everyone knows the difference between right and wrong. It's just sometimes people have problems doing the right thing because it may interfere with what they may want to do, and consequently people get hurt. I have had to defend myself against these views.

Now between you and me, I asked this guy on the radio after that *Sports Illustrated* article, "Isn't it a fact that 70-80% of the active players are black?" He said, "Yes." I asked, "Well, isn't it a fact that 70-80% of the retired players are white?" Again, he said, "Yes." "Then what the hell is wrong with that quote?" I asked him. I can remember ten or twelve years ago people were saying there weren't enough black players, black coaches or black executives in the league. Well, that has changed, but the point is if I came out with a White Miss America contest or a Cloud Magazine instead of a *Jet Magazine*, a White Broadcasting Network instead of *BET*, I would have Al Sharpton and Jessie Jackson pounding on my door.

Why is it, politically *incorrect* for me to mention a factual statement? There is a cultural difference in the league now and it transcends race; it is beliefs and values. It is a *me* generation of kids and of players. It's all about *me.* What I said in that article is that there is a cultural difference between the players of yesterday and the players of today. Values and beliefs have been transcended, and much like the rest of America, the league has become a *me* league. It's a *me* generation, whether you're a ball player or not. I don't give a good goddamn if a person is white, black, Chinese or whatever. It is still a *me* generation and a *me* league.

Race has nothing to do with the me generation?

The *me* generation is based on belief and values. The difference is what our generation believes in and what *this* generation believes in. Many of us still take care of our parents where this generation probably has enough money that they will send their parents to nursing homes. It's the *me* generation versus the *we* generation.

Do single parent households have anything to do with it?

Shit, no. That has nothing to do with it. There are a lot of people who come from single parent households. Anyone who is looking for an excuse or rationale can find one for anything.

Conrad, from what I've seen, America has become an overly sensitive country. We have to watch everything we say, all the time. If we disagree with the status quo, we are in the wrong. It is a dangerous trend for our country.

Yes it is and I say fuck it.

He paused to get the last of the Nicorette.

With the sense of entitlement and all this *me* shit, where's the compassion? Simple honest compassion -where is it? There is no excuse for not being compassionate, none. It *is* expected. I don't think this new *me* generation has any idea what it's like to be compassionate. Larry Johnson of the Kansas City Chiefs has bragged about his three hundred thousand dollar watch; why does he do that? I would much rather give away three hundred thousand dollars because I'd feel better about myself at the end of the day. Bragging about that watch will only get him killed on the streets where he hangs out.

Do you think this bodes well for the future of the league?

Well, the league is seeing, or they certainly would like to see, some of these stories go away, but the league knows the public is fickle and that today's news is today's news, and tomorrow's news is tomorrow's news and no one will remember what happened yesterday. The phrase that's been used is *delay, deny and hope we die.* Every day another one of us old fucks dies off and, sooner or later, there won't be many of us around to say anything. Commissioner Goodell is making 11 million a year, Upshaw 7 million a year. Remember the color of law in America *is green.* If you have enough *green*, you can make the law read anyway you want. The NFL and the NFLPA have a hell of a lot more green than we do. We couldn't find a lawyer to represent us because any lawyer who is smart enough will know that they will be broken, just by the amount of paper work the teams of opposing lawyers will throw at them. The union and the league will flood him with so much paper work that we won't be able to afford to pursue them; do you understand what I'm saying?

Sure, I do. Many other retired players have said the same thing; "They keep us so busy with paperwork that nothing gets done." That's the delay part of the phrase, I imagine.

Yes, it is, so nothing gets done. Anybody who sues, or the

attorneys, have to pay the people to do all the paperwork.

I had some of the best lawyers in the nation. They battled the tobacco companies. They were so flooded with paperwork from the NFL that they were overwhelmed. They went through the entire Collective Bargaining Agreement and said to me, "We could spend millions to tell the NFL that the CBA is wrong but nothing is going to change." Then they asked, "What would they get out of it?"

Their lawyers overwhelmed your lawyers?

Fucking right! Lawyers have to make money or pay someone to do all that paperwork. If they see that, regardless of how much paper work is filed or gets pushed around, nothing will ultimately change. Then they, too, will say, "Fuck it." We have to do it ourselves, we, the huddled crippled masses of games past. *Give* us your poor and huddled crippled masses like the Statue of Liberty only NFL-style this time.

Have you been turned down again on your disability?

Shit, I've been turned down more time than the beds at the Marriott down the road.

Good one. Are you still 90%?

It is well known that I was ninety percent disabled from all the injuries I sustained playing the game. I was over two million dollars in debt, without a job, and doctors were telling me that I could work. The NFL screwed me bad and the NFL overwhelmed my attorneys. I have had seven knee transplants, over all. My second knee transplant lasted only five years. Shit, I've had tires that lasted five years. Dan Dierdorf has had the cycle. Tom Banks has had two hips and two knees replaced. Bob Young is dead. This is just one offensive line that played together for a couple of years in St. Louis on that Astroturf. What the *fuck*! Jim Hart has nothing to bitch about. He was sacked only seven times in one season. Shit... Whoops! I keep forgetting your wife is there.

Yeah, but she…

Shit. Tell her that fuck just means *f*ornicating *u*nder the *c*ontrol of the *k*ing.

Fornicating. That's a good scrabble word.

In my disability case, my lawyers have been back and forth with this form and that form and this hearing and that. I'm doing better but with these knees and all this battering and bruising shit; my body is pretty well beat.

In courtrooms or statehouses, if you flood your opposition with so much paperwork that they have too much to do so nothing gets done at all, then maybe the problem is forgotten and goes away.

Like I said, Rob, the real power in America today is the color green and any lawyer knows that. They will be overwhelmed by the power of the green produced by the NFL and the NFLPA if they pursue any action against either of them. The NFLPA and NFL scare away any lawyers who may try to litigate a case against them.

Watch them, the NFL or the union, when the stories start getting bad about how shitty the retired players are being treated. The league or the union will make some small announcement at a press conference stating how much they have given or will give to retired players. But they won't tell you how much will go to guys like me, or Dierdorf, us older broken *and* broke guys. We still get shit as Gene gets 7 million. Watch them.

We haven't talked much about your NFL days. You were drafted in 1972 in the fifth round. It was a good draft that year. Ahmad Rashad, Franco Harris and Reggie McKenzie came into the league that year. You started as a rookie?

No. I didn't get any real playing time until my third year, 1974, with Bob Young, Dan Dierdorf, Mel Gray and Jim Hart. We had a good team in those years.

You made three pro-bowls, '75, '76 and '77. You scored one touch down. How'd you do that?

That was on a Monday Night game in 1977. That would have been against the Giants I think. I'm glad it *was* a Monday night game because that Saturday before, my buddy got married and I got drunk and was hung over real bad. I'd never have been able to play on a Sunday. Any way, we were on their two-yard line or so and we fumbled. It bounced into the end zone and I pounced on it. Believe it or not, a fight ensued.

No! A fight?

Yea a fight. I'm proud to say that everywhere I went I made an impact though. We had those great teams in St. Louis. Jim Hart was hardly ever touched. When I went to New Orleans, they had their first winning season ever. When I came to Buffalo, I was part of that team that beat the Dolphins.

A number of years ago your wife, Joy, had an accident, something that could happen to any of us. She was climbing into a hammock and fell out landing on her neck. She knew it was broken right away and is now a quadriplegic. How is she doing?

She is doing okay. You know, I can't believe it's been seven years now.

How did you meet?

I was doing some lectures for a drug abuse hospital and they had a convention in New Orleans. She was a nurse there.

How long have you been married now?

Too long. Twenty years. We believe that all will okay though. Upshaw is an ass but I guess this world is supposed to have them too. Joy and I will be just fine. I won't lie. It's difficult some days but the sun will rise again.

Sources

Chapter 1

Facenda, John, "A Time For Glory", The Power and The Glory, NFL Films Inc., 1998

Chapter 2

Baez, Joan, "The Night They Drove Ol' Dixie Down," The Complete A&M Recordings, A&M, 2003

Chapter 3

"Man Against The Poppers", Time Magazine, Time Inc. December 1957

Chapter 4

Facenda, John, "The Heroes of the '60's", The Power and The Glory, NFL Films Inc., 1998

Chapter 5

Facenda, John, "Winds of Victory", The Power and The Glory, NFL Films Inc., 1998

Chapter 6

Byrds The, "Turn, Turn, Turn", The Byrds Greatest Hits, Sony, 1999

Chapter 7

Temptations The, "Don't Look Back", The Ultimate Collection: The Temptations, Motown, 1997

Chapter 8

Facenda, John, "November", The Power and The Glory, NFL Films Inc., 1998

Chapter 9

Will, George

Chapter 10

Thorogood, George and The Destroyers, "Get a Haircut", Anthology, Capitol, 2000

Eskenazi, Gerald, "Pro Football; After Bills' Era of Mediocrity, Success is Sweet for Smerlas", New York Times, Times Inc., January 1st, 1989

Chapter 11

Tasker, Steve, "Kelso The Savior", Tales From The Buffalo Bills, Sports Publishing Inc., page 51

Chapter 12

Days of Our Lives, Irna Phillips, Ted Corday, Betty Corday, NBC Television, Sony Pictures, 1965

Printed in the United States
204494BV00002B/1-99/P

9 781432 728540